CLAREN...ET

M king Films in Contemporary

Hollywood

Making Films in Contemporary
Hollywood

Alan Lovell and Gianluca Sergi

Hodder Arnold

A MEMBER OF THE HODDER HEADLINE GROUP

First published in Great Britain in 2005 by
Hodder Education, a member of the Hodder Headline Group,
338 Euston Road, London NW1 3BH

www.hoddereducation.co.uk

Distributed in the United States of America by
Oxford University Press Inc.
198 Madison Avenue, New York, NY10016

The advice and information in this book are believed to be true and
accurate at the date of going to press, but neither the authors nor the publisher
can accept any legal responsibility or liability for any errors or omissions.

British Library Cataloguing in Publication Data
A catalogue record for this book is available from the British Library

Library of Congress Cataloging-in-Publication Data
A catalog record for this book is available from the Library of Congress

ISBN-10: 0 340 80983 3
ISBN-13: 978 0 340 80983 9

1 2 3 4 5 6 7 8 9 10

Typeset in 10/13 Adobe Garamond by Servis Filmsetting Ltd, Manchester.
Printed and bound by Gutenberg Press, Malta.

What do you think about this book? Or any other Hodder Education title? Please send your comments
to the feedback section on www.hoddereducation.co.uk.

Contents

Shooting a movie is as much a study in desperation as it is in inspiration. But more desperation because the pressure is too intense, the time-frame too short, the financial risk too great and the egos too fragile . . . a group of mostly strangers has been assembled, often in an inhospitable location, and asked to work in harmony under demanding circumstances. The shooting days are limited, the budget closely monitored, the cast quarrelsome. Each individual is guarding his turf . . . (Peter Bart and Peter Guber – at various times, studio executives and producers)

Moviemaking is a very expensive, high-risk kind of gamble. There's a whole lot of things that are enormously important. I'm talking about the politics of movies and I don't mean the politics of kissing a director's ass or not. I mean the hierarchical politics of the people who make movies and how they make them is enormously important. (Michael Chapman – cinematographer)

Acknowledgments

Gianluca would like to thank all his colleagues, past and present, for their help with this project. In particular, I would like to thank Mark Jancovich for his continuous encouragement and support, and Julian Stringer for his never-failing ability to provide constructive remarks. I would also like to say a big thanks to all my students who helped me structure my thinking around some difficult topics and issues: you were a fantastic audience for my own test screenings! I would also like to thank Gary Rydstrom for his support and help with trying to understand what motivates filmmakers and spurs their creative efforts.

As ever, I owe my biggest thanks to my wife Cathryn and my family in the UK and Italy. You all provided me with the kind of love and support that made all this possible, even when I kept on blabbering about things that probably don't figure quite so high on your agenda . . . Thanks for being so patient and caring!

Alan would like to thank Jim Kitses, Daphne Edwards, and John Manuel for their support, suggestions and criticisms. I'd also like to remember the late Paddy Whannel who first set me thinking about the issues dealt with in this book.

We would both like to thank Peter Kramer for his constant support and insightful comments. We also owe thanks to our 'producers', Lesley Riddle and Abigail Woodman, whose support, suggestions and considerable patience helped ensure the project remained on track, if not entirely on time!

And finally . . .

We would like to dedicate this book to our children (in order of appearance): Tessa, Howell and Monica. You are the best muses we could ever wish for!

chapter one

Introduction

Fig 1.1 On the set of *Titanic*, 1997. (Photo: 20th Century Fox/Paramount/Digital Domain/The Kobal Collection)

How do films get made in Hollywood? To provide a context for our investigations, we describe how three very different films came to be made.

Blade Runner

1968   Philip K. Dick's science fiction novel, *Do Androids Dream of Electric Sheep?*, is published. It does not attract much interest from filmmakers. Martin Scorsese, then an up-and-coming director, shows an interest but does not option the book.

1974   An independent production company, Herbert Jaffe Associates, does take out an option on the book. A script is written but the project progresses no further than this.

1975   A third attempt is made to turn the novel into a film. It founders almost as soon as it begins. Hampton Fancher, an independent filmmaker and actor, approaches Dick about the film rights. Dick is discouraging; Fancher more or less abandons the project.

1977   Fancher suggests to Brian Kelly, an old friend, that he can further his ambitions to be a producer by acquiring the rights to Dick's novel. Kelly does so and commissions Fancher to write the script.

1978   Kelly uses Fancher's first draft (called *Dangerous Days*) to involve Michael Deeley, an established and successful British producer (*The Italian Job*, *The Man Who Fell to Earth*, *The Deer Hunter*), in the project. Deeley suggests a rewrite, which he sends to a number of potential directors, including Adrian Lyne, Michael Apted, Robert Mulligan and Ridley Scott. Mulligan is the only one to express interest.

   After a few months Mulligan's enthusiasm for the project wanes and he drops out. The search for a director for *Dangerous Days* continues; Deeley is especially keen on Ridley Scott.

1980   Having initially turned the project down, Scott changes his mind. In February, he agrees to direct it.

   His involvement has an unfortunate consequence. CBS Films, who had expressed an interest in financing *Dangerous Days*, feel that Scott's ideas for developing the project suggest a higher budget than it can afford. CBS withdraws.

Filmways, an independent production company, agrees to back the film. It suggests a budget of US$13 million. Scott believes that this is unrealistic; he thinks the likely budget will be around US$20 million. Filmways will go no higher than US$15 million.

Scott and Deeley look for other sources for the extra US$5 million. Unable to find any, they agree to go ahead with the US$15 million budget.

Scott sets about putting a crew together. One of his first signings is Syd Mead, an artist and industrial designer, to work on the visual design of the film. He also looks for an actor to play the lead role. Dustin Hoffman shows serious interest but after two months of discussions decides not to go ahead. Harrison Ford is signed to replace him.

By July, Fancher, working closely with Scott, produces a new draft of the script under a different title, *Blade Runner*. Over the next few months Fancher and Scott work to refine this draft. When serious disagreements emerge between them, Scott and Deeley decide to hire another writer.

David Peoples is signed and, by the end of the year, he produces a new draft. Hampton Fancher officially leaves the project.

Financial problems re-emerge. In December, Filmways withdraw their backing.

1981 By early January, Deeley has found new backers: The Ladd Company, Sir Run Run Shaw and Tandem Productions. The Ladd Company is an independent production company, which has support from Warner Brothers. Sir Run Run Shaw's company is a major Asian production company. Tandem Films is mainly a television production company. Tandem acts as the production guarantor for the film. The budget is now set at just over US$21 million.

A cast and crew are assembled. They include actors Rutger Hauer, Sean Young and Daryl Hannah, along with Jordan Croneweth as cinematographer, Lawrence G. Paull as production designer and Terry Rawlings as editor.

David Peoples produces a new version of the script in February.

Shooting begins in March on the basis of this draft. After two weeks Scott decides to reshoot everything he has already shot because he thinks the images are too dark. The film quickly goes over budget and behind schedule.

During shooting there is a good deal of tension between Harrison Ford and Scott, and between Ford and Sean Young. Tandem

Productions becomes alarmed at the way the film is developing. It is particularly worried about the budget and schedule overruns because of its responsibility as the production bond guarantor.

Shooting eventually finishes in June. By this time *Blade Runner* is US$5 million over budget.

Tandem is by now very anxious about the production. Scott and Deeley are fired. Their dismissal is more a mark of the company's frustration than a serious act, because Scott and Deeley continue working on post-production.

Douglas Trumbull's Entertainment Effects Group starts work on the special effects in August. Their work is not completed until the end of the year.

In December, Vangelis is signed to write the music.

Tandem is not happy with the rough cuts it sees. It pressures Scott to add a voice-over.

1982   The film is given audience previews in March in Denver and Dallas. It is very badly received. As a result, the voice-over narration is much extended and the ending is made more upbeat.

A third preview is held in San Diego, where the film gets a much better reception.

In June, *Blade Runner* receives its first public showing. It fares badly both with the critics and the public. The film gets two Oscar nominations – for best art direction and best visual effects.

Blade Runner's final budget is US$28 million. It takes $14 million on its first theatrical run. 298 people worked on the film.

Up Close and Personal

1988   The film producer John Foreman is asked to explore the possibility of making a film of *Golden Girl*, a biography of Jessica Savitch.

Jessica Savitch was a well-known television news personality in the late 1960s and 1970s. She was ambitious, unstable and had a drug habit. Sexually ambivalent, her most important relationship was a long-lasting, abusive one with a television producer, who acted as her mentor. Savitch drowned in 1983 after a freak car accident.

Foreman contacts Joan Didion and John Gregory Dunne, two screenwriters he is friendly with, and asks them to write the script. Didion and Dunne's involvement makes the project more viable.

In November, Foreman persuades Disney to take an interest in the project.

1989   In discussions with Didion and Dunne, Disney executives express their main worry about the project. They think the story is too negative and downbeat. They are especially concerned that the central character should not die at the end. Didion and Dunne agree to write a draft that takes account of these concerns.

        The writers deliver the draft in November. Disney still thinks the story is too downbeat mainly because the characters are not sufficiently sympathetic.

1990   By the summer Didion and Dunne have written four more drafts in which they attempt to address Disney's concerns.

        In September, fearing that the project is going nowhere, they refuse to sign a new contract unless a director is hired. Disney refuses to do this.

        A new writer, James Andrew Miller, replaces Didion and Dunne.

1991   Having done a rewrite, Miller leaves the project. Over the next couple of years, Disney makes unsuccessful efforts to re-engage Didion and Dunne in the project.

1993   The producer, Scott Rudin, expresses an interest in *Up Close and Personal* to Disney. He is willing to develop the project on condition that he can start from the very first draft of the script and that Didion and Dunne are willing to become involved again. Disney agrees and, after some hesitation, Didion and Dunne rejoin the project.

1994   By February, Didion and Dunne have written three drafts for Rudin. He sends the third to Disney whose response is along the same lines as previously. Rudin suggests to the writers that these criticisms should be ignored.

        In collaboration with Rudin, Didion and Dunne write another four drafts. Rudin sends the last to Disney and also approaches John Avnet to direct the film.

        Rudin believes the film must be star-driven. In September, Robert Redford and Michelle Pfeiffer are signed to play the leads.

        Because of disagreements about the character of the drama, Rudin, Didion and Dunne find Avnet increasingly difficult to work with. The disagreements are sufficiently strong for Rudin to leave the project in October. Didion and Dunne follow suit soon after.

        Avnet signs Anthony Drazan to do a rewrite.

1995 Both Redford and Pfeiffer express dissatisfaction with Drazan's rewrite.

Didion and Dunne are persuaded to meet with Avnet and Redford to see if there is a basis on which they can work together. Redford's approach is sufficiently sympathetic for Didion and Dunne to re-engage.

Helped by notes from both Redford and Pfeiffer, a shooting script is finally produced. It is the 26th draft of the script.

Shooting begins in March in Miami and, proceeding without great difficulties, is completed in July.

Audience previews are held in San Diego and Ventura County during August. In both previews, the response is favourable.

1996 *Up Close and Personal* opens at the beginning of the year. Its critical reception is mixed but by September it has taken US$100 million at the box office.

The film has cost US$60 million to make. It gets one Oscar nomination – best song. 438 people had worked on it.

Titanic

1995 James Cameron begins negotiations with Twentieth Century Fox to make a new version of the Titanic story. Initially, he asks Fox for US$2 million to dive on the wreck of the real ship and shoot some footage. His record as a director is strong enough for Fox to agree.

On the basis of Fox's offer Cameron organizes the dive and begins work on his 'scriptment' (a hybrid of novel and screenplay) for the film. Fox is impressed with the material Cameron shoots and agrees to support further development of the project.

A production team is put together. Cameron's first choices are people who can help him design the ship. Peter Lamont is hired as production designer, Tommy Fisher as physical effects supervisor and Rob Legato to look after the special effects. By the end of the shoot they will have built seven different models of the ship. Two Titanic historians are also employed to advise on the authenticity of the ship's design. Jon Landau becomes Cameron's co-producer.

The search for actors to play the two central characters begins at the same time. Gwyneth Paltrow, Claire Danes and Gabrielle Anwar are considered for the female lead before Cameron decides to cast the young British actor, Kate Winslet. After lengthy negotiations, Leonardo DiCaprio agrees to play the male lead. Kathy Bates and Bill Paxton are signed for two of the main supporting roles.

1996   Fox is sufficiently happy with these choices to give the final go-ahead in May. Cameron's first budget estimate is US$125 million; Fox will only agree to a US$110 million budget.

In order to limit its exposure, Fox enters into a co-financing agreement with Paramount. Each studio will provide half the budget and split the revenues on the same basis.

In July, preliminary shooting begins in Halifax, Canada, on the present-day scenes that are to open and close the film. By the time this work is completed, Cameron is dissatisfied with the approach of his cinematographer, Caleb Deschanel, which he thinks is too refined. He has him fired.

The shoot goes a week over schedule so there is a budget overrun. Worried by this development, Paramount renegotiates its deal with Fox so that its contribution to the budget is capped at US$65 million.

Principal photography begins in Rosarito, Mexico, in September. Adam Greenberg replaces Deschanel as cinematographer.

Almost immediately, the budget again becomes a concern. Cameron is committed to making the ship look authentic and its sinking realistic. He believes previous versions of the story were not as exciting as they might have been because there were too many compromises in these areas. His commitment creates immense technical problems, which means that a day's shooting costs around US$250,000. By October 1996, US$75 million has been spent.

To contain the overspend, Fox suggests a number of cuts in the script. The studio also thinks that the producer, Jon Landau, is too close to Cameron and is not exercising sufficiently tight control over the spending. Martz Katz is appointed as supervising producer so that more control can be exercised.

At a meeting with Fox on 23 December, Cameron reassigns his profit participation to the studio to help with the budget problems.

1997   By the time shooting finishes in March, US$150 million has been spent.

Post-production takes place during the spring and summer. Cameron is closely involved in all its aspects. He effectively edits the film, even though two experienced editors, Richard Harris and Conrad Buff, have been employed.

James Horner is hired to write the music. On his own initiative he writes a song, which he persuades Celine Dion to record.

> *Titanic* is test screened in Minneapolis on 14 July. The audience is very enthusiastic. Further screenings in Portland and Anaheim produce similar responses. After minor adjustments, the finished film receives its first public screening at the Tokyo Film Festival on 1 November.
>
> *Titanic* goes on general release in December. Its final budget is US$200 million.
>
> 1998   *Titanic* wins 11 Oscars (best picture, director, cinematography, film editing, art direction, visual effects, sound, sound editing, song, score and costume).
>
> The film takes over US$1 billion in the domestic and international box offices. Approximately 994 people worked on it.

The size of budgets, financial instability, the number of people involved and the complicated artistic process – all these features are highlighted in our descriptions of the making of *Blade Runner, Up Close and Personal* and *Titanic.* The starting point for this book was our increasing awareness, especially when we were teaching a university course about modern Hollywood filmmaking, of how inadequately such features were dealt with in existing accounts.

We were most struck by the failure to confront the collective nature of Hollywood filmmaking. One of the most evident facts about Hollywood film crews is that they are made up of large numbers of people: actors, carpenters, cinematographers, composers, costume designers, directors, editors, electricians, hairdressers, painters, producers, production designers, scriptwriters, sound designers, and stunt men and women. These people contribute a wide variety of skills to the production of a film, but critics of all kinds focus predominantly on one contribution, the director's. Other contributions are marginalized. As we continued teaching and researching in this area, we became increasingly curious about those 'other contributions'. This book was written, as much as anything, to satisfy that curiosity.

The reason for such an exclusive focus on the director is not hard to find. Direction has been identified as the creative heart of filmmaking. This is a belief that can be found almost anywhere film is discussed: in newspaper articles and radio and television programmes just as much as in academic books. By now the belief has a taken-for-granted quality. David Bordwell and Kristin Thompson's statement of it, in their influential textbook, *Film Art,* has the advantage that it is supported by a clear and concise rationale.

> Most people who study cinema regard the director as the film's 'author'. Although the writer prepares a script, later phases of production can modify the script beyond recognition. And although the producer monitors the entire process, he or she seldom controls moment-by-moment activity on the set. It is the director who makes crucial decisions about performance, staging, lighting, framing, cutting and sound. On the whole the director has most control over how a movie looks and sounds.

... For the most part it is the director who shapes the film's unique form and style, and these two components are central to cinema as an art.

(Bordwell and Thompson, 2001: 33)

The justification for recognizing the director as the author of the film is the control he/she has over the key aspects of filmmaking: staging, lighting, framing, sound and cutting. It is through the use of these that films are given the qualities that establish them as an art form.

The identification of the director as the key figure does not automatically mean that the contributions of other filmmakers will be ignored but it certainly has encouraged neglect of them. Films are routinely discussed as if the director was also the cinematographer, editor, writer, production designer, etc. Bordwell and Thompson (2001), for example, provide discussions of five films (*His Girl Friday*, *North by Northwest*, *Do the Right Thing*, *Breathless* and *Tokyo Story*) as demonstrations of how film criticism should be approached. Apart from the directors of these films, the work of only one other filmmaker is referred to (cinematographer Raoul Coutard's contribution to *Breathless*).

This account of filmmaking is one that, by now, has a long history. The basic assumptions come from the ideas developed in the magazine, *Cahiers du Cinema*, in the late 1940s and 1950s. It is a tribute to the power of the *Cahiers* of that era that its ideas are so strongly present in a textbook such as *Film Art*, the latest edition of which was published in 2001. But it is also disconcerting that they should have such a recognizable presence, given the way they have been argued about and criticized over the past 40 years.

Thomas Schatz, to take just one of the most obvious examples, in *The Genius of the System*, has provided a convincing account of Hollywood filmmaking in the 1930s, 1940s and 1950s in which he shows that the director's role was often far from the central one. But accounts like Schatz's, although their quality has been recognized, have failed to change the basic framework. As the quotation from *Film Art* suggests, *Cahiers*' ideas still provide the dominant framework for film criticism and theory. Concepts such as *auteur* and *mise-en-scène*, key parts of that framework, have become staples of writing about film by both academics and journalists. Explanations of them are central topics of introductory courses for film students.

The *Cahiers*' critics were writing at a time when both the cinema's cultural status and its distinct identity were still uncertain. Their first project was to give the cinema cultural legitimacy, to put it on an equal footing with the traditional, high-prestige arts such as painting, the novel and classical music. Their starting position was that great art was a form of personal expression. It was therefore necessary to demonstrate that there were individual filmmakers whose work had the same kind of personal expressiveness as the work of great painters, musicians, poets and novelists. Filmmakers whose work had this quality were *auteurs*.

Their second project was to give the cinema distinctiveness as an art form. They did this by arguing that a film was much more than its script (because this would tie cinema too closely to literature). The quality of a film was to be found in its images. A film was written in its images, not words. If this was the case, the person responsible for the character of the images (what the *Cahiers*' writers called its *mise-en-scène*) would be the creator. The director was the key figure, not the writer.

In the context in which they were developed, *Cahiers'* ideas were undoubtedly liberating. However, we believe that they have left a legacy of problems that ought now to be confronted, especially for anybody interested in Hollywood cinema. The most obvious one is that the commitment to the individual artist discourages interest in the collective nature of film production. Our central aim in this book is to encourage interest. To do so we have investigated filmmaking from different perspectives, asking ourselves a range of questions: what contributions do the cinematographer, the editor, the sound designer and all the others involved make to a film? Are their roles principally supporting ones? How do they relate to each other? Is it accurate to describe them as technicians? What do they think about the work they do?

Our overall ambition is to understand the dynamics of filmmaking. To do so properly, we found it necessary to place the contribution of individual filmmakers within the larger framework of film production – the framework indicated by our narratives of the making of *Blade Runner, Up Close and Personal* and *Titanic*. As a result of doing so, we became dissatisfied with an aesthetic position that makes personal expression its central value. In most forms of cinema, but especially Hollywood, there are a variety of well-known constraints on personal expressiveness. If they are recognized, the attachment to personal expression as an artistic value condemns the cinema to be a second-rate art.

There were two other issues that concerned us:

1   the identification of images as the creative dimension has encouraged a dogmatic belief that cinema is a visual medium. As a consequence, the role of sound has been neglected or downplayed;

2   discussing cinema in the general context of 'art' has produced myopia about its commitment to 'entertainment'. It is this commitment that poses some of the most interesting problems about cinema as a form of modern cultural production.

These are important issues, which we do not have the space to deal with adequately in this book. They do have a presence, shaping our discussions in a variety of ways.

We chose contemporary Hollywood cinema for our exploration. By this, we mean the period from the early 1970s (*The Godfather, Jaws, Star Wars*) to the present day. This is, for us, a distinctive period in filmmaking that might well be called post-studio Hollywood because the character of the studios had changed so much; they were now owned by large business conglomerates. Where once studios had been all-embracing filmmaking enterprises, they were now commissioners of projects. There were other important changes. Movie-going was no longer a regular habit; it was now an occasional choice. A new generation of filmmakers had emerged whose ideas about filmmaking had been strongly influenced by the French New Wave. These filmmakers were freelances rather than studio employees. New technology (sound, visual effects) increasingly affected the way films were made.

There were two substantial reasons for choosing this period. First, the issues we are particularly concerned with are highlighted by the large crews and sophisticated technologies that have become so characteristic of contemporary filmmaking. Second, the sources of information about the period are particularly rich. We have been greatly helped by interviews with filmmakers, descriptions of the making of individual films and the DVD commentaries that are now so freely available.

There was a third reason for choosing contemporary Hollywood cinema – our own enthusiasm for the films. We are conscious that this engagement gives the book two themes. We are interested in some general critical problems and we are also interested in the character of contemporary Hollywood cinema.

We do have a thesis that unites these themes. Film scholarship has certainly changed since the *Cahiers'* critics first made their intervention. Marxism, semiology, psychoanalysis, feminism and post-modernism have all left their marks. Despite this, writers about film are still heavily dependent on concepts originating in *Cahiers du Cinema*: *auteur, mise-en-scène,* personal expression, film as a visual medium and cinema as art. We think those concepts are unhelpful for understanding most forms of cinema, but especially a cinema such as contemporary Hollywood. Contemporary film scholarship needs a new critical framework.

chapter two

The politics of filmmaking

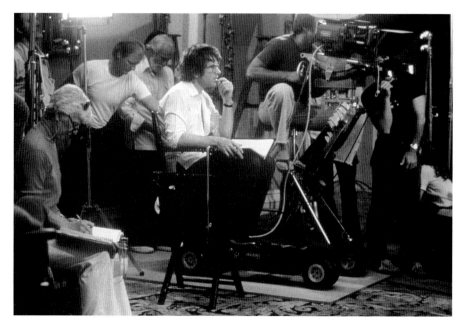

Fig 2.1 On the set of *Heaven Can Wait,* 1978. (Photo: Paramount/The Kobal Collection)

Walter Murch, with his vast experience of filmmaking as both a sound designer and an editor, asks:

> How do you get 150 temperamental artistic types to work together on the same project, and make something that not only comes in on schedule, on budget, but that has an artistic coherence. It's simply beyond the ability of a single person, a director or a producer, to cause that to happen by any series of direct commands. It's so complicated it just can't be done. The question is: how does it happen?
>
> (Ondaatje, 2002: 84)

Murch does not answer the question. In fact the process is not nearly so open as he makes it appear. When a film is being made, 150 individuals do not confront each other on equal terms. Most importantly, a division of labour exists. A crew is divided into separate departments that are organized around particular skills (cinematography, editing, sound, etc.). Each of these departments has a hierarchical structure. So, for example, cinematography is structured along the lines shown in Figure 2.2 (depending on the film's budget):

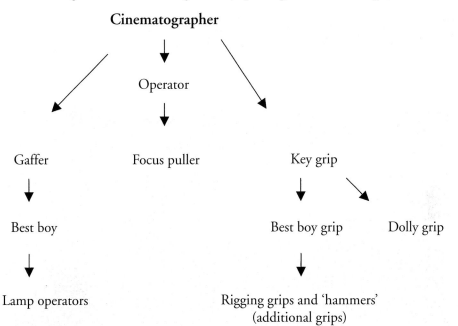

Fig 2.2

There is, of course, an overall structure into which individual departments fit. This is much harder to describe formally because it changes from film to film. It often looks like that shown in Figure 2.3.

Director

Writer–Actors–Production designer–Cinematographer–Editor–Sound designer–Special effects–Composer

Fig 2.3

The structure is not quite so flat and shallow as this figure makes it appear. Making a film is a dynamic process. At different stages in the production of a film the relationship between the director and the other filmmakers changes. Some figures come into the foreground as others drop back. In pre-production the dominant relationship is likely to be between the director and production designer; during shooting the director/cinematographer relationship replaces it, while in post-production the relationship between the director and the editor is the strong one.

There are also two contributors who complicate the structure and can disrupt it. The producer is a significant figure in Hollywood filmmaking, as later chapters will indicate. However, the producer is absent from Figure 2.3. The reason is that producers perform their role in different ways. The one thing they have in common is general responsibility for financial and administrative issues. Some producers confine themselves to these areas; unless the film goes significantly over budget, they are unlikely to limit or challenge the director's authority. However, other producers play a much more substantial role. They may initiate the project, hire the writer, contract the stars and choose the director. Some producers go even further and exercise close control over all phases of the making of a film: writing, casting, shooting and editing. Consequently there are a number of different places where a producer could be placed in the figure.

As well as producers, stars can destabilize the situation. As actors they are formally under the director's control; however, because of their status as stars, they have the *de facto* power to intervene at any stage of the film's production.

So the answer to Murch's question is that the 150 artistic types can work together because they work within a hierarchical structure that is similar to that found in the military, with a chain of command; the director or producer does not have to tell each of the other 149 people directly what they should be doing. The structure is sufficiently stable for most films to be made successfully. However, one of the reasons filmmaking is a fraught activity is the presence of destabilizing forces within the system.

Of all the people involved, who, besides the director, makes a significant creative contribution? The way in which budgets are drawn up suggests one answer. A distinction is made between costs that are above the line and costs that are below the line (the 'line' being a purely formal distinction that indicates how budgets are drawn up). Payments to stars, directors, writers and producers are above the line; payments to all the other contributors are below the line. Above-the-line payments are much larger than those below the line. The distinction appears to have been established on the basis of two rather different measures. Power is one. The distinction signifies who has the most power in the making of a film and, on this basis, it makes sense. Stars, producers and directors certainly have more power than any of the other contributors – though writers are a different kettle of fish!

The second measure is creativity. The distinction appears to mark off those contributions that are considered creative from those considered technical. It is significant, for example, that none of the above-the-line contributors have a direct relationship with technology in the way that below-the-line contributors, such as cinematographers or editors, do. On this basis, we do not believe that the distinction is a helpful one. It is based on an outmoded idea that craft and technology are separate from creativity. The most superficial examination of the work of cinematographers, sound designers, editors or production designers reveals that the nature of their work is just as creative as that of writers, stars or directors.

We think William Goldman's discussion of the issue is more helpful. Goldman suggests that the significant creative contributions should be widely spread and that altogether ten contributions should be taken into account:

1 Actor (Star)

2 Cinematographer

3 Composer

4 Director

5 Editor

6 Producer

7 Production designer

8 Sound designer

9 Writer

10 Visual effects.

Goldman's choices seem to us to be intuitively correct. All of these contributors make decisions that are easily recognized as creative ones. A cinematographer makes decisions about the quality of light, an editor about the rhythm of a scene, a production designer about appropriate colours . . . Decisions such as these are not simply a matter of pressing buttons or repeating what has been done many times before.

Goldman's choices also help to clarify the structure of filmmaking since they cover all areas that contribute to a finished film. Seven of the contributors (cinematographer, director, editor, producer, production designer, sound designer, visual effects) are responsible for groups of people. If these groups are added together, more or less the entire film crew is accounted for.

What kind of people perform the roles Goldman suggests are the primary creative ones? Lacking the resources for a substantial, systematic survey, we carried out a limited one by noting details of all the filmmakers (171) we came across in the course of our research. The picture that emerges is, to a large extent, predictable. The filmmakers are predominantly white; coloured people are especially noticeable by their absence (we only came across three coloured filmmakers). The group is also predominantly male, with women making up only 11 per cent of the total. Its members are generally well educated – 70 per cent had some form of higher education. They are also well prepared for work in the movies by the education they had received. Approximately half of the filmmakers entered the industry having taken courses that prepared them for their future careers. Those who did not take such courses had often been prepared through work in similar professions, such as stage, radio or television. A relatively small number (7 per cent) entered the industry directly and received on-the-job training.

The overall figures disguise great variations within particular areas. We did not come across any female cinematographers, for example, but just over 30 per cent of production designers are female. Writers were less likely to have had an education that related to their future career – only 17 per cent had taken a relevant course – but they were more likely to have attended elite universities. In contrast, well over 90 per cent of production designers and cinematographers had taken relevant courses.

There is little research with which we could check these figures but what there is supports the picture that emerges from our work. In their survey of producers, directors and writers in the period 1965–82, Stephen Powers, David J. Rothman and Stanley Rothman draw a similar portrait of a group dominated heavily by white males. Interestingly, their research suggests that the political and cultural attitudes of the group were predominantly liberal. In her research on the position of women in Hollywood, Martha Lauzen discovered that 19 per cent of the executive producers, producers, directors, writers, cinematographers and editors working on the top box office films of 2001 were women. She also discovered that there had been no substantial change between 1987 and 2001 in the number of women who directed (3 per cent in 1987, 6 per cent in 2001) or wrote (7 per cent in 1987, 8 per cent in 2001) one of the top 100 films of those years.

The most substantial research done in this area is Emmanuel Levy's study of stars. For our purposes, the study has obvious limitations. It covers only one group of filmmakers and its main focus is on a different period (1930–84) from ours. This is a pity, because Levy studies the social background of stars in a detailed and informative way. In so far as any conclusions can be drawn from his research about the period we are interested in, stars appear to be an idiosyncratic group in some important respects. Although males very obviously dominate, females have, for obvious reasons, a stronger presence than amongst other groups of filmmakers. Also, stars as a whole are less likely to have had higher education than members of the other groups. Levy also makes the interesting point that stars as a group come from a wider social class base than do elite groups in other industries. We did not, unfortunately, have the information to check how this compares with other groups of filmmakers.

The only (mild) surprise that comes out of the overall research is Powers' and Rothmans' finding that producers, directors and writers are generally liberal in their social attitudes. It would be interesting to see if this applies to all the filmmakers we are concerned with. The overall picture is of a homogeneous group. The typical figure is a white male who has had some form of higher education, either of a general character (university degree) or a professional character (film or art school training). It seems likely that this homogeneity amongst the major creative contributors is another reason why Murch's '150 temperamental artistic types' find it possible to work together.

chapter three

What do filmmakers think about filmmaking?

Fig 3.1 On the set of *Insomnia*, 2002. (Photo: Alcon Entertainment/Section Eight Limited/The Kobal Collection/Rob McEwan)

How do filmmakers understand their roles, the challenges they face and their relationships with each other? We investigated their self-consciousness about the filmmaking process. In our desire to give them a strong presence, we have tried as much as possible to allow them to express their attitudes in their own words.

Producers

The producer's role in filmmaking has always been an elusive one. It has become increasingly so over the past 30 years, as producer credits have begun to proliferate: executive producer, associate producer, supervising producer, line producer, etc. Many of these credits do not indicate that a person has played a substantial role in the actual making of the film. They may do no more than acknowledge that, at some point, that person had something to do with the film. For example, the head of the company that finances the film may be credited as an executive producer, or the agent of a star may be credited as associate producer.

How do those producers who do make a substantial contribution describe their role? Reflecting on his experiences as a producer, Art Linson says his function is to be 'the mayonnaise in the sandwich'. However, when he describes in detail how he works, the metaphor seems a misleading one. Take his account of how he produced *Great Expectations*. Linson had a deal to produce films for Twentieth Century Fox. His son suggested that a version of *Great Expectations* set in the present day would be a good idea for a movie. Linson liked the idea and worked with a writer, Mitch Glazer, to develop it. Linson then chose the director, Alfonso Cuarón, cast Gwyneth Paltrow and Ethan Hawke in the main parts and persuaded Robert de Niro to play a cameo. A satisfactory script had not been completed before shooting began. Linson had to mediate between the writer and director when differences emerged about how the problems should be solved. He also had to deal with the film falling behind schedule and going over budget. When the editing of the movie was finished, it was clear that there were holes in the story and that a narration would be needed to cover them. Linson got David Mamet to write the narration. All of these decisions had to be made in the context of getting and maintaining the support of Twentieth Century Fox. In such a situation, it would be more accurate to say that, rather than being the mayonnaise, Linson was the chef both making and mixing it.

Lynda Obst describes the challenges faced by a producer as a consequence of this:

> That film noir thriller the director wants to make is the buddy picture the studio wants (well, two guys are in it). The psychopathic loner the actor wants to play is the same guy as the crusading cop the studio wants (well, he changes). You must convince every party that you want what they want and what they (the big 'they') want is what he wants, and you must march all of them toward the goal line more aware of what they have in common than what they will later discover they don't.
>
> This will be your job for the rest of the show. (For the rest of your life.) The danger here is obvious. If you're papering over an abyss too wide, you'll fall through. You will spend the rest of the show fighting these competing notions and stretching yourself like a human canvas over the gaping chasm. Believe me, this is an extremely unpleasant sensation.
>
> (Obst, 1996: 66)

There are some significant differences between producers, especially regarding their relationship with the director. Loretha Jones describes one view when she says, 'I want to make sure that the director's vision of it [the film] is protected' (Kent, 1991: 202). Albert Ruddy elaborates on this:

> You must build a wall around [the director] so that he can address the greatest possible amount of his creative energies to the execution of the film and not be concerned with a lot of other pressures.
>
> (Kent, 1991: 202)

George Lucas takes a different view. Discussing the making of the early *Star Wars* trilogy, he explained:

> They were done . . . with me as executive producer, casting them, writing the scripts, determining the look, everything. I shot second unit and I was there every day to approve everything. *Empire* is Kersh's movie, he was a huge creative force on it, but if he strayed too far off the path, we wouldn't go there. It was a collaborative thing. It wasn't like I was off in an office someplace and they delivered a movie. It wasn't really out of my control at all. The deal was that they would handle the daily operations on the set and I would be the overseer.
>
> (Solman *et al.*, 2002: 32)

In a much more aggressive fashion, Don Simpson stated this view of the relationship when he described how he and his partner, Jerry Bruckheimer, approached the making of a film:

> We don't take a passive role in any shape or form. Some directors who shall remain nameless do regard movies as an extension of their internal emotional landscape, but Jerry and I decide on the movie we want to make. We then hire an all-star team who can implement the vision. I don't believe in the *auteur* theory.
>
> (Fleming, 1998: 44)

Producers are also divided about their goals. Lynda Obst articulated her goals in this way:

> . . . our work is meaningful when we make movies about the things that move us, provoke us, inspire us, that *engage* and compel us . . . If the products of our efforts reach the screen, the bookstore, the public in any way – regardless of whether they are hits or flops – and they have some kernel of fineness, some ineffable, original first-rateness that only *we* could have provided, it all will have been for something worthwhile.
>
> (Obst, 1996: 235)

Challenged about the kinds of films he makes, Joel Silver expressed a very different set of goals:

> I love these kinds of movies, and so do the audience. Why do you perceive *Lethal Weapon* as a lesser kind of movie? Why is it lesser than something else – because it doesn't have a *message*? The message is entertainment, that's what our movies are about, *entertainment* . . . That's what we *do*, entertaining movies, why must they be perceived as something more?
>
> (Thomas, 1992: 76)

Screenwriters

Screenwriters' attitudes to their work mark them out in significant ways from all other contributors. The most obvious difference is the great anxiety they display about the cultural value of screenwriting. Richard Price expresses this anxiety in its most extreme form:

... Screenwriting – there's no reason to do it except to make money. I would take the crummiest novelist over the best screenwriter as a talent, as a legitimate artist. I mean it's a job, screenwriting is a job.

(Schanzer and Wright, 1993: 82)

Larry McMurtry expresses the same attitude in a more measured way:

In the first place, screenwriting is *not* hard work, intellectually or physically. It is a form of piecework, generally done in collaboration with other people, so that even the labor of conception is shared. Take the best screenplay ever written – if you can find it – and compare it, say, with *Middlemarch*, or with *The Origins of Totalitarianism*, to use a couple of admittedly disparate examples. Which looks like hard work, which like fun and games? And the comparison is not meant to denigrate the screenplay, merely to draw a distinction. The screenplay is only secondarily a *written* thing; it is an elaborate notation, or, put another way, a kind of codified visualization. It is the kind of work that does not require the writer to wrestle overmuch with his psyche. It can be written quickly and fortunately, rewritten quickly, as the director, in wrestling with *his* psyche, discovers that he needs the visualization refined.

(McMurtry, 2001: 56)

This sense that screenwriting is always overshadowed by 'literature' runs through all screenwriters' comments on their work. William Goldman characteristically quips, 'movies are not Chekov' while Callie Khourie says she does not think that 'screenwriting is great literary writing'.

There are few positive statements of the value of screenwriting to set against these denigrations. When screenwriters make such statements, they tend to appeal to different criteria; to the influence their work might have rather than its cultural value:

As a screenwriter, you have the opportunity to talk to the world. You have to decide, given that opportunity, what you want to say. To me, that carries with it an incredible weight and responsibility. If someone were to come up to you right now and give you a microphone that keyed into every television on the planet, what would you tell people?

(Schanzer and Wright, 1993: 110)

But even this affirmation of the value of screenwriting is compromised. In the same interview, Bruce Joel Rubin still feels the need to acknowledge the superiority of literature. Screenwriting, he says, 'allows you to do just enough good writing to make you feel like a writer. But not so much that you think of yourself as a novelist, a real writer'.

Screenwriters' uncertainty about the value of their work is heightened by their sense of insecurity. Unlike any of the other contributors, screenwriters are aware (1) that they are likely to be replaced by other writers; and (2) that even if they remain on the film throughout its production, their work is likely to be changed by directors, actors, producers or studio executives. William Goldman sums up the prevailing attitude of writers to this situation:

Few of the powers out there know what a cameraman does, but they know they can't do it. Occasionally a cameraman gets replaced, but not often. The same for the other technicians.

They don't know what we do, either, but they do know the alphabet, and they also have lists of dozens of other writers who can change what we've done.

(Goldman, 1985: 402)

As well as having strong feelings of insecurity and inferiority, screenwriters have a profoundly divided awareness about where their position is in the creative process. Many see themselves as secondary to the director and believe that the nature of filmmaking means that the director is the dominant creative figure. Ron Bass is unequivocal that 'the storyteller in film is not the screenwriter, it's the director' (Schanzer and Wright, 1993: 23). Judith Rascoe takes a similar view, 'I believe very strongly that I'm a member of the director's crew, I am not the co-author of the film' (Schanzer and Wright, 1993: 149). Bass elaborates on this position:

You can't do everything by committee and one person's vision has to tell the story . . . you have a different role when you are writing for screen, and you're always going to be disappointed if you can't accept that. Unless you find a director who's your identical twin, his vision will be personal and it will always be different from yours.

(Schanzer and Wright, 1993: 23)

Other writers want more emphasis to be placed on the writer's contribution. Discussing her contribution to *Edward Scissorhands*, Caroline Thompson complained:

. . . screenwriters work really hard at what we do, and it's a very distinct job. I did feel hurt by the pieces written about *Edward Scissorhands* when it was always Tim Burton's vision, or ninety percent of the time it was Tim Burton's vision. There was a lot of me in that movie, and anybody who knows me can see me in it. But to the public at large, it wasn't mine at all, it was Tim's completely.

(Schanzer and Wright, 1993: 238)

Joe Esterhas pushes the logic of Thompson's claim even further and suggests that the contribution of the screenwriter is more important than that of the director:

I have dealt with the same themes in *Jagged Edge* and *Betrayed* and *Music Box* and *Basic Instinct*. The themes are: do we ever know the people we love? What part of us remains private and inviolate? How do we manipulate each other? Where is deceit in the context of love? Now, okay, those are four pictures. The first was directed by Richard Marquand, the second was directed by Costa-Gravas, the third was directed by Costa, the fourth was directed by Paul Verhoven. If you look at these movies as a body of work, to whom do these themes belong? Do they belong to the three different directors on those pictures? Or do they belong to the man who wrote all four pictures?

(Schanzer and Wright, 1993: 273)

Not all screenwriters want to make the choice between director and screenwriter or regard their two contributions as privileged ones. William Goldman has been a forceful and articulate spokesman for collective authorship. As we have already noted, Goldman asserts that filmmaking is a group endeavour and suggests that there are approximately ten contributors whose work is crucial to the success or failure of a film. He believes that 'to elevate any single element in a film is simply silly and wrong. We all contribute, we are all at each other's mercy' (Goldman, 1985: 102).

Another area that marks screenwriters out from the other contributors is a concern with entertainment. They are more likely than any of the other contributors to talk about it directly. They speak eloquently about the thrill they get from seeing an audience being entertained by a film they have written.

> The best part was sitting in an audience, listening to the girls do those puppy responses, 'Aawwwhhh'. I loved listening to the laughing and I loved it when I could hear the crying at the end; I just loved it. It still gives me goosebumps to think about it. It was a really great first experience. [Caroline Thompson on *Edward Scissorhands*].
>
> (Schanzer and Wright, 1993: 234)

However, while screenwriters acknowledge the importance of entertainment as part of the movie-going experience, there is almost always an undertone when it is discussed as an artistic goal. Reservations are implied and suggestions made that a film needs to be more than entertaining:

> Not that you can't just tell wonderful entertainments, not that you can't tell good frightening and thrilling movies, but I think if you feel there's a higher purpose involved, your film is going to have a greater richness and a greater impact.
> [Bruce Joel Rubin] (Schanzer and Wright, 1993: 110)

Rubin is effectively making the traditional art/entertainment distinction. It is a distinction that nearly always has a presence when screenwriters discuss their work

Unlike most of the other contributors, technique is not something that preoccupies screenwriters. There are certainly references to it but little sense of a systematic concern. In particular, the 'three act structure', which is much referred to by screenwriting teachers and by critics, does not seem to be a matter of great interest. It comes up only when interviewers ask screenwriters about it directly. Opinions are, predictably, divided about its value.

Directors

How do directors conceive their work? They certainly make it clear how wide-ranging their involvement in the making of a film is likely to be. It is also clear, however, that they are involved at different levels of intensity. James Cameron involves himself (or tries to) intimately in every area of production. Few directors are as ambitious as this. Even Steven Spielberg, who has a wide-ranging technical competence, is content to leave the responsibility for some areas to other people:

Now I delegate happily the functions that I feel there are people much better equipped to execute than I am – functions like makeup and set construction and composing music. These are things I used to do myself, but now I delegate them to people with whom I feel very secure – and I never look back. But there are other functions that I continue to get involved in – where the person is either my surrogate or my sounding board, and I pretty much work directly with these functions through the person that I hire.

(Friedman and Notbohm, 2000: 62)

When asked what their most important tasks are, the majority of directors highlight the work they do in pre-production:

The principle [sic] job of a director is to first get his script and get it right and get it playable and get it almost foolproof. Then his job is to cast it as perfectly as he can.

[George Roy Hill] (Goldman, 1985: 392)

Most directors reply in similar terms, especially in relation to the script. For some, this means that directing and writing are intimately linked and are best done by the same person. Anthony Minghella says he 'can't imagine wanting to write a film and not direct it because they are such an organic activity' (Kagan, 2000: 20).

Coming to terms with the script is a demanding task. It is necessary to make sure that it works in obvious dramatic terms – the plot is coherent, the characters are well defined, the dialogue is lively, the action is varied, etc. However, there is a second stage. Sidney Lumet says that the most important decision he has to make is 'What is this movie about . . . what is the theme of the movie, the spine, the arc?' (Lumet, 1995: 10). Having decided on this, he says, he then knows how it should be cast, how it will look, how it will be edited and scored.

Mike Nichols describes the process in more grandiose terms than Lumet but also sees it as crucial for the success of a film:

It seems to me that, to a greater extent than a play, a movie's artistic success, success as an experience, depends on the power of the metaphor that is the central engine of the movie. If you have a powerful metaphor, if the audience knows why you're there, you can soar very high. If you don't have that metaphor, no amount of cleverness with the camera or talent on the part of the actors can lift it, because the engine that is the metaphor is everything.

(Smith, 1999: 18)

And when asked where the metaphor came from he replied, 'It's in the story – it's as simple as that. The story either contains it or it doesn't' (Smith,1999: 18).

Having decided what the movie is about, what its metaphor is, directors see themselves facing a second key task. It is important that everybody working on the film understands what the theme or metaphor is. Sidney Lumet describes this as making sure that 'the costume designer is not doing *Turandot* when the rest of us are doing *Prince Igor*' (Smith, 1992: 60).

Most directors regard production as the most difficult part of filmmaking. They repeatedly complain about the intense pressures created by the need to make a lot of decisions very quickly, knowing that these decisions could have serious consequences for the quality of the film.

> ... a director is asked five million questions every single day. And you've got to make all those decisions very fast. And over the course of eight, nine, ten weeks, an accumulation of the wrong choices and your movie is fucked up!
>
> [Spike Lee] (Breskin, 1997: 179)

The common attitude to the different stages of filmmaking is well expressed by Steven Spielberg:

> The conception of the story is the most exciting part about making a picture for me. The second most exciting part is assembling the film. The most nerve-wracking part of the movie, the process that I most dislike, is the actual shooting and directing of the picture.
>
> (Friedman and Notbohm, 2000: 16)

Production is most likely to be discussed in terms of images and actors. Although they are rarely explicit about it, most directors take the widely accepted view that cinema is a visual art. Predictably, Tim Burton is the most up-front about this:

> Cinema is a visual medium so everything that you do – even if it's not blurting out to the audience on a completely conscious level: 'This is what I am' – everything is meaningful in terms of the look of things.
>
> (Burton, 1995: 38)

However, what directors contribute to the creation of images varies enormously. At one extreme, Steven Soderbergh feels the process is so important that he has become his own cinematographer. At the other, Jonathan Demme says that he leaves the creation of the images entirely to his cinematographer.

There are only a few exceptions to the emphasis on visuals. Barry Levinson highlights the importance of dialogue:

> I've always been very strong on dialogue, period. My feeling has always been that the dialogue is, in fact, action if you handle it correctly and you don't need to 'employ' some kind of visual circus to keep the audience involved. If you can kick it right, then people become involved in it . . . If you handle dialogue well, give energy to it, show the shadings of it, then it's exciting.
>
> (Thompson, 1992a: 35)

More broadly, David Cronenberg says he does not think film is specifically a visual medium and that visuals are just one of the many elements a director has at his disposal.

Acting is an area that creates problems for directors. There are directors, especially those who have been actors or who have had extensive experience in the theatre, who have no problems in handling actors. But many directors express anxiety about this task. Most of this anxiety comes from a sense that acting has its own special language and methods about which they are ignorant. Also there is no common agreement about the best way of preparing actors during production. For some, such as Sidney Lumet, a rehearsal period before production begins is essential. For others, such as Barry Levinson, rehearsal can be counterproductive:

> There are certain directors who like to have extensive rehearsal periods, then do a couple of takes and move on. For me, personally, I find that nice, professional work which doesn't have an edge to it, it seems too pat. I prefer to let the actors be almost struggling with their lines and worrying about how they are going to cope with certain things, and then out of the takes that we are doing you shape a kind of behavior.
>
> (Thompson, 1992a: 43)

Few directors make explicit or self-conscious claims to be artists. However, the claim is made in an implicit way. Like writers, directors make the art/entertainment distinction. What is particularly striking about the way they make the distinction is their consistent downgrading of entertainment.

> I just was so challenged by *Schindler's List* and so fulfilled by it and so disturbed by it. It so shook up my life, in a good way, that I think I got a little taste of what a lot of other directors have existed on through their careers – people like Altman, people like Kazan, even people like Preston Sturges, who made fiercely independent films. I suddenly saw what some of the tug was to the real filmmakers, who are always drawn to the subject matter because it's dangerous. I made *Schindler's List* thinking that if it did entertain, then I would have failed. It was important to me not to set out to please. Because I always had.
>
> [Steven Spielberg] (Friedman and Notbohm, 2000: 176)

Coming from a director whose films are so linked to entertainment, Steven Spielberg's confession is illuminating. On the good side are 'real filmmakers' who choose 'dangerous' subject matter. On the bad side are 'entertainers' who aim to 'please'.

Spike Lee makes the art/entertainment distinction in just as radical a way as Steven Spielberg. He claims that most films use

> ... the same old tried and true formula, and at the end of the movie everything is wrapped up in a nice little bow. And very rarely do these movies make you think, and once you leave the theatre, by the time you're back on the subway or driving home, you've forgotten what you watched. It's like disposable entertainment. You sit there for two hours, and it washes over you and that's it. . . . I think we don't demand enough of the audience. No subtlety, playing down to the lowest common denominator, making films for an intelligence level of retarded twelve-year olds.
>
> (Breskin, 1997: 75)

What is particularly interesting about Lee's response is his awareness that questions are inevitably raised about audiences when distinctions are made between art and entertainment. In his interviews he consistently comes back to the question of the audience, shifting between blaming Hollywood for underestimating the audience and wondering whether Hollywood is right in its estimate:

> Well, I would say that with ninety-five per cent of the films put out by the studios, everything is tied up in a neat little bow. Maybe it's my duty to be that quirky five per cent where everything isn't done like that. Of course, that's going against the grain, and a lot of times audiences resent that. Maybe you're making them work too much, or think too much.
>
> (Lippy, 2000: 70)

Rather surprisingly, Steven Soderbergh, one of the most commercially successful directors in recent years, supports Lee's low view of the audience. When Soderbergh asked Dick Lester why he stopped directing films, Lester said that he felt out of touch with audiences. Soderbergh responded,

> I think filmmakers in my generation – or whatever you want to call it – feel ourselves divided further and further from the audience. For the most part, it's not an audience we feel is very discerning.
>
> (Soderbergh, 1999: 107)

Ridley Scott is much more sanguine about audiences:

> Two absolutely essential considerations are critical to the success of any so-called Hollywood movie. The first is that the end result of any film is communication with its audience. And the second is, the larger the film, the larger your budget – which also means the larger the audience you have to consider. I think a lot of people actually don't realise that.
>
> So what you've got to set in your mind, right up front, is what kind of audience you're hoping your subject will reach. Therefore, unless you're a fool you construct your story and budget and the scope of your film accordingly. In other words if you're going to end up in an art cinema, you should stay within the confines of a small budget movie, which will allow you to explore most any esoteric idea you wish. But if you're going to follow along the path of a Spielberg, then your choice of subject matter and the way you're going to explain and communicate your story to that larger audience is, of necessity, going to be on a slightly more simplified level. I wouldn't say on any less intelligent level, just less esoteric.
>
> (Sammon, 2000: 380)

Few directors are as up front and articulate about their views of the audience as Steven Soderbergh and Ridley Scott. For most of them, the audience is a source of anxiety, a necessary but elusive part of the filmmaking process.

Stars

Stars form a group that is different in character from the others. They are a subsection of the overall group constituted by actors. As a group, actors have an enormous amount in common.

Star and non-star actors do the same kind of work and that work is based on a common stock of ideas. They are divided into separate groups not by the work they do but by the different status given to actors who play leading roles as against actors who play supporting roles. Star actors have a status that gives them the power to be major contributors in the making of a film. Non-star actors do not have the same status and, as a consequence, are minor contributors.

In the initial stages of filmmaking the script is crucial for stars. Asked what her criteria were for choosing a film, Meryl Streep said 'the script, the script, the script. I'll only take jobs if I like the screenplay' (Norman, 1989). Robert de Niro's reply was similar, 'A good script, number one' (Cardullo *et al.*, 1998: 285). However, he added that he also wanted a say in the casting. For some stars, the director is more important than the script. Asked what his criteria were, Jack Nicholson replied, 'I look for a director with a script he likes a lot but I'm probably after the directors more than anything' (Cardullo *et al.*, 1998: 308).

Whether they value the script over the director or *vice versa*, once the project gets under way the star's key relationship is with the director. Whenever stars discuss their work, this relationship is a main theme. It is, however, discussed in a different way from that in which other groups, such as cinematographers or editors, discuss it. There are almost no references to the 'director's vision'. The discussion is much more of an operational kind. Much of it relates to the general problems actors face and is not specific to stars. What kind of support should a director provide? There are some stars, such as Harvey Keitel, who want to discuss every detail with the director before they play the role. Most stars do not want this kind of detail, but simply a general indication of how the director sees the character. Stars may differ over the amount of preparatory work that is necessary but they are united in demanding the freedom to shape their performances in the way they see fit. Jeff Daniels gives a good account of the consensus:

> But whenever it's possible, I'll ask the director what he wants. I'll listen to what he says, and take that and try to do it in my own way. Then, we'll both be heading in the same direction. . . . I also don't think it's good to walk into a scene that you're shooting with the attitude that there's only one way to play it. . . . If I've done some research I know some basics, I have some skill and some craft, and the director and I agree about the character in a general way, then I try to give the director and the editor four or five different spins on each scene. That way, the director and editor can have a good time picking which one they want.
>
> (Cardullo *et al.*, 1998: 256)

That stars' relationships with directors are often difficult is well known. Stars provide some vivid accounts of such difficulties. Susan Sarandon's account of her relationship with George Miller on *The Witches of Eastwick* and Dustin Hoffman's account of his relationship with Sidney Pollack on *Tootsie* are two of the best examples. Some stars see the conflicts that arise as helpful. Jack Nicholson says, 'It's through conflict that you come out with something that might be different, better than either of you thought to begin with' (Cardullo *et al.*, 1998: 306). However, Jeff Daniels points out that such conflicts can escalate into a struggle for artistic control of the movie. Dustin Hoffman has been most forthright in discussing the situation from the star's point of view:

I think that some directors are close minded about what an actor can contribute. You'll hear directors say sometimes, 'Yes, I got a performance out of that actor; I had to push him. I had to push him further than he thought he could go'. Well, there are probably a lot of uncredited occasions where actors have pushed directors in areas that they haven't gone before, and I think there have been more than a few occasions where a picture is better because of an actor who is in it. They will say, 'The actor is subjective – only cares about his own part'. Not so. An actor is as capable of considering 'the whole' as the director, and often does. Sure we care about our own parts, but we have a responsibility to the entire film also, and I don't think many of us ignore that responsibility. And, believe me, I know some very subjective directors, who focus mostly on covering their ass.

(Cardullo *et al.*, 1998: 295)

While few stars are as forthright as Hoffman, questions of authority are always present when the star/director relationship is discussed.

Although critics often suggest that there is a particular aesthetic of star acting, stars show little awareness of what it might be. In general, their ideas about acting are the same as those of non-star actors. The most widely shared approach is one clearly influenced by Method ideas. Lindsay Crouse is one of the most articulate exponents of these ideas:

There is always something going on. Some people call it subtext; to me it's the quintessential thing that you're doing. That's where the art of acting lies – something has to come out of my mouth, which may be the opposite of what I am really doing. I have to be doing that second thing so strongly that you know it, that it's clear, even though I'm saying something entirely different. That's why Lee (Strasberg) says that the text is your enemy. Because in that sense, you are not there to act out the text. You are there to bring out, with all the force of your being, that action of the play.

(Zucker, 1990: 20)

Two important issues emerge from this account. The first is that the script has a provisional basis, 'the text is your enemy'. An actor who believes this will clearly not be bound by the script and will feel free to make changes. Robert de Niro estimates that 20–25 per cent of the finished film will be different from the screenplay. The second issue is that such an approach favours a particular kind of drama, one where the characters have psychological depth.

Along with the concept of subtext, another concept that is frequently referred to is 'being in the moment'. Jennifer Jason Leigh links the two when she says that, 'You can't play subtext . . . but if you're honestly in the moment, all of that will be there' (Smith, 1990: 56). The concept of 'being in the moment' suggests an actor should play a scene as if it were happening for the first time, approach the scene without preconceptions and be alert to the particularities of the situation. A constant refrain is that an actor is most likely to be in the moment if he/she 'listens' to the other actors in the scene and does not take what they say and do for granted.

'Playing the subtext', 'being in the moment' – these are means for getting the actor to their ultimate goal, which is usually characterized by words such as 'honesty' and 'truth'.

> You know, you have to be very honest. As an actor, I work on that probably more than anything else. I say, be honest, be honest, be honest. Come to it with the truth, don't lie. And that's from within, because it's all lying, in a way. Acting is lying, because we're not in 1963 at a rally but in 1991 at a staged set, but there is an area within the acting itself that is honesty. Within that given world that you have re-created, you have to try to be honest and truthful.
>
> [Denzel Washington] (Lee, 1993: 116)

For Robert Duvall this commitment to truth marks an important development in Hollywood acting.

> I always wanted to be as truthful as possible, and I felt that many of the old actors were not very truthful – except for a guy like Spencer Tracy, who was just marvellous, and Walter Huston too. I think we helped the actors who came after us.
>
> (Smith, 1997: 35)

However, Duvall also expresses an awareness that the commitment creates a dilemma for the actor. He describes what the director, Ubu Grosbard, said to him about his role in *True Confessions*:

> 'You don't have to worry about getting anywhere, just see where it goes, forget about energy.' Usually, it's the other way round – directors want [snapping fingers] energy, pace – which is what's wrong with so many movies: you just see everybody up there trying to do something.
>
> (Smith, 1997: 33)

When he came to direct a film himself, Duvall discovered that the choice between energy/pace and truth is not easily made. He wanted the actors to be truthful in their work but he found himself asking them to keep the story moving as well. As a result he was forced to pare down some scenes and cut others out.

Michael Douglas found that combining the roles of producer and actor produced the same dilemma. Describing his work on *Romancing the Stone*, he said:

> . . . we take a nice leisurely time setting up the character, Joan Wilder, as a romantic novelist – and we reshot all that. We had to reshoot the whole opening, with Kathleen as the writer. My job was to come in and create – I could check off responsibilities, pick up the pace of the picture, bring in a sexual element or a conflict, bring some humor and action and edge. It may be, as far as energy level, that I am not selfish enough to slow down.
>
> (Thomson, 1990: 19)

Jack Lemmon is one of the few actors who have articulated a different position from the dominant Method-inspired approach. Crucially he does not see acting as an attempt to express truth:

But I am firmly of the belief that it is not only legitimate, but a matter of duty, for an actor *not* to try to be honest about how a character should basically be played because I don't think honesty has anything to do with the theater. (I thought so, when I was very young.) An actor is there for only one purpose: to perform in front of people that must be amused on the highest possible level. And by amusement I mean *Some Like It Hot* or *Hamlet* or *Othello*. That audience is there to be amused. If you can legitimately bend a character, if you can make him behave in a certain way, so long as it's logical that he *could* behave that way, and if that way is dramatically or comically more exciting than standard behavior pattern, then I say bend that character. It's the actor's duty to find out the most exciting way a role should be played, then to play the role to the hilt. This could mean bits of business, like those we've discussed, it could be underplaying, it could be climbing up and down the walls, it could be chewing up the scenery, but if he doesn't give it hell, make his characterisation as complete and compelling as possible, he isn't fulfilling his function as an actor.

(Cardullo *et al.*, 1998: 271)

Production designers

Production designers are divided over the centrality of their work. Some do have a strong sense of its importance. Richard Sylbert says confidently: 'I take care of how the picture looks. The cameraman takes care of the lighting. And the director takes care of the emotions' (Heisner, 1997: 143). Others have a sense of being more marginal, an attitude well captured by Albert Brenner's wry comment that: 'The production designer is in charge of everything that's either out of focus or doesn't move' (Heisner, 1997: 113).

There is a strong acknowledgement that a production designer's most important relationship is with the director. 'Basically, it's the director's film' is a generally shared view. However, there is also an acknowledgement that this relationship is mediated through other relationships:

The director has the vision, and you are interpreting his vision. The DP [director of photography] is putting it on film, and you are both contributing to the visual style of the film; it's an incredibly intense and personal relationship. We're in one of the most collaborative arts . . . A production designer and the DP should be working on the same wavelength, which comes from the director.

[Mel Bourne] (LoBrutto, 1992: 104)

The other important relationship is with the producer:

You find yourself dancing in this funny world, appeasing the money guys, appeasing your own visual needs and the visual needs of the director. On every film I do, the first three or four weeks are spent grappling with the budget. While creation and designing is waiting in the wings, I'm locked in rooms with producers saying, 'Okay, it's going to cost you half a million dollars to do all this.

If you don't have that, then we're going to have to start paring back on what the director wants and you as producers are going to have to tell him what he can have'.

[Kristi Zea] (LoBrutto, 1992: 244)

Polly Platt points to the complications that can arise in these relationships:

Mostly you go to the producer with your problems. Hopefully, the producer trusts his director, and the director is king. When that doesn't happen, they become adversaries. And you can get caught in the middle. It takes skilful negotiating in critical, powerful situations. That's why many crew members have a tendency to disappear. It's too dangerous, you can get ground up in the powers rolling around. Grist for the mill.

(Brouwer and Wright, 1990: 184)

The general aesthetic position of production designers is a familiar one. Films should be transparent and organic. Paul Sylbert expresses this view clearly and precisely:

You cannot impose a style on a film. It must grow out of a vision arising from the script and a knowledge of how to form the various scenes into a whole, and it should, like the film itself, have its own movement. Style in film results from every part of it, and those parts must cohere, and they must be directed at some effective result. Design is not self expression. It is an expressive use of objects, forms and colors in the service of the script.

(LoBrutto, 1992: 85)

Mel Bourne echoes Sylbert's view in a more pragmatic way:

My philosophy is to give the director an emotionally appropriate spatial environment in which an actor can tell a story. I don't want it to intrude; I don't want it to make a statement.

(LoBrutto, 1992: 115)

The belief that production design should be unobtrusive, that an audience should be unaware of it, is a mantra of production designers. This unobtrusiveness is best achieved when the film is organic: any one element should be intimately related to all the others. As Paul Sylbert suggests, the script is key to the development of this organic quality. There's general support for Sylbert's view, as well as an awareness that scripts do not always provide the necessary support:

One of the big challenges for this movie [Silence of the Lambs] was, how do you depict some of the shocking scenes described in the screenplay. Like when the police officers burst into the room in Memphis to discover their fallen partners. Ted (Tally) wrote 'What greets them is a snapshot from Hell'. Thanks Ted.

(Heisner, 1997: 159)

However, the aesthetics of the organic and transparent are frequently undermined in practice. Designers tend to describe in broad terms the challenges they face as making the literal situation into an interesting one:

> . . . I can't simply read the script and do what it says: 'This is a bedroom'. Two walls is a bore. I can't do that. I have to make it interesting for me as well as doing what the script says.
>
> [Albert Brenner] (LoBrutto, 1992: 99)

Clearly, once a move is made beyond the literal, transparency may be undermined. This conflict between the 'literal' and the 'interesting' is highlighted strongly in Ferdinando Scarfiotti's account of his approach:

> When you have an idea, you really have to follow it through, exaggerating a little bit so that it has a visual impact. Otherwise, it only becomes the usual venetian blinds which you see in every office, but if you make this image strong and you move across the room in a very surreal way, that creates a certain unsettling feeling and it becomes something. You can't leave it there half-dead; you have to make it strong and give it some extra point.
>
> (LoBrutto, 1992: 145)

Such an approach pushes production design towards an expressionist aesthetic, though production designers do not discuss it in those terms.

Cinematographers

Asked how he conceived his role, cinematographer John Bailey replied,

> The director is really the key to whether the film works or not and if the director's vision isn't realised somehow, the film really doesn't have any chance at all. So that's where my responsibility is.
> *So you're basically implementing the director's vision?*
> Yes.
>
> (Schaefer and Salvato, 1984: 52)

The director's vision determines the success of a film. The cinematographer's responsibility is to help the director realize that vision. This is one of the most widely held beliefs of cinematographers. However, although they acknowledge the dominance of the director, cinematographers are also well aware that their relationship with directors is not a simple one of command and execution. Michael Chapman, discussing the influence of Gordon Willis, points out that directors do not always know what their 'vision' is:

> Another thing that Gordy demonstrated by his work and his personality was that you have to have an overriding point of view. He's always very careful in interviews, to say that you absorb that point of view from the director. But a lot of times you don't. Hopefully you do, but sometimes the director doesn't necessarily have one or he wavers in his point of view. But if you can be

unwavering in your point of view, whether you got it from him or you made it up on your own, or, as inevitably happens, there is a combination of the two, if you can have that point of view for the length of the film and not allow yourself to waver, it's one of the most important things.

(Schaefer and Salvato, 1984: 101)

Cinematographers also complain that the relationship can become problematic because directors may have a limited awareness of how cinematography works. Nestor Almendros remarks that 'Communication between a director and a cinematographer is sometimes ambiguous and confused, because many directors know nothing about the technical and visual aspects' (Almendros, 1985: 55).

There is a tension between the identification of the director as the dominant figure in filmmaking and an insistence that the script is crucial for the success of a film. When asked how they chose which films they would work on, John Alonzo, John Bailey and Owen Roizman all said their choice was determined by the quality of the script. John Bailey explained:

The more experience I get the more I see that a problematic or mediocre script in the hands of a brilliant director is still going to have problems. A brilliant script in the hands of an okay director can still be a very good film. I'm coming to have more and more respect for what that script is.

(Schaefer and Salvato, 1984: 68)

Even those cinematographers, such as Nestor Almendros, who use the director as the basis for deciding which films they will work on, acknowledge the importance of the script. Almendros says that what determines his choice is 'the director's artistic personality, his cinematographic sensitivity' but that 'reading the script is of prime importance' (Almendros, 1985: 43).

Cinematographers have a strong sense of themselves as technicians, but they also have a sense that cinematography is more than technique. There is an uncertainty about what that 'more' is. To describe it, words such as 'taste' and 'sensitivity' are used, words that belong more to art than to technique. The following exchange with Gordon Willis is a good example of this issue:

Do you have any techniques that allow you to maintain depth of field at low light levels? Because there is a lot of depth in many of the scenes in The Godfather I and II. It may be dark but there's detail in the foreground and also detail back on the wall too. How do you do that?
Lighting detail you're talking about?
Right.
Well, again it goes back to the principle we were just discussing. It's knowing what's black and what's not really black. Do you know what I mean? What gives the impression of being dark but is not really dark? It's knowing the relativity of lighting ratios and what you're finally going to end up with on the screen. The application of that is taste.

Some people have bad taste; some people have good taste.
Right. Selznick once said, 'There are two kinds of class: first class and no class.'
And it's the same thing with visual taste. You can teach certain principles to
people but the application of those principles may not function for them.

(Schaefer and Salvato, 1984: 289)

The exchange begins with a specific technical question and the answer ends with taste. It is a particularly revealing exchange because Willis always expresses a no-nonsense attitude to filmmaking and insists that it is fundamentally a craft activity. Michael Chapman, who worked as an operator for Willis, is much more emphatic about the non-craft dimension of cinematography:

The amount of unconscious material that you're involved with in shooting – I
couldn't believe it, when I started shooting, how much there is. I always knew
there was in operating, because I've done a lot of it. Operating is very much a
matter of existential choices; I mean, you're out there floating and you're making
choices at twenty-four frames a second. But it's easier to demonstrate, in a way,
how existential operating is. But shooting is too. And you deal with a lot of
unconscious material. I can't explain why or how but it's true. I can't explain
why, if I'm lighting your face, why the light being here or being there makes a
difference but I do know it does.

(Schaefer and Salvato, 1984: 125)

Two themes dominate in cinematographers' discussions of the aesthetics of cinematography. One is the problem created by improvements in technology. There is a feeling that film stock is now so fine-grained and lenses so sharp that the resulting image is too perfect, that it has a picture-postcard quality. Various strategies are employed to 'degrade' the image. Conrad Hall vividly describes the struggle:

Disliking saturation, I was struggling with the primariness of color. I didn't like
blue to be strong blue, you know. I didn't like pure green or those vivid kinds of
colors. I didn't see light that way and there's always atmosphere between color
and me in the form of haze, smog, fog, dust. There's a muting of color that goes
on in life. There was none of that in certain kinds of printing colors in film. And
so I objected to that. I couldn't stand that kind of primary color and I tried to
change it. I experimented with filters and fog filters. I used desaturation when we
had imbibition printing. I tried all kinds of things: underdeveloping, overexposing
and various lab techniques. The overexposing was a way, I felt, of destroying the
color.

(Schaefer and Salvato, 1984: 157)

The second theme is a more traditional one. What role does beauty play in the creation of the image? Some cinematographers, such as Bill Fraker, are out and out advocates of beautiful images, 'I think movies should be romantic. I think people on the screen should look pretty. I don't think people with a forty-foot face up there on the big screen should be ugly . . .'

(Schaefer and Salvato, 1984: 145). Fraker goes on to argue that films should be escapist, not realist. This conflict between beauty and realism runs through nearly all discussions of the aesthetics of cinematography. It creates an illuminating, though unacknowledged, tension in Nestor Almendros's accounts of his approach. In one interview he said: 'I start from realism. My way of lighting and seeing is realistic; I don't use imagination. I use research' (Schaefer and Salavato, 1984: 5). However, in his autobiography he writes, 'One must try to discover a different and original visual atmosphere for each film and even for each sequence, to obtain variety, wealth and texture in one's use of lighting' (Almendros, 1985: 32).

It is a recurring complaint from cinematographers that audiences only notice images that are heavily coded as beautiful, such as sunsets or exotic landscapes. There is general agreement that an audience's main interest is in the story and that the challenge is to help tell it as well as possible. The consensus is that audiences are not very aware of the cinematography; that if they are, it is at a subconscious level:

> The general audience does not know, really, the difference between good lighting and bad lighting or good composition and bad composition. But it's a psychological subconscious feeling that's transmitted to them by the cinematography. And if it's not very good, the audience walks out feeling that it was average. If there's something really special about it, they can feel it. They may not know what it is but they can feel it. And I feel it enhances the film.
>
> [Owen Roizman] (Schaefer and Salvato, 1984: 218)

Editors

Editors share with cinematographers the same view of the structure of filmmaking. The director is the central figure. It is the job of the other contributors to support the director to express his/her vision. Michael Kahn describes how the director/editor relationship works:

> I like to know the point of view of the scene. I like to know if he has any preferences as far as take selections of performances and how he wants to deal with the scene transitions. I have to be on his wavelength because he shoots with something in his mind's eye, and maybe I can embellish it, make it better. He's the man I work for. A director makes or breaks a film. The man does everything on a film and I'm one of those spokes on a wheel, but I've got to know where he's at.
>
> (LoBrutto, 1991: 173)

However, editors see themselves as having a different status from the other contributors:

> I believe the job of the director is really to synthesize everybody's best work, although I think the only other person who really has an overview of that is the editor, who spends the second longest amount of time on a film.
>
> [Alan Heim] (Oldham, 1995: 379)

Because of this position editors carry a particular burden:

> The picture editor is responsible for the film being a success, period. No matter what it takes. Sure, he can hide behind the director and the writer and the producer, but the mandate is simple. He's just supposed to make it work, and if it was shot wrong, he's still supposed to make it work. If it was misconceived, he's still supposed to make it work. And if it was miswritten, yep, he's supposed to fix that too. There is really no limit to the responsibility, in the ultimate sense, of the film editor.
>
> [Peter Frank] (Oldham, 1995: 238)

There is some agreement amongst editors that their position has changed over time, that they now occupy a more central position than they once did. Richard Marks describes the changes that he thinks have taken place:

> I think there was a point when the nature of how films were made changed the editor's role. The difference in the editor's role reflected the change in filmmaking, and that probably came about when they started recording on mag stock rather than optical tracks. They started shooting more and coverage became different. More and more directors came to rely on the editing process to create scenes that at one time were created in one sweeping take, where they would rehearse something for three days, shoot it and get it right. All of a sudden they only had a day to shoot four scenes and they would shoot it in pieces. As the shooting became more complicated, the need for relying on the editorial process became more apparent. Editors were no longer a pair of hands cutting off slates, they were people who had to think, have opinions, and have some feelings for the material. The process became more dramatic choice than automatic, mechanical response.
>
> (Oldham, 1995: 364)

Like cinematographers, editors put a high value on the script. Carol Littleton says flatly, 'If you have a bad script, there's no place to go. The film is rarely ever going to rise above the level of the script' (LoBrutto, 1991: 223). Sheldon Kahn also acknowledges the importance of the script but allows the editor some latitude in dealing with it:

> I think the most important thing is the script and when you get a good script and those words come out of the actors' mouths, it is absolute magic. There are times when an editor can take a bad script and make it better, but it's very difficult to make a good script bad. A well-written story is very difficult to turn into a bad movie. There are times when through a good editor's vision you can take a not-too-well-written story and make a much better story out of it, usually by what you leave out as opposed to what you put in.
>
> (Oldham, 1995: 26)

Editors also frequently describe their work in terms of writing. Sometimes this is in a literal way:

> It's like writing the drafts of a screenplay. Working with Walter [Hill], we joke that editing is the final rewrite. We can take out or add any lines of dialogue we want or rearrange the structure of entire scenes or sections of the film.
>
> [Freeman Davies] (Brouwer and Wright, 1990: 364)

At other times the account is more metaphorical:

> ... editing is a lot like writing. You are rewriting a film. You have a script but you're rewriting the script with the film. It's not like editing in publishing. It is not a matter of omitting and corrections. It's very different, I think. You become a writer, but you're writing with images, you're writing with music, you're writing with performances, you're writing with all the things – intangible things as well – that make an emotional event.
>
> [Carol Littleton] (Oldham, 1995: 64)

Although editors have a keen awareness of themselves as technicians, they are insistent that editing is much more than the application of the appropriate technical knowledge. Editors often compare themselves to musicians and describe their situation as that of the musician who must not only play the score but also put feeling into their playing. They repeatedly emphasize the elusive, mysterious nature of editing and the difficulty of giving a rational account of the decisions they make. Walter Murch eloquently expresses this view of editing:

> When you're putting a scene together, the three key things you are deciding over and over again, are: what shot shall I use? Where shall I begin it? Where shall I end it? An average film may have a thousand edits in it, so: three thousand decisions. But if you can answer these questions in the most interesting, complex, musical, dramatic way, then the film will be as alive as it can be.
>
> For me the most rhythmically important decision of the three is the last: where do you end the shot? You end it at the exact moment in which it has revealed everything that it's going to reveal, in its fullness, without being overripe. If you end the shot too soon, you have the equivalent of youth cut off in its bloom. Its potential is unrealised. If you hold a shot too long, things tend to putrefy.
>
> (Ondaatje, 2002: 267)

Descriptions like these make it easy for editors to claim to be artists rather than technicians. Sidney Levin makes a strong claim for this status:

> I'm an artist and I believe that many of the people I work with are artists ... Editing requires a certain kind of technical facility. All art does, but technique is just the icing on the cake. What is important is the *humanity* of the work. We're not machines.
>
> (Oldham, 1995: 294)

There is a kind of humility evident in editors' discussions of their situation, which presumably comes from their awareness that the material they work with has already been well worked by directors, writers, actors, cinematographers and production designers. One sign of this humility is the mantra is that editors should not impose themselves on the material, that they should allow the film to tell them how to treat it. It is not surprising, therefore, that the strongest aesthetic position that emerges from editors' reflections is transparency:

> Editing should never call attention to itself. The experience of seeing a movie should be an experience that is divorced from its technique. Anything that suddenly pulls you out of the totality of the experience, a beautiful shot, a gorgeous piece of photography, even a *tour de force* performance, can hurt the overall effect. The dramatic experience should be the smooth seamless integration of everybody's work on the film.
>
> [Evan Lotman] (Oldham, 1995: 231)

However, there is evidence that this is a formal, taken-for-granted position rather than a guide to practice. Michael Kahn suggests that changes in the cinema have produced a different aesthetic, one that foregrounds editing:

> The early directors like George Cukor shot a nice frame and stayed on great actors. They said 'Action', they would go, and then say 'Cut'. The editor takes the scissors and cuts the slates off, but the director has locked himself in and it better be good. Today, people are not going to sit there and languish over a hunk of film, even in a drama. They want energy, something that's going to motivate them. A good angle change will do that; you need pieces. That's why an editor today is more important than he was years ago, because we have more footage to work with.
>
> (LoBrutto, 1991: 176)

Visual effects artists

Although the creation of visual effects has been part of filmmaking since its early days, it is only in the last 30 years that it has stopped being marginal. For many years the status of the work was indicated by the tendency to call it 'special effects'. *Star Wars* certainly provoked a change in that status. From the mid-1970s onwards, visual effects became a central part of filmmaking with more and more resources at its disposal. However, the area has not yet fully developed. There is no figure who focuses all the different activities in quite the way a production or sound designer does. The discussion of their work by visual artists is still limited and likely to concentrate on technicalities. However, it is possible to see the beginnings of a more general discussion.

Realism is frequently referred to when visual artists reflect on their work. But the commitment to it as a goal is consistently undermined by the artists' sense that the way they work is close to the way magicians work. John Dykstra says visual effects are all 'smoke and mirrors'. So 'realism' often appears to be a synonym for 'believable' or 'plausible'. This uncertainty can be seen in Rob Legato's discussion of the issue:

I am constantly driving home the concept of making things not only look real but feel real for the specific scene . . . If it feels real, then the audience will accept it even though they may intellectually know better . . . In *Titanic*, for example, you know in your heart some of the shots aren't real, but they are just real enough so that you don't really care they were artificially produced.

(Rogers, 1999: 209)

Making their work less 'special' and more an integrated part of films is a major preoccupation of visual effects artists. Richard Edlund comments:

There are special effects movies that are, to me, very self-conscious because every time you cut to an effects shot, it is absolutely classically composed, done with a locked off camera, elements placed perfectly, and probably 'a castle on the hill'. These effects become self-conscious. It's the 'look at this shot!' mode.

(Rogers, 1999: 121)

There is a consciousness that audiences have a more sophisticated awareness of visual effects:

In the recent past there has been a succession of films that exist more for the existence of effects – not the story that audiences need to be told. Audiences might flock to the 'effects' film, on the first weekend. But since they will be tired of 'effects' over 'story' we find the attendance will drop off. What would keep an audience in the theatre, at least for the first hour, pales to impossible to watch when it gets to video. Audiences are getting too sophisticated.

(Rogers, 1999: 50)

In general there is a strong, shared conviction that film is a narrative art. John Dystra is very clear about this:

You have to be adaptable, to be able to design the resource to fit the storytelling requirement. It isn't about using the latest computers or sophisticated mechanical devices. It is about storytelling.

(Rogers, 1999: 89)

If film is about storytelling then visual effects artists need to integrate their work into the narrative.

When you discuss a sequence that involves effects, the first thing you have to understand is how the shot fits into the fabric of the film. You can't use effects as a be-all and end-all, but as a tool to advance the story telling process.

[Rob Legato] (Rogers, 1999: 209)

There is less self-consciousness on the part of visual effects artists about their relationship with the other collaborators. This may well be because they are much less likely to be hired as individuals. The effects for a film are usually contracted to a company – Industrial Light and Magic are the prime example. A team of people then does the work. There is a recognition of the centrality of the director. There is also a recognition that directors may well not know much or be sympathetic to the area.

> Directors are often horrified to find out how much time and prep it takes to get the job done. If they are actor performance-oriented . . . they can quickly become adversarial to the needs of the effects people whom they perceive as stealing away their quality time with the talent.
>
> [John Van Vliet] (Rogers, 1999: 324)

Some of the most interesting reflections on the status of visual effects come from matte artists, perhaps because what they do is close to what painters traditionally have done and because many matte artists have an art school background. Chris Evans places matte painting firmly within the overall art tradition when he says that '. . . filmmaking and, specifically, the matte painting process is the end of the line in the progression of Western art fooling the eye' (Chell, 1987: 309).

This proximity to a high-status art form produces some of the anxieties that writers express: Chris Evans accepts that a matte painting, like all the other visual effects, should be transparent:

> A well-designed matte shot will go right by the audience, no matter how awesome it really is. It should be integrated into the other images.
>
> (Chell, 1987: 301)

He goes on to explore the consequences of this:

> Anonymity is a sign of the matte artist's success. What really makes an individual artist is his style. But if you are watching a film and a shot comes up that has the style of a particular artist in it, you know it's not real and all of a sudden the whole illusion is shattered.
>
> (Chell, 1987: 302)

He concludes:

> Matte painting can be very satisfying work for an artist, but you are always fulfilling a filmmaker's ideas for the telling of a story. You are using your skill and your craft, but you aren't always using your deeper creative vision.
>
> (Chell, 1987: 307)

This downbeat assessment of the role of visual effects artists is probably a minority view. There is, among most visual effects artists, a growing sense that the importance of their role is being recognized.

> Today, producers and directors are seeing visual effects people as an important element from the beginning. They cast their cinematographers, production designers, costume people early. They do the same with effects people, giving that department the credence and level of respect an equal partner gets.
>
> [Scott E. Anderson] (Rogers, 1999: 49)

Sound designers

'Sound designer' is a new credit, one that first emerged in the mid-1970s. Like 'Production designer' it marks the reorientation of an existing area. There have been people responsible for sound since its introduction in the late 1920s. The emergence of this new credit marked a stronger and more coherent interest in the area. This interest was stimulated by new developments both in recording and reproduction technology. Because the reorientation is a recent one, sound designers discuss their work in a more exploratory and uncertain way than do the other contributors.

Like most of the other contributors, sound designers acknowledge the director as the central figure. Wylie Stateman is clear about this, 'You need to be instrumental in bringing the director's vision to the screen sonically' (LoBrutto, 1994: 254). However, a more characteristic formulation of the relationship between the sound designer and the director is expressed by Richard Anderson, 'In the end what we do is please the director or whomever is the creative control person' (LoBrutto, 1994: 161). The kind of qualification marked by '*whomever* is the creative control person' is frequently made. There is a sense of distance from the director in most sound designers' discussions of their work and a suggestion that other people may be in control. From a sound designer's perspective, one of the most important reasons for this is that few directors are sound literate. Jim Webb suggests that there are only about a half a dozen directors who seriously think about sound. As a consequence most directors do not involve themselves deeply in the construction of the sound track and are content to delegate detailed supervision of it to somebody else.

Descriptions of the construction of sound tracks suggest the process is handicapped by a lack of authority and cohesion:

> ...That was a good collaboration; it doesn't happen very often. More often the composer, the sound editor, and the sound effects people in particular end up competing for any given scene. When you're working on a film, you're working in your own universe. You have a given scene; you want to make it work because doing effects is your job. So you pour everything you can into it so it works with the sound effects by themselves, despite the fact that you know down the line there is going to be music. You keep editing and editing until it's all covered, and there's detail, rhythm, pace, contrast and dynamics to the scene. These are all the same things that the musician uses. The composer takes this scene and throws everything he can into it until it works for him with just the music. He's trying to make it emotional in the same way you are. Now you have these two complete things, where really both need to be there 50–50. Then in the mix you meet in this big collision.
>
> [Gary Rydstrom] (LoBrutto, 1994: 232)

There is a general agreement that it would help if sound designers were involved much earlier in the production process. Walter Murch argues:

> For a film to really take advantage of sound, it even has to be in the script stage. Sound is not something that should be applied later on as a coat of paint; it

really has to be like certain stains that penetrate the wood. Sound needs to be part of the script.

(LoBrutto, 1994: 98)

The changes that have taken place in sound recording and sound reproduction technology have strongly encouraged sound designers to rethink the place of sound in movies. As a consequence, no settled, well-defined aesthetics of sound emerge from their discussions. There are some areas of agreement, some where there are different emphases and some important disagreements.

Most sound designers believe that their work should be transparent:

If it's good you shouldn't notice the sound – it should draw you into the movie without drawing attention to itself. It's the *movie* you should remember.

[Cecelia Hall] (LoBrutto, 1994: 199)

They also believe that dialogue is the dominant element in the sound track, at least in the sense that nothing should interfere with the audience's ability to hear the track:

I think you should hear all the dialog. In a movie you are trying to tell a story. The first thing you think if the dialog can't be heard is 'I didn't hear what they said' and now you are no longer in the movie, period. You need to suck them in and keep them in.

[Bruce Stambler] (Sergi, 2004: 172)

Views on the importance of the sound track in the overall movie are clearly changing. The traditional view was that the sound was secondary to the visuals. That view still has strong support. Cecelia Hall, for example, speaks of 'reinforcing what the filmmakers are trying to do visually' (LoBrutto, 1994: 189). However, sound designers increasingly have started to assert that sound is an equal partner:

. . . you have two levels of a film: you have the visual side that is giving you some information and you have the sound side. They are really two aspects to the film and they are equally important and equally able to convey information.

[Gary Rydstrom] (Sergi, 2004: 228)

Connected to this re-evaluation of the importance of the sound track is a new view on the relationship between the different elements of the sound track. The traditional position was that dialogue and music were the key elements and sound effects a minor one. Tom Fleischman succinctly expressed this position, 'the dialogue is king, the music is the queen, and the sound effects fill in' (LoBrutto, 1994: 180). Gary Rydstrom expresses a different position:

What I find happens when people think about sound, including sound people, is that they think that the dialogue is the literal part of the track, you get the information from dialogue, and then you have music at the other end of the spectrum that is pure emotion and that is really not connected to anything, and a lot of soundtracks have dialogue and music and really don't make use of this vast area in between, in what the rest of the track can be, which is some combination of literal and figurative sound that can always be doing something to set mood and to get you inside a character's head and to be dramatic.

(Sergi, 2004: 227)

It is this interest in the creative potential of sound effects that is the most distinctive in the way sound designers discuss their work. The interest is clearly encouraging a less naturalistic, more expansive aesthetics of sound:

A great key for me was to be abstract and really get off the obvious, get off what you think it has to be. I forced myself out of that pattern. The real sound is not necessarily the right sound. Sound is an element that is easy to apply abstractly. Once you realize the capability, you're really painting the sound.

If I had any one sound in my repertoire, it was the sound of nothing – that's the strongest sound in the world. If you've got the guts not to do anything, you can really make a statement. Jacques Tati was one of my biggest inspirations. He used silence better than anyone.

[Frank Warner] (LoBrutto, 1994: 30)

Composers

There is strong agreement amongst composers that their crucial relationship is with the director. James McNeely expresses that consensus very clearly:

It's ultimately about pleasing the sensibilities of the director. He made the film – it's his vision. He has been on the movie for a couple of years. He has controlled almost everything in the movie up to this point. And, now, at the very end, here comes the composer. So the more you get inside this guy's head, the better the film will be.

(Schelle, 1999: 266)

There is also a sharp awareness that the relationship may not be an easy one. Directors may have little understanding of music or have conventional ideas about it. They may want to give their movie 'class' by having an orchestral score. They may want to use music to cover their failures – a scene that does not work, an actor who has performed badly. At worst they may want it to save an unsuccessful film. But composers are clear that whatever objections or disagreements they have, the director is the person in charge:

Collaboration implies equality, and I don't think the situation between composers and directors is one of equality. I think 'employee' is a more accurate term. And I don't think that's a bad thing, I think you just have to *know* that.

(Morgan, 2000: 49)

More than any of the other contributors, composers are philosophical about their situation. They know very well they are hired to perform a specific task and that normally means they have to respond to the needs of the director. But they also know that the director is not totally in control of the film. They have a strong sense that other people – producers, studio executives – may make different demands on them. Those demands are usually perceived as negative ones.

> But yes, those phone calls *do* come from producers. Working on *Ice Storm* they did, and working on *Ride with the Devil* they were even more intense, and in fact I kind of caved on that one. They got what they wanted, which was a big, overblown orchestral score. It wasn't what I wanted to do for the film originally, but the pressure was extremely intense (as a lot of other composers would attest) and I did start questioning my concept.
>
> [Mychael Danna] (Morgan, 2000: 255)

The first impression created when composers discuss their work is eclecticism. Musicians come from a wide variety of musical backgrounds; classical, contemporary classical, jazz, rock and pop, and there appears to be no agreed strategy about how music should be used. However, this is deceptive. There are some common preoccupations. The vast majority of composers are agreed about the central challenge they face – how to create a complex relationship with what is happening on the screen. What needs to be avoided at all costs is a simple relationship where all the music does is reinforce what is happening on the screen – happy music for happy scenes, sad music for sad scenes. The terms they use to express the kind of relationship they want vary. Some talk about creating a 'subtext', some about giving the film a different 'dimension', some about trying to express the 'ambience' of the film. But however they express their position it is very clear what their general perspective is:

> When the music is more about sub-text – adding an element that isn't on the screen – that's the most satisfying. The most simple minded scoring is what you get in most B-movies and bad television, where they want happy scenes made as happy as possible, love scenes made as loving as possible, and action scenes made as fast and furious as possible. It's not as creative, and it doesn't leave much room for your imagination, except to try to find some *new* way to write the same old music anyway, a generic, same old score that isn't going to tax anybody.
>
> [David Shire] (Morgan, 2000: 1)

To a certain extent, this search for a complex relationship between music and image is part of a reaction against 'old' Hollywood, which is characterized in terms of simple relationships, music with nineteenth-century classical roots and a big orchestra.

The relationship between the different elements on the sound track (dialogue, music effects) is a major preoccupation. Composers have to consider how their music relates to the other two elements. The music/dialogue relationship is the easier one to handle because of the general assumption that dialogue is the privileged element. Composers know their role is the junior one. The challenge in creating a good relationship is caused by the nature of the human voice, which has many musical characteristics.

Writing for dialogue is a terrific challenge. You have to take into account the personalities of the characters and the actors who play them. A good example would be Gregory Peck. He has a wonderful deep voice and a very slow delivery with marvelous cadences. When working with dialogue, you isolate the tone of the character's voice: is he a tenor or a baritone? We're not talking about exact notes, obviously, there's always a range. And then you write the music to that central voice – under it, over it.

[John Barry] (Schelle, 1999: 8)

The way in which music and dialogue are recorded also creates a challenge. Barry suggests that the nature of the image can be powerfully affected:

How the dialogue is recorded is also critical to where the music fits in: is the dialogue what I call 'front screen' – right in your face, right in front – or is it off to the left or the right? If the dialogue is 'front screen', the sax needs to sound as if it were coming from off stage, otherwise you're in trouble. The instruments can move the actors – push them back or move them forward. By being aware of dialogue duration and distance, you can create a cushion behind the whole thing.

(Schelle, 1999: 9)

The music/effects relationship is a more troubling one. There is no agreement that one should be privileged against the other so they frequently end up competing. Almost every composer has strong views about the relationship. For some there is an inevitable conflict between the two elements. A choice has to be made for one or the other:

Well, you have ninety tracks of sound effects but like two tracks of music! You not only have sound effects and ADR and foleys (all those little scritchy-scatchy things whenever somebody moves their arm against the side of their body), so when you've written this beautiful love theme and the beautiful girl in the Edwardian dress sits down on a settee, you hear all this scritchy-scratchy stuff that's so damn noisy you've already cut through half the score.

I'm not averse to sound effects; I'm averse to directors thinking they can balance everything out instead of just having 'That's sound effects, great; that's music, great'. But when you try to stuff it all into one bag, it might give you the *feeling* that it's right, but if you really had selected either one you'd be much more happy. It would give you much more sense of clarity.

(Morgan, 2000: 231)

John Barry acknowledges that there can be such a conflict. Discussing the sound tracks of some action movies he says:

It's just a jumbled mess – incredibly loud effects and loud music at the same time. You can't tell the difference between the two sound sources. When the effects are *that* loud, there's no way you can work around them. Seriously, you can't. Range extremes – adding high piccolos, xylophones, bass trombones, tubas, contrabass clarinets, that kind of thing – is really the only way to try to

find a register that's not being eaten up by the effects. But it's still too much
sound. A lot of composers will write a loud, full orchestra tutti against the
effects and then nobody wins. Even worse, now they throw synthesisers into the
mix – synthesised effects, synthesised music – all with the orchestra and natural
sound effects, which produces just a huge fusion of way too much sound
information. You can't tell who's doing what. It totally loses its dramatic impact.
It's supposed to be very exciting, but it becomes boring.

(Schelle, 1999: 24)

However, for Barry, such a conflict is the result of bad choices rather than some elemental
conflict between music and effects. When he composed for the *James Bond* movies, he says he
always worked closely with the sound people and tried to blend the effects and the music so
that they reinforced rather than competed with each other.

The majority of composers support Barry's view. They often indicate that some of the
problems in the relationship are caused by practical considerations. They believe the time
available in post-production is insufficient for them to establish a proper relationship with the
sound department. In addition they often feel excluded from or unwelcome at the final sound
mix. Those who do attend do not always find it a happy experience. Carter Burwell describes
the mix as 'a battlefield' with everybody fighting his or her own corner. At best, he says, the
composer can try to anticipate what is going to happen and 'make sure the music isn't too
badly bruised' (Lippy, 2000: 51).

Audiences have a ghostly presence in composer's discussions of their work. References to
them are casual, with little detailed discussion. This seems to be because few musicians think
their work will have much effect on a film's success with audiences.

Box-office is never really a consideration for me. I really figure that that has
little to do with me. Actually, at the end of the day, it has very little to do with
anybody in the postproduction end. There are so much bigger forces at play in
terms of whether a film fares well at the box office.

[Mark Isham] (Schelle, 1999: 209)

Explicit discussion of the audience is most likely to emerge when the need to avoid simple
relationships between music and image is being argued for.

And all we're doing the entire time is manipulating their perceptions, and
through their perceptions, their experience. But of course, one 'dark side' of this
manipulation is when you discount everything that a person brings to the theatre
with them – when you just assume everybody is the same. 'Oh, we'll get them to
cry by playing a solo violin here.' 'We'll scare them by having a loud crashing
cymbal here.' It's not even evil: it's just sad, because it underestimates the
audience so much.

(Lippy, 2000: 49)

Common themes

How much agreement about the nature of filmmaking emerges from this account of the different contributors' attitudes? The most widely shared points of agreement are that the director is the central figure and that his/her vision shapes the film. Some qualifications need to be made about this belief. First, as we have seen, some producers do not share it. Although they form a small group of all the people involved in filmmaking, their disagreement is significant because of the power they wield. Second, there is a strong current of opinion that favours the script as fundamental in the making of a film. For filmmakers holding this opinion, the film's vision may well be located in the script rather than in the director. Finally, although the word 'vision' is very frequently used, it is rarely elaborated upon. Different contributors appear to mean different things by it. Some use it in the same way that film critics do. 'Vision' indicates a director's distinctive insight into human existence or a philosophical point of view. Others mean 'having something to say' or 'a message'. There are yet others who give the word a weaker, more operational meaning. For them, making a film is a complex process so somebody needs to have a clear view of its purpose.

Apart from the belief in the director's vision, it is not easy to define a common aesthetic approach that unites all of the filmmakers. There is general agreement that the making of a film should be transparent, that an audience should not be aware of the cinematography, the editing, the sound, etc. But this often appears to be a formal belief, one that is not a strong guide to practice. Evidence of the disconnection can be seen in our account of production designers' attitudes where, effectively, designers argue that if the set is too transparent, there will be no dramatic effect. The same disconnection can be seen in the attitudes of editors. They express a commitment to 'invisible' editing at the same time as they express an awareness that, in modern cinema, the editing is much more on display.

▶ chapter four

Oscars and aesthetics

Fig 4.1 On the set of *Gangs of New York*, 2002. (Photo: Miramax/Dimension Films/The Kobal Collection/Mario Tursi)

Scholars have mostly assessed Academy Awards, or Oscars as they are more familiarly known, from two points of view. Most have routinely described the Oscars awards ceremony as a rather glitzy event, inconsequential in critical terms. Others have underlined the relevance of the awards to marketing and sales (i.e., winning Oscars increases exposure and therefore increases sales). However, few seem to have looked into whether there is, in fact, more that can be learnt from the list of Academy Award winners over the decades. In particular, with the exception of work on how specific studios and other Hollywood establishments have fared over the years, little statistical analysis has been done to ascertain whether any 'patterns' emerge in the way the Academy has awarded their accolades.

Our interest in the Academy's choices arises from wondering whether there are any such interesting patterns and what light they may shed on the relative weight that filmmakers themselves place on those categories of filmmaking that we have identified as 'key' to making movies in Hollywood. We are not so much looking for answers to specific questions, rather this is an attempt to highlight attitudes that may become evident from our statistical analysis. In the past, scholars have indeed looked at the Oscars as a means of identifying attitudes. One of the most popular views about Hollywood, that it considers 'serious' dramas as artistically more worthy than comedies, is often correlated with the ways in which the Academy has bestowed the Best Picture award. Available data support this impression. In the period 1970–2002, only 15 per cent (5 of 33) of movies that won the Best Picture Oscar were in the Comedy/Musical category. The remaining 85 per cent (28 of 33) were categorized as Drama. Data alone cannot answer the question whether Hollywood filmmakers hold any substantial view in relation to artistic worth and hierarchical structures (other sections of this book attempt to do this more substantially). However, data can be helpful in highlighting patterns, especially if these strongly confirm or disprove widely held views and beliefs. In this sense, awards also serve the purpose of establishing and/or confirming a hierarchy within the different contributions to films of all the main collaborators.

This view would seem to be endorsed by the way in which the Academy understands its role in the film community, as the following quote strongly emphasizes (our emphasis):

The Academy of Motion Picture Arts and Sciences, a professional honorary organization of over 6,000 motion picture professionals, was founded to *advance the arts and sciences of motion pictures*; foster cooperation among creative leaders for cultural, educational and technological progress; recognize outstanding achievements; cooperate on technical research and improvement of methods and equipment; provide a common forum and meeting ground for various branches and crafts; *represent the viewpoint of actual creators of the motion picture*; and foster educational activities between the professional community and the public-at-large. What it does not do is promote economic, labor, or political matters.

(The Academy of Motion Picture Arts and Sciences, available at: http://www.oscars.com/legacy/history.html; accessed 15 April 2004)

The Academy's pronouncement about supporting art and representing the viewpoint of filmmakers unequivocally reflects the filmmakers' desire to let their colleagues and audiences know what their general attitudes towards filmmaking are, what practitioners think should be called the best (or at least be nominated as part of the year's elite). Traditionally, commentators have strongly criticized, even ridiculed, most aspects of the awards decision-making process: from the artistic merits of the Academy's choices to the political wrangling linked to the attempts by studios to influence the voting, the prevailing view would seem to be that the Oscars are a populist, artistically pointless, cynical enterprise.

The fact remains that, together with the awards given by various filmmakers Guilds (more about the Guilds below), the Oscars are the only awards *for* filmmakers *by* filmmakers; the other major awards in the US calendar are voted for either by critics (The National Board of

Review, The National Critics Association and the two 'crix' organizations, The Los Angeles Critics and The New York Critics) or by the Foreign Press (The Golden Globes). There are other elements that should sound a note of caution in dismissing the Awards-giving process as irrelevant: (1) the career of many filmmakers has been either significantly boosted or reignited by Oscar wins; (2) Oscar nominations and wins are routinely employed as a means to advertise a film's 'quality' and 'prestige'; (3) nearly 6000 practitioners are eligible to vote for the Academy Awards; (4) every year the Oscars race is the subject of unparalleled media and popular attention (no other award of any kind receives close to the same coverage in the news as does the Academy Awards). To gain a more rounded sense of these indicators of attitude amongst Hollywood filmmakers, we will also look later in this chapter at the manner in which the various professional filmmakers' Guilds claim a stake in the filmmaking process (and thus at the negotiating table), and at the ways in which pay scales confirm or contradict the filmmakers' opinions and views about the existence of a hierarchical structure in Hollywood filmmaking.

Before we look at the data and their potential implications, a few words on how the Academy actually reaches its decisions. On their official web site, this is how the Academy answers the question 'How does a film or performance get nominated for an Academy Award?':

> Awards are presented for outstanding individual or collective efforts of the year in up to 25 categories. Up to five nominations are made in most categories, with balloting for these nominations restricted to members of the Academy branch concerned. Directors, for instance, are the only nominators for Achievement in Directing . . . Best Picture nominations and final winners in most categories are determined by vote of the entire voting membership of over 5,700 individual filmmakers.
>
> (http://www.oscar.com/legacy/faqs3.html; accessed 15 September 2003)

In other words, in deciding who is nominated, the Academy opts for a 'members only' approach whereby only the members of each category choose the nominees for that category (i.e., editors choose the films to be nominated for the 'Best Editing' category, cinematographers choose the Best Cinematography' nominees, etc.). The votes are cast for 14 categories or 'branches': Actors, Art directors, Cinematographers, Directors, Documentary, Executives, Film editors, Music, Producers, Public relations, Short films and Feature animation, Sound, Visual effects and Writers.

Meaningful relationships and emerging patterns

It is difficult to make sense of the remarkable amount of data available when taking into account all the variables involved in the decisions of the various award-giving bodies. We have chosen to highlight some of the most significant relationships that suggest strong (or weak) associations between different categories or that highlight meaningful discrepancies. This is obviously not meant to be an exhaustive analysis, but we have looked at an extensive number of records. We looked at three decades of data, from 1970 to 2002. This period is an arbitrary choice, but one that follows two main logical guidelines. First, 1970 is a useful starting point as it marks the beginning of a crucial decade for Hollywood that was to transform the industry substantially. Second, the period chosen includes the production and release of the three films we discuss in Chapter 6; and the year 2002 is the last for which a full set of data was available to us. Although we have chosen to focus on the Academy Awards, we also looked at a variety of award-giving bodies to gain a better sense of the award-giving process. In particular, we investigated two main categories of film awards: (1) those awarded by industry filmmakers (Academy Awards and the various Guilds' awards) and (2) those awarded by critics and the press (Golden Globes, the National Film Critics Awards, The National Board of Reviews, The New York Film Critics and The Los Angeles Film Critics). In other words, we have chosen to focus on the awards that have traditionally been deemed the most significant in terms of signalling industry trends but also in influencing taste formation and quality judgements.

The Academy Awards (Oscars)

The most significant relationship emerging from a statistical analysis of the period we have chosen concerns the relationship between the Best Picture award and that of Best Director. Of the films that won Best Picture between 1970 and 2002, 82 per cent also won the award for Best Director. Interestingly, these results also mirror those of the Directors Guild of America (DGA), the most powerful and influential organization of its kind in Hollywood. Although this is not surprising (almost all of the 360+ directors who select the five films for the Best Picture category also belong to the DGA) it is still interesting to note that, in the history of the Academy Awards, only on six occasions have the Oscars and DGA awards gone to different directors (five of those six times actually occurring in the 1970–2002 period). Whatever the political considerations clouding the Oscar vote, data indicate that in the less publicly scrutinized world of the Guild's Awards directors would seem to share similar attitudes to those expressed by the Academy. The message from both organizations is clear: only in exceptional circumstances can the terms 'Best Picture' and 'Best Director' be separated.

The only other category scoring a high degree of correlation with the Best Picture prize is Writing. There are two Writing awards (one for Best Original Screenplay and the other for Best Adapted Screenplay) in both the Academy Awards and the Writers Guild of America (WGA) awards. The correlation between Best Picture and one of the two Best Screenplay awards is 73 per cent. This is perhaps not as high a proportion as it may at first appear, if we take into account the two Writing awards (thus doubling the chances for a positive match). Nevertheless, the match remains high. When compared with the WGA choices, however, it is interesting to note that, unlike the case of directors, the Academy and the WGA have often disagreed. In 21 of the 33 years we have looked at, the WGA and the Academy disagreed on one or both of the Best Screenplay awards (64 per cent). Again, the dual category classification goes some way to explain the high value (it is simply more likely to occur) but it is clear that writers and the Academy do not often see eye to eye.

Before moving on to the relationship of the other categories with Best Picture, it may be worth noting that the strong links in the minds of filmmakers between Picture and Director and Writer are confirmed by the very high score of films winning all three awards in the same year. Indeed, of the more complex relationships we looked at (i.e., three awards or more for the same picture), the most significant is undoubtedly the Picture/Directing/Writing triangulation: 58 per cent of films winning Best Picture awards also won Directing and Writing.

The figures above begin to make sense when put in context with other meaningful filmmaking relationships. Cinematographers hold very strong views about the importance of their work. Directors have often confirmed these views: if cinema is a visual medium, then images are of fundamental importance. However, this widely held belief has no statistical confirmation. Indeed, quite the opposite. We looked at the most common statistical occurrences of wins in relation to the Best Picture award. In the period under consideration, only 27 per cent of films were awarded both Best Picture and Best Cinematography. This also includes a remarkable (and unprecedented) 12-year period from 1970 to 1981 when no film awarded the Best Picture Oscar won also the Best Cinematography Oscar. (In fact, the period to which we are referring began in 1967; i.e., it actually lasted for 15 years.) In other words, in the late 1960s and throughout the 1970s the Academy Awards dissociated the words 'picture' and 'cinematography', at least as far as their awards were concerned.

Music is another surprise. It figures even less frequently than cinematography in relation to the Best Picture award. Despite being often cited by directors as key to setting the mood, highlighting tension and providing pace, only 24 per cent of films winning Best Picture also won Best Music. As for Sound (see below), we looked only at the Best Original Score award, which is an award for the whole score rather than a particular section of it, as is the case for Best Song. The 'performance' of both the Music and Cinematography awards is in stark contrast with other categories that are less frequently indicated as of key importance. Editing, in particular, is an interesting example: aside from Directing and Writing, the Best Editing and Best Picture combination is the most frequently observed with 45 per cent of films that won Best Picture also receiving Best Editing. Most other categories fall in a 'middle band', scoring averages from 30 per cent (Costume Design) to 33 per cent (Sound) and 36 per cent (Art Direction and Best Actor). (Note that we included only Best Sound, and not the Best Sound Editing category, as the latter is a relatively new addition to the programme of Academy Awards.)

However, the lowest of all correlations with the Best Picture award is currently Best Actress. Whilst Best Actor scores a respectable 36 per cent, the Best Picture and Best Actress combination scores the lowest percentage of all the relationships we looked at. Indeed, at 18 per cent, it is safe to say that for an actress hoping to win the Best Actress award it is advisable to avoid any film that may have a chance of winning the Best Picture award!

Table 4.1 provides a full breakdown of the key permutations, by decade.

Table 4.1 Relationship with Best Picture: the chance of a film winning Best Picture and at least one other category in the same year

Best Picture & Direction

1970s	1980s	1990s	2000 (up to 2002)
9/10	8/10	9/10	1/3
Overall occurrence: 82%			

Best Picture and Writing

1970s	1980s	1990s	2000 (up to 2002)
8/10	9/10	6/10	1/3
Overall occurrence: 73%			

Best Picture and Cinematography

1970s	1980s	1990s	2000 (up to 2002)
0/10	3/10	6/10	0/3
Overall occurrence: 27%			

Best Picture and Editing

1970s	1980s	1990s	2000 (up to 2002)
5/10	3/10	6/10	1/3
Overall occurrence: 45%			

Best Picture and Sound

1970s	1980s	1990s	2000 (up to 2002)
2/10	4/10	3/10	2/3
Overall occurrence: 33%			

Table 4.1 (*cont.*)

Best Picture & Music

1970s	1980s	1990s	2000 (up to 2002)
1/10	3/10	4/10	0/3
Overall occurrence: 24%			

Best Picture and Art Direction

1970s	1980s	1990s	2000 (up to 2002)
3/10	4/10	4/10	1/3
Overall occurrence: 36%			

Best Picture and Costume

1970s	1980s	1990s	2000 (up to 2002)
1/10	4/10	3/10	2/3
Overall occurrence: 30%			

Best Picture and Leading Actress

1970s	1980s	1990s	2000 (up to 2002)
2/10	2/10	2/10	0/3
Overall occurrence: 18%			

Best Picture and Leading Actor

1970s	1980s	1990s	2000 (up to 2002)
5/10	3/10	3/10	1/3
Overall occurrence: 36%			

To gain a better sense of the patterns emerging beyond individual category relationships we also looked at more complex relationships (involving three or more categories). We mentioned earlier the Picture/Director/Writer combination. Its score of 58 per cent becomes particularly significant when compared with other combinations. For an industry that is regularly understood, described and taught as a 'visual medium' it would be legitimate to expect a high score for the Directing/Cinematography/Art Direction combination, as all three deal with the visual contribution to a film. However, the data substantially counter this expectation: only 21 per cent of films in the 1970–2002 period shared the Directing/Cinematography/Art Direction trio of wins. This is one of the lowest results in complex relationships involving the award of Best Director.

Less obvious combinations score higher, as is the case for the Directing/Editing/Sound combination and the Directing/Writing/Editing trio, both scoring 27 per cent of occurrences in the period under consideration.

Patterns therefore begin to emerge. Although the filmmakers' choices underline the relevance of the pre-production process, and in particular the relationship between producers, directors and writers, they appear to reflect a far less well-determined opinion about a film's visual production team (director, cinematographer and art direction). Indeed, what appears to be the case is that any meaningful combination, focusing on either production (Art direction, Cinematography, Direction: 21 per cent), post-production (Sound, Editing and Directing: 27 per cent) or acting (Actor, Actress, Direction: 6 per cent; in fact only two films, *One Flew over the Cuckoo's Nest* and *The Silence of the Lambs*, achieved this combination in the period we studied), does not get even close to the importance of the early decision-making team in the eyes of filmmakers. The different Guilds' results also confirm those choices, especially those of the two most influential Guilds, the DGA and the WGA.

The issue of credits and the 'place' of the director

One of the key ways in which audiences, critics and even filmmakers understand the issue of filmmaking hierarchies is the thorny issue of film credits. This is a highly politicized issue amongst the various filmmakers' Guilds and other professional associations and it is an issue worth considering, for it can be rather revealing of attitudes towards filmmaking. Not surprisingly, the Directors Guild of America, for example, has exercised its remarkable power and influence over the years in shaping film credits. Indeed, the DGA has a special department, the Credits Department, to deal with all issues concerning film credits. In its 'basic agreement' with employers the DGA stipulates that:

> There are minimum requirements guaranteed by the Basic Agreement. For example, a Director is guaranteed credit on screen on a separate card on the last frame before the picture. This prominent placement is an appropriate acknowledgment of the creative contribution made by the Director.
> (Available at: http://www.dga.org/thedga/gi_credits.php3; last accessed 1 May 2004)

The political and economic relevance of the DGA's position is further emphasized later in the basic contract agreement for directors:

2. RESTRICTION ON THE USE OF WORD 'DIRECTOR': No use of (other than for the director of the film), any credit which includes the word 'director', 'direction' or any derivation thereof.
(Available at: http://www.dga.org/thedga/gi_credits.php3; last accessed 1 May 2004)

Far from being just a means of arranging the names of the various collaborators, credits become a tool to ensure that a hierarchy of roles is maintained. In particular, the strict link between films and their directors is protected, indeed enshrined in contractual form. In this sense, the case of the 'possessory credit' dispute is an example of the attitudes of the two most influential Guilds, the DGA and the WGA, and the relationship they have enjoyed with studios and the labour market since the 1970s:

Directors receive possessory credits because they have the primary responsibility for making a movie. Much as filmmaking is a collaborative art form, ultimately, the vision reflected on screen is that of the director. And the best directors have a signature style, artistry and a level of quality that audiences recognize as a particular brand through a possessory credit.
[Michael Apted, President of the Directors Guild of America] ('DGA amends contract provisions regarding possessory Credit', 9 February 2004. Available at: http:///www.dga.org/news/pr_expand.php3?358; last accessed 8 May 2004)

The complex situation surrounding the so-called possessory credit ('a film by') is a particularly interesting example in that it both (1) highlights the tension at play between directors and writers (and hence the DGA and WGA, respectively), and (2) reminds us of who sits at the 'top table' when it comes to discussions of overall responsibility. In 1973 the WGA attempted to improve the position of their members, and writers in general, by claiming that, in some circumstances, the possessory credit should be awarded to the writer, not the director. The DGA (successfully) pushed for the Alliance of Motion Picture & Television Producers (AMPTP; the labour organization representing the studios and regulating most contracts in Hollywood) to recognize the right for a director to negotiate the possessory credit directly with the studio. This provision to the existing agreement was effectively targeted at sidelining writers on this matter. The fight that followed, involving the DGA, the WGA and the AMPTP, still resonates 30 years later in the 2004 negotiations. Indeed, embedded in the text of what is meant to act as a conciliatory statement by the DGA about the recent new agreement (see below), the aforementioned 1973 provision is referred to thus: 'The provision was added after the DGA beat back an attempt by the Writers Guild of America, West, to take away the credit from directors such as Alfred Hitchcock, Frank Capra, David Lean and King Vidor and assume total control of the credit'.

The language and tone, far from being conciliatory, actually reflect the animosity between writers and directors, and confirm the strong belief amongst directors of a 'pantheon' of authors whose rights are clearly to be protected. This latter part, the belief in authorship, would appear to be perfectly aligned with the critical discourses about authorship. Apted's remarkable claim that 'the best directors have a signature style, artistry and a level of quality that audiences recognize' is in this sense particularly meaningful. He does more than claim the existence of a canon of directors whose work shows such quality as to make it evidently above that of their peers: Apted, thus also the DGA, believes that audiences actually recognize this superior quality. It is therefore not surprising that, despite the (partial) retreat the DGA had to perform in 2004 following the serious threat of a strike by writers, the Directors Guild is still inextricably linked to the notion of great directors whose work exhibits a 'signature style of filmmaking'. Indeed, this is seen as such a crucial point as to make it one of the clauses whereby studios can assign directors a possessory credit:

> Several non-binding guidelines are also spelled out in the sideletter for the Employers to consider when they are weighing whether to grant the possessory, such as whether a director has established a marketable name, a substantial body of work consisting of three or more films or a *signature style of filmmaking.*
>
> (our emphasis)

Although in the past the WGA has referred to the possessory credit as the 'vanity credit', this history of negotiation and conflict cannot be dismissed, as it often is, as mere ego. Both directors and writers know that professional status (hence contractual power, financial remuneration, but also high ranking in the filmmaking decision-making process) is at stake. Indeed, in this sense, the writers' position is actually closer to that of directors than it might at first sight appear. The WGA's 'Committee on the Professional Status of Writers' is the group that has argued the WGA's corner in the possessory credit dispute. In its reaction to the new 2004 agreement, it states that:

> This committee, which held the talks on the vanity credit issue, also entertains a wider agenda. The movement of the theatrical writing credit from the 'third position' on-screen to the 'second position' was negotiated in this forum in 1995 and progress in the implementation of this provision has been evident. Contracts in place when the provision took effect in 1995 that guaranteed a producer the 'second position' credit are allowed to remain in effect, so the effect of this provision is still, gradually, being realized.

Here the full implications of the credits issue become apparent. The quote speaks loudly about the relative positions within the filmmaking hierarchy. In particular, it highlights the virtual stronghold that producers, directors and writers have on contractual power. The WGA does not argue in favour of full recognition of the collective nature of filmmaking; it argues for a higher credit position on screen. All other aspects of filmmaking are clearly deemed as 'less relevant'. In some cases, the contractual power of the DGA results, wittingly or otherwise, in a gatekeeping exercise. Perhaps the most notorious of these examples is sound. Deemed a 'technical' (i.e., not 'artistic') credit, sound credits are relegated to a sort of credits limbo, stuck somewhere between the 'third driver to Mr Cruise' and the 'thanks to the population of what-is-its-name for their support in making this movie'. In this sense the WGA's attitude to the issue is misleading: this is not an issue of vanity, but rather one of substance.

However, what is the position of the other Guilds and associations representing the other, less 'powerful', areas of filmmaking? Overall, the picture that arises from looking at how Guilds state their aims and philosophy seems to confirm the views expressed in interviews with individual filmmakers that would appear to underwrite the DGA's position. Of most relevance to this study is that there would seem to be a well-defined narrative of professionalism that works to frame the more craft-specific comments contained in such statements. This narrative is usually divided into two main stages. In the first, most Guilds reiterate their view of filmmaking as a collaborative effort. This almost immediately leads on to statements about the relative importance of the Guild's specific area (e.g., costume design, editing, etc.). For example, in their opening statement the Costume Designers Guild expresses the view that:

> Film is the great collaborative art. The design triumvirate – the director of cinematography, the production designer and the costume designer – struggle to create an invented world to help the director tell his story. A film is one gigantic jigsaw puzzle. A movie is an enormous architectural endeavor of sets and lighting and costumes for one time and one purpose.

Similarly, the Art Directors Guild suggests in their main statement that:

> Production Designers have one of the key creative roles in the creation of Motion Pictures and Television. Working directly with the Director and Producer, they must select the settings and style to visually tell the story.

However, in the second stage of these narratives, Guilds customarily revert back to a more deferential position with respect to direction. Statements such as 'Sometimes a glamorous entrance may be inappropriate and destructive to a scene. The costume designer must first serve the story and the director' (Costume Designers Guild) and 'Our members create the visual concepts for storytelling which support the director's vision' (Art Directors Guild) are, in this sense, good examples and a clear indication of attitude. A variation on this theme comes from those areas of filmmaking that see themselves as still fighting for the right to sit at the same negotiating table as the other Guilds. The case of sound, substantially penalized by the DGA's position with respect to credits, as we mentioned earlier, is significant. In the Motion Picture Sound Editors' (MPSE) opening statement, the 'prime objective' is indicated as being 'The improvement of prestige and recognition of its members through the education of both the entertainment community and general audience to the importance and artistic merit of the sound track'. Similarly, other associations of filmmakers have expressed concerns at the possibility of being sidelined, both financially and industrially. Elmer Bernstein once famously remarked on behalf of the Society of Composers and Lyricists (one of the largest non-unionized associations of film composers) that 'Composers are being abused in the workplace in terms of work procedures, and are certainly being abused economically . . . the composers are very disadvantaged'.

The difficulty in dealing with this kind of material is not so much whether it is possible to find any meaningful degree of consistency across the Guilds' statements. The issue is more one of interpretation: do filmmakers refer back to the traditional 'the director is in charge' line because they always believe this to be the case regardless of circumstance, or do they employ this as a means of establishing a common framework of reference applicable across all crafts? We believe that the answer has a little of both. On the one hand, filmmakers are clearly aware of the contribution of their specific craft to any given movie. It would be illogical to suggest that they could ever fully agree with the concept of the director as the only real author of a film, but they could easily still hold a contradictory position on this matter. On the other hand, filmmakers are fully aware of the political and cultural dimensions within which they operate. The DGA represents not only a significant craft in filmmaking but a very powerful one too. Regardless of whether filmmakers buy into the director-as-author argument they all agree on one point: directors are powerful people in their industry. Most importantly, directors can hire them and directors can fire them. Directors are, indeed, powerful. In this sense it should not come as a surprise that other filmmakers should show some measure of deference towards them.

However, there is a potentially more significant reason for filmmakers to return to notions of centralized authorship to which all crafts need ultimately to defer. In a complex, highly specialized labour environment such as Hollywood filmmaking, the need to identify a central authority is less of an artistic choice than an industrial necessity. Without a recognized/acknowledged centre of gravity the risk of centripetal creative forces spinning away from a strong sense of a commonly shared project would be substantial. In this sense, it is interesting to note how different crafts working in isolation from or in competition with each other have often been quoted by filmmakers as an issue of central concern: directors do not consider enough the needs of editors in the way they shoot a film; production designers do not think of the needs of cinematographers in the way they build their sets; composers do not take into account the needs of sound re-recording mixers when they compose their music, etc.).

The work of the Guilds, of institutions such as the Academy, and their awards would thus seem to underwrite a belief amongst filmmakers in the need for a hierarchical structure and a common professional framework as a necessary pre-condition for the whole industry. However, it is also clear that under this layer of apparent unity over the role of directors and the existence of an agreed hierarchy there brews a fragmented universe of skilled individuals who vie for attention for their own skills and ideas. We believe that in this (very human) desire to claim an individual stake within the larger hierarchy lies one of the keys to the understanding of the way Hollywood filmmakers operate. This negotiation is at the heart of how filmmakers understand their own contribution to filmmaking, both in terms of their own individual effort and how this impacts on the collective project.

chapter five

Observations: *Bonfire of the Vanities, Up Close and Personal, Heaven's Gate*

Fig 5.1 On the set of *That Darn Cat,* 1997. (Photo: Walt Disney/The Kobal Collection)

There are a number of books that describe the making of individual films in modern Hollywood. The best of them provide insights into and valuable information about the production process. We have chosen three, *The Devil's Candy* by Julie Salamon, *Monster* by John Gregory Dunne and *Final Cut* by Steven Bach, because of the different perspectives on filmmaking they provide.

The Devil's Candy (*Bonfire of the Vanities*)

The Devil's Candy is perfect for our purposes because Salamon's aim was 'to illuminate the filmmaking process'. Brian De Palma, the director of *Bonfire of the Vanities*, gave Salamon *carte blanche* to observe the making of the film and, generously, imposed no restrictions on her. A film critic and journalist, Salamon knew where to look and what questions to ask. An adaptation of Tom Wolfe's best-selling novel, *Bonfire of the Vanities* was a big-budget, prestige production. Salamon was not overwhelmed by the size and glamour of this kind of filmmaking. She is generally sympathetic to what the filmmakers were trying to achieve but this does not prevent her from making critical judgements. The book's greatest strength is the comprehensiveness and detail of Salamon's observations of the filmmaking. The quality of those observations does indeed 'illuminate the filmmaking process'.

Not surprisingly, Salamon is most informative about De Palma's contribution. His support provided her with a unique insight into the way he engaged with the film. For anybody interested in getting a precise sense of what a modern Hollywood director contributes to a film, *The Devil's Candy* is a key document.

De Palma's contribution to the film, as it emerges from the book, was wide-ranging but far from comprehensive. There were areas where he exercised close, detailed control; in others he was much more distant. At the pre-production stage he was involved in almost every area. Those to which he devoted the most energy and attention were the script, casting and finding locations.

De Palma worked closely with Michael Cristofer on the script. Before De Palma was hired by Warners, Cristofer had already written a first draft. It was not much liked, mainly because Cristofer was thought to have 'softened' the story more than was necessary, especially by the way the main characters were finally redeemed. De Palma suggested to Cristofer that, in the next draft, the novel's plot should be reinstated and that the story should be told partly through a voice-over narration. Having established a basic framework, he continued to work with Cristofer on refinements to the script, more or less until shooting finished.

Some of Salamon's most vivid descriptions reveal the substantial amount of energy and time De Palma devoted to casting. He took an active part in the choice of actors for both major and minor roles. His control over the choices for the major roles was limited. Tom Hanks had already been cast as Sherman McCoy, the story's protagonist, before De Palma was hired. He wanted Uma Thurman for the main female role but opposition from Hanks prevented her from being cast. De Palma was, however, happy with Melanie Griffith as a replacement. The casting of the other central male character, Peter Fallow, was made on pragmatic grounds. In Wolfe's novel, Fallow is English. In the script, Fallow had become the narrator and De Palma felt that American audiences would be drawn into the film more if the narrator's voice was American. Bruce Willis had shown an interest in playing the part. Although the studio executives did not think he was the ideal choice, they knew that a star with Willis's popularity could only improve the film's audience appeal. So, with De Palma's approval, Willis was cast.

The casting decision that caused the most problems was finding an actor to play Judge Kovitsky. De Palma believed it was important to get an actor who could bring out the sympathetic qualities in the character. He originally wanted Walter Matthau but Matthau was too expensive. De Palma thought Alan Arkin would be a suitable replacement and Arkin was signed up. However, Lucy Fisher, the Warner Bros executive responsible for the film, began to worry about how the different ethnic groups were treated in the script. The main white characters were portrayed more sympathetically than they had been by Tom Wolfe; his satirical and critical portrait of the black characters remained unchanged. De Palma did not at first respond to Fisher's concern but he became increasingly anxious about the bleak emotional tone of the drama. He decided it needed a more sympathetic quality. Fisher and De Palma finally agreed that casting Morgan Freeman would meet both of their concerns. Freeman replaced Arkin.

The third area of pre-production in which De Palma was deeply involved was choosing locations. In one of the best chapters of her book, Salamon provides a vivid account of the care he took in evaluating a Bronx location, to see if it was an appropriate setting for the crucial event that sets the action rolling. He was just as demanding about the choice of a courtroom, the setting for the climax of the drama. The search for a suitably appropriate one became a substantial drama in its own right, creating great tension with the studio and adding substantially to the cost of the film.

During shooting, most directors work closely with the actors. De Palma was no different in this respect. He was always willing to have a large number of takes if he was not satisfied with a shot, although his main concern seemed to be with establishing how the overall scene was working rather than worrying about the details of a particular performance. His chief preoccupation, however, was with the visual quality of the film. He did not want the film to look like television and regularly expressed a horror of visual clichés, particularly in the presentation of New York. This meant he was always looking for ways of being visually creative. Together with Cristofer he had, for example, invented an opening scene that depended on a long and technically demanding tracking shot. At one point during shooting, when he and his cinematographer, Vilmos Zsigmond, were worrying about the effect of some unusual angles they had chosen, Salamon quotes him as saying, "What are we, Vilmos, old fogies? Let's go for it' (Salamon, 1993: 233).

In post-production, De Palma was much less involved in the day-to-day work. While shooting he had a good idea of how he thought the film should be edited. He gave storyboards to the editors, Bill Pankow and David Ray, at the beginning of their work to indicate what he wanted and then let them get on with it. He made occasional checks on what they had done. In making these checks he did not engage in much discussion but gave precise instructions about changes he wanted. His approach to music was similar. He knew what kind of music he thought would be appropriate for the movie and chose a composer, Dave Grusin, who he thought could provide it. He then gave Grusin rough indications of where and what kind of music would be helpful. With sound other than music, De Palma had a more distant relationship. He does not appear to have established a general strategy but contented himself with commenting on the work that had been done.

As well as providing an invaluable account of how De Palma worked on *Bonfire of the Vanities*, Salamon's account is also helpful about more general issues. As we have suggested in a previous chapter, a director's impact on a film is often discussed in terms of his or her 'vision', though it is often not clear what the word means. Although Salamon does not discuss the issue directly, it is possible to identify De Palma's 'vision' for *Bonfire of the Vanities* from her account. She reports that when he was first being considered as the director of the film, he explained to the Warner executives that he would treat the story 'as a broad satire, a dark farce on the order of Stanley Kubrick's "Dr. Strangelove"'. To do this, he thought, he would have to find a filmic equivalent of Tom Wolfe's hyperactive prose style.

This 'vision' of the film as satire and farce guided him in all the work he did on the film. This is most evident in two areas, the script and the images. In the script, the basic strategy was to introduce farcical elements into scenes; in the images, it was to find unusual camera angles. From Salamon's reports of her discussions with De Palma's collaborators, it is clear that he successfully communicated to them what his 'vision' was and that they were sympathetic to it. However, her account also makes it clear that it is not easy for a director to communicate in specific terms how this 'vision' should be translated. She describes how De Palma explained to Zsigmond and Sylbert what he wanted: '"Acrylic!" he said. "It should be acrylic."' She goes on to comment that Zsigmond's reaction was that there was no such thing as 'acrylic' lighting (Salamon, 1993: 78). The kind of problems this creates can be seen in De Palma's reaction to some of the costumes. Following De Palma's 'vision', Ann Roth, the costume designer, exaggerated some of the characteristics of the costumes for bystanders in the crucial scene in the Bronx. De Palma complained that the costumes made the extras look like clowns.

The conflict between art and commerce usually has a taken-for-granted quality in discussions of Hollywood filmmaking. Because of her access to De Palma, Salamon is able to strip away some of that taken-for-grantedness. Her account of a Hollywood director seriously engaging with the conflict is absorbing. De Palma's approach to filmmaking had been formed in the 1960s when directors were being powerfully identified as artists. An artist expressed a personal vision and did not compromise, even if his work was provocative and unsettling. De Palma had started out making films in New York on very low budgets, which made personal expression possible. But he wanted to work on the larger scale that Hollywood allowed. To do so he had to reconcile his sense of himself as an artist with the demands of the box office.

His films had mixed success with audiences. Some, such as *Carrie* and *The Untouchables*, were big successes. Others, such as *Blow Out*, failed. *Casualties of War*, which he had directed immediately before he became involved with *Bonfire of the Vanities*, had been very much a personal project and was a big commercial failure. Consequently, he was anxious that *Bonfire of the Vanities* should not be another. The dilemmas this created for him came to a head when Lucy Fisher suggested that a black actor be cast as Judge Kovitsky. As we have already indicated, De Palma did not at first think such a change was necessary. But then it occurred to him that an actor such as Morgan Freeman could bring sympathetic warmth to a film whose satirical and farcical approach might easily alienate audiences. Salamon reports his reflections on the situation:

> He wasn't sure where integrity stopped and compromise began and where irresponsibility fit into the mix. The bigger the movies got the more they felt like an enterprise and the less they felt like artistic expression. This movie had become very big, and because he was in charge he found himself seriously considering these ideas the studio executives kept harping on, ideas that seemed to him entirely irrelevant to the production of a work of art: *likeability. Empathy. Racial balance.* Racial balance. What was he, the ACLU [the American Civil Liberties Union]?
>
> (Salamon, 1993: 109)

By the end of the movie the problem appeared even bigger:

> You get your aesthetic judgement swamped . . . One day I'm going to say, 'What am I doing this for? Wrestling with these people trying to do something unusual and different, and they want something mediocre and stupid . . . You sit in New York and say, 'That's a piece of junk. Why do they make movies like that?'
>
> (Salamon, 1993: 315)

But he also showed some awareness that the problems were not simply caused by the limitations of studio executives:

> Then you come out here, and you can begin to understand how they can make movies like that. The fact is, people pay money to see them.

The Devil's Candy is impressive in its comprehensiveness. Salamon takes account of everybody who made a substantial contribution to the making of the film. While the book is most illuminating about how a modern Hollywood director operates, it also illuminates other areas. Salamon's description of Tom Hanks's and Bruce Willis's contributions provides a sharp insight into how star power operates. Salamon describes the two actors as, personally, almost complete opposites. Hanks was open and friendly, happy to socialize with other crew members. Willis kept to himself and was always surrounded by his own entourage. But both, at different points in the film, exercised their power. In the early stages of pre-production, Hanks made it clear that he would not accept Uma Thurman as the female lead, despite De Palma strongly favouring her. During shooting, when he was acting in one of the scenes, Willis made criticisms of how it was being played and started to redirect it.

On the face of it these are two routine examples of how stars interfere in the making of a film. What makes them worth noting is that they both go against the established idea that stars interfere in arbitrary and egotistical ways. Hanks's belief that Thurman was wrong for the role was an astute judgement, as De Palma eventually conceded: 'She's a great actress, but she isn't comedic. She didn't have the comic timing – you either have it or you don't. Tom's a natural comedian and he wasn't able to play off her' (Salamon, 1993: 18). Willis's interference was also based on an astute judgement, even if he was undermining De Palma in the way he expressed it. His point was that the scene was losing its effectiveness because it was being played too slowly. Once De Palma had talked to Willis and reasserted his authority as director, he accepted the point and speeded the scene up. In both cases, the stars' judgements were as much in support of the overall quality of the film as they were in support of their own performances.

One of the most valuable results of Salamon's comprehensiveness is the light she throws on the work of studio executives, a group whose work does not often receive serious attention. The conventional wisdom about modern studio executives is that they have a business school mentality that leads to a preoccupation with figures, not movies. They are contrasted unfavourably with the old moguls who are said to have loved movies. Salamon's depiction of them does not support this view. Neither of the executives involved with *Bonfire of the Vanities* had a business school background or displayed a business school mentality, unless trying to keep control of a budget that was rapidly escalating up from US$29 million is a sign of such a mentality. Mark Canton, the executive in charge of production at the studio, had a traditional Hollywood background. His father had been Alfred Hitchcock's publicist. Canton's own career had been in show business. He had begun in the music business and established himself in the film industry by producing goofy comedies. Lucy Fisher, the executive most directly responsible for the film, was a Harvard graduate whose special responsibility at the studio was for culturally ambitious projects such as *The Color Purple.*

In this context a third person must be taken into account. Peter Guber, who initiated the project, had spent his career shifting between being a studio executive and an independent producer. Technically, at the time the film was first proposed, he was an independent producer, with an exclusive production deal with Warner Bros. Guber did have a background in Business Studies (an MBA at New York University). Paradoxically, despite this background, his approach was similar to the old-style moguls, somebody who depended strongly on his instincts in his choice of projects. It was his idea to make a film of Tom Wolfe's novel. The decision was a risky one. Because of its sprawling plot and generally unattractive characters it was generally thought not to be a good box office prospect. Guber was prepared to take the risk because he was confident in his ability to overcome the difficulties, especially by putting together the right cast and crew.

Guber and Fisher were primarily responsible for deciding how Wolfe's novel should be approached. They wanted it turned into a 'big entertainment' movie rather than an art movie. To achieve this the main characters should be given redeeming qualities and generally the characters and the narrative should be made less complex. In Fisher's words, 'You have to figure out a way not to de-ball a great book, yet figure out a way to give yourself a line through it in which people are maybe slightly less complex' (Salamon, 1993: 15). The writer, Michael Cristofer, was encouraged to think in these terms when he set out to adapt the novel. The choice of Tom Hanks to play the main character was a result of this approach. Hanks was not the ideal choice – he certainly did not look like the rich, white, Anglo-Saxon protestant Wolfe had invented – but Guber thought he would bring a quality of likeability to the part. The choice of director proved more difficult to fit into this perspective. Somebody like James L. Brooks would have been ideal but he (and other directors who had worked in the same kind of dramatic territory), was not available. No other director demonstrated any interest in the project until Brian De Palma did.

Salamon's description of how Guber and Fisher approached the film raises some general issues. First, it is striking how unconcerned they were about the politics of the novel. They showed none of the political caution that is supposed to be ingrained in Hollywood studio executives. Wolfe's book has a wide range of targets: modern capitalism, New York's upper class, municipal politicians, the legal system, black activists and the media. Some of these are politically very sensitive yet there was no attempt to change or soften them. The only political intervention was Fisher's suggestion that Kovitsky should become a Black character and not the white Jew he is in the novel. This could be seen as an example of executive caution, a way of protecting the film from political flak. It could also be glibly dismissed as an example of political correctness. But it could just as well be seen as a sensible artistic judgement on Fisher's part about the process of adaptation. If changes are made in the central character, the consequences of those changes for all the other characters need to be taken into account.

A second issue that is raised is that Guber and Fisher's approach was as much a 'vision' of the film as was De Palma's. There were, in fact, two visions shaping the production. They were not irreconcilable but neither were they an easy fit; the demands of a 'big entertainment' and those of a 'dark farce' were always likely to create tension. Also, even if there is only one vision, practical difficulties often make it hard to put it into effect. Guber and Fisher found, in Michael Cristofer and Tom Hanks, a writer and a star with the kind of qualities they were looking for, but Brian De Palma was something of a forced choice. If you were looking for a director who would bring out warmth and sympathy from a rather downbeat story, his certainly was not the first name that would come to mind!

If any film demonstrates the importance of the work of a producer, *Bonfire of the Vanities* does. The film did not have a properly recognized producer. Peter Guber, the original producer, dropped out when he and his partner, Jon Peters, were hired by Sony to run Columbia Pictures. Warners were unable to replace him quickly and the film went into production without a producer. By default, the producer's role was split between De Palma and Fred Caruso, the line producer. Caruso performed most of the producer's duties but he lacked authority, both with De Palma and with the studio executives. The result was an ill-defined situation that did not help the production. De Palma suffered the most. He had the additional burden of dealing directly with the studio executives when substantial problems arose and he had no one with whom he could discuss his concerns. The executives were apprehensive because they believed there was no proper control of the production, and Caruso was left unclear as to exactly what his responsibilities were.

The difficulties this caused are evident in Salamon's description of the consequences of hiring Morgan Freeman in place of Alan Arkin. This had an immediate effect on the budget. Arkin had to be paid off and Freeman was about four times more expensive. Because of Morgan Freeman's other commitments, he had to stay in New York and was not able to go to Los Angeles at the time scheduled. This meant further costs because the courtroom set, which was already being built on the studio lot, had to be abandoned. The contracts with some of the supporting actors also had to be renegotiated. A replacement courtroom had to be found in New York. De Palma was very demanding about the character of this courtroom. One of his strongest concerns about the film was to avoid it being what he called a 'talkfest', so he wanted a place where he could stage the conventional legal exchanges but also some more elaborate action. The search for a suitable location led to some sharp conflicts with the studio about the cost implications of some of the proposed choices. In the end, Salamon estimates that the decision to hire Morgan Freeman added US$2 million to the budget.

As there were cost overruns in other areas, the budget became a major source of concern for the studio executives. (Overall the budget increased from an original US$29 million to a final US$40 million.) The result was battles between De Palma and the studio executives that led to restrictions on the money available for staging some of the later scenes. The presence of an established producer would not have guaranteed the solution of all the problems but, at the very least, the burden De Palma carried would have been shared.

The final invaluable service that Salamon provides in *The Devil's Candy* is information about what people earn. The information is far from complete but it is helpful for understanding the financial (and power) structure of filmmaking. It confirms graphically the well-known fact that male stars dominate. Tom Hanks and Bruce Willis both received US$5 million. In comparison, Melanie Griffith received only US$1 million. For a supporting role, Morgan Freeman earned US$650,000. After Hanks and Willis, Brian De Palma was the most highly paid, earning US$2.5 million. The writer, Michael Cristofer received US$600,000; rights for the book cost US$750,000. The production designer, Richard Sylbert, received US$190,000. It is worth putting these figures into more general contexts. They indicate that the budget was heavily weighted towards the above-the-line talent. Out of a total budget of US$40 million, almost one third was spent on payments to the principal actors, the director and the writer. The gap between the payments made to the writer and to the production designer is also worth noting. Writers often bemoan how little valued they are, yet Michael Cristofer, a middle-ranking writer, was paid three times as much as Richard Sylbert, one of the most highly regarded production designers in Hollywood.

Audiences stayed away from *Bonfire of the Vanities*; critics did not like it. Does Julie Salamon's account make it possible to understand why the film was such a failure? Although she does not address the issue directly, her account suggests that what most undermined the film was the uncertainty created by the existence of two visions, the 'big entertainment' and the 'dark farce'. In a general sense, this appears to be a clash between commerce and art, the kind of clash that is thought to be emblematic of Hollywood. Salamon's detailed description of the ideas and motives of the main people involved makes the clash more complex and interesting than it is usually taken to be.

Guber and Fisher wanted to attract a large audience. Although it was a best seller, the readership of Wolfe's novel was small compared with the numbers of filmgoers needed for a large-scale film to be successful. Because of its scope, it was not the kind of story that could easily be done on a small scale. There were good reasons for thinking that the book, unchanged, would not provide the basis for attracting a large audience. Much of its appeal depended on the reader having some background knowledge of the economic and social world of New York in the 1980s. It had a complicated sprawling plot, with a large number of characters. Also its view of the world could be seen as being rather misanthropic. It could be argued that it simply was not suitable to be made into a film, but equally, a case can be made that it was brave to attempt to do so since its commercial prospects were always likely to be uncertain. When he visited the film at a late stage in its production Peter Guber summed up the risks it ran:

> This picture has to operate between a nine and a ten. It can't operate at a seven and succeed. Straight comedies, or action, they can operate at a five. But this one – nine! Probably closer to nine point five. To really work and bring in the audience, it has to be unique in all its qualities. This is the film that will put the cap on the eighties.
>
> (Salamon, 1993: 315)

De Palma saw the film as a dark farce. However, this did not mean that he did not recognize the need for it to be big entertainment. Apart from anything else, it was important for his career as a director that the film should be a box office success. But Salamon's description of his state of mind suggests that he was not able to think creatively about how to marry the two visions. Instead, his awareness that the film needed to be a big entertainment undermined his judgement and made him insecure, as his reflections on casting Morgan Freeman vividly demonstrate. His general insecurity made it almost impossible for him to score as highly with the film as Guber thought was necessary. The absence of a producer with whom he might have discussed his anxieties did not help. De Palma used Michael Cristofer as a sounding board but Cristofer does not seem to have been able to help much; he was not the most suitable person for this role. According to Salamon, he was hired initially as much because he was a willing workhorse as for his writing skills. It is interesting to speculate about what the film would have been like if Guber had stayed on as producer.

As the reactions of the audiences at the previews indicated, the big problem with the film was its tone. In the novel, Tom Wolfe combined a high-spirited comic tone with a moral purpose. In the film, farcical comedy and morality did not combine so successfully. Wolfe himself made an acute judgement of the film. Salamon says he

> . . . couldn't really understand what kind of farce De Palma wanted 'Bonfire' to be. 'It wasn't a bitter farce and it wasn't a bedroom farce and it wasn't a sweet farce or an agreeable movie', he said. 'As far as I can tell they didn't take on a point of view and cleave to it. I'd be pretty hard put to tell you what the point of view is . . . . It was as if Brian De Palma said "Well, I've got to do something extraordinary to pull this off in two hours, so I'm going to try all kinds of things. I'm going to try this 'Dr. Strangelove' approach. I'm going to try the most extreme camera angles I've ever used."' . . . If you're going to exaggerate, it has to be done just so, as in 'Dr. Strangelove'. The slightest false note can boomerang.
>
> (Salamon, 1993: 409)

Monster (*Up Close and Personal*)

John Gregory Dunne's *Monster* has the advantage of being written by someone who was directly involved in the making of a film. Dunne (with his partner, Joan Didion) wrote the script for *Up Close and Personal*. In his book, he is mainly concerned with the setting up of the film. This took eight years to do and, by the time it was finished, Dunne and Didion had written 27 drafts of the script. Dunne provides a detailed narrative of how and why the process was so protracted. Although Dunne is writing from a different viewpoint from Julie Salamon, his account raises many of the same issues.

Dunne's own view of filmmaking is made clear by the title of his book. It is derived from a story about a meeting between studio executives and a couple of filmmakers. The executives had suggested some changes to the script that the filmmakers were disputing. The chief executive suddenly and surprisingly announced that he would be forced to take the monster out of the cage. He then explained what the monster was – 'It's *our money*' (Dunne, 2000: 15).

If *Monster* was simply an account of the conflict between money and art, philistines versus artists, crass studio executives versus creative filmmakers, it would be a less illuminating book than it is. In fact, its description of filmmaking is richer and more nuanced than the title suggests.

The key issue that faced the filmmakers of *Up Close and Personal* is the same one faced by the filmmakers of *Bonfire of the Vanities*. How do you make a film that will be attractive to audiences? The source material for *Up Close and Personal* – a biography of the television presenter, Jessica Savitch – posed the same kind of problem as Tom Wolfe's novel. The material was dramatic, but uninviting. As we noted in the Introduction, Savitch's story was a bleak one. The Disney studio executives thought that a straight dramatization was not the kind of story that would attract audiences. They suggested that the positive elements in the story – Savitch's rise from obscurity to national fame – should be emphasized; the negative elements should be diminished, if necessary by changing biographical facts. Did the protagonist need to die in the end? One of the reasons for such a protracted period to set up the film was that the Disney executives were hard-nosed about giving the story a positive spin. They were particularly encouraged to be so by their success with *Pretty Woman*, a film whose original downbeat script had been transformed into a romantic, Cinderella story.

However, is their hard-nosed attitude simply an example of philistinism? One of the most interesting documents that Dunne quotes is a rather naive memo from one of the creative executives at Disney. Its very naivety provides a sympathetic insight into the issues with which studio executives try to grapple:

> I struggled to define for myself the best way to mold all the good material into the kind of material that would attract mainstream audiences, without sacrificing the integrity of the piece. I thought about such very good recent movies as *Bugsy, Thelma and Louise*, and *GoodFellas*, pictures that were not big commercial successes. I feel in these films the heroes and/or heroines, though they were often likeable, did things that went against the grain of our accepted moral standards, and audiences couldn't identify with them. On the other hand some very good recent films like *Rainman, Good Morning Vietnam* or, in the past, films like *Funny Girl, Terms of Endearment, The Way We Were*, and *Love Story* were all huge hits, *with* bittersweet endings and complex characterisations. They dealt with different kinds of love, but, in all cases, the leading characters put themselves at risk one way or another, to help someone they loved. Therefore audiences could get deeply involved on a positive level and identify with the characters.
>
> (Dunne, 2000: 98)

It is easy to make fun of such ideas and Dunne is generally dismissive of the executives' interventions. Nevertheless, he and Didion did respond to their concerns and, crucially, in doing so they provided a script for a film that found an audience and made a profit. One of the weaknesses of the book is that Dunne does not properly explain why, despite his derision of the executive's suggestions, he and Didion put so much effort into dealing with them.

Like Julie Salamon's, Dunne's discussion of the contribution of the two stars, Robert Redford and Michelle Pfeiffer, does not support the idea that stars are only egotistically interested in their own roles. In an effort to sort out the script, Dunne, Didion and the director, John Avnet, met with Redford. Of Redford's contribution to the meeting, Dunne says that his main concern was with making the film work and that, 'his remarks were always those of a director, not an actor counting lines'. Dunne is just as positive about Pfeiffer's contribution and, in describing it, he illuminates the relationship between stars and writers:

> ... Michelle had meanwhile sent us eight pages of notes on our last draft. It is always interesting to see how much work a good actor does with a screenplay. She had scoured our available early drafts for lines and incidents that could be dropped into the shooting script. Shorten the airport scene, add the pick-up truck scene; lose the line regarding her menstrual period, it's dated ... On the basis of her notes, Michelle ... seemed to like more direct confrontation between the characters than we did, the indirect being the altar at which Joan and I prefer to worship, and to favor obligatory scenes, which we tend to avoid if at all possible, but these were just matters of personal preference that she would work out with Jon, and Jon with us. It was Michelle Pfeiffer, after all, who was going to be twenty-five feet tall up there on the big screen in a darkened theater, not us.
>
> (Dunne, 2000: 154)

The producer's role is another issue that *Monster* shares with *The Devil's Candy*. 'What producers do is rarely understood, and seldom appreciated', writes Dunne. *Monster* is particularly valuable for its portraits of producers and its accounts of how they operate. John Foreman was responsible for developing the project in the first place and it was a tribute to his persistence that, after it was turned down by a number of studios, he persuaded Disney, the most unlikely studio of all for such a project, to take it on. When the project seemed to have collapsed and Foreman himself had died, Dunne vividly describes how Scott Rudin's energy and enthusiasm revived it in a way that encouraged him and Didion to return to work on it. Dunne's portrait of Rudin emphasizes the creative role a producer can play. Rudin was both very clear about the kind of film he thought *Up Close and Personal* was, and strong and decisive in his dealings with the Disney executives. Dunne completes his gallery of portraits of producers with one of Don Simpson. While the *Up Close and Personal* project was dormant Dunne and Didion worked on a script for Simpson and Jerry Bruckheimer. Dunne's portrait of Simpson is as vivid, if not quite so sympathetic, as the one of Rudin. It also highlights the positive qualities a producer can bring to a project, particularly creative energy and decisiveness.

Final Cut (*Heaven's Gate*)

Final Cut by Steven Bach is particularly distinctive because it is written from the point of view of a studio executive. For anyone wanting to understand the role played by studio executives and the ideas and ambitions that motivate their actions, the book is a priceless document. The story Bach tells is, by now, a well-known one. In 1980, United Artists agreed to finance a Western, *Heaven's Gate*. The studio lost control of the budget. The original estimate was that the film would cost US$7.5 million; the final cost was US$40 million. *Heaven's Gate* was very badly received, both by critics and audiences. As a consequence of all this, Transamerica, the company that owned the studio, sold it to MGM. So United Artists, a company with a very special place in the history of Hollywood, lost its distinctive identity.

Bach could not have had a better view of what happened since he was a United Artists executive intimately involved in the production of the film. His story has many of the elements of a best-selling novel. The characters were playing for high stakes; their actions were marked by ambition, deception, miscalculations, vanity and fear. Because of this, it is very easy to see the book as confirming all the usual disparaging assumptions about the nature of Hollywood film production. This would be a mistake. Bach's self-aware, thoughtful account provides rich and varied evidence that undermines many of these assumptions.

The delineation of the basic problems faced by studio executives is one of the most valuable aspects of his book. Bach does this in a way that undermines characterizations of them as basically philistine: 'suits', 'accountants', 'bureaucrats'. Of all the studio executives he discusses, only Andy Albeck, the president of United Artists, in any way conforms to this stereotype. However, it is worth pointing out that Bach's description of his methods and attitudes is particularly sympathetic. The work of studio executives begins from the recognition of one obvious fact: no one can be sure what film will be successful: 'James Bond? Who could have predicted that *Dr No* with an obscure English [sic] actor would spawn the most successful series of pictures in the company's [United Artists] history?' However, Bach goes on to suggest that, faced with this unpredictability, the challenge for studio executives is not to surrender to irrationality. He points out that people in the industry often talk glibly about the importance of 'gut instinct', forgetting that it can produce failures as well as successes.

> It sounded often like a lazy reliance on luck, on a roll of the dice, a substitute for analysis and clear thinking. If the dice couldn't be rigged or analysed into control — and there was ample evidence they couldn't — at least the odds could be computed, and the risks minimised.
>
> (Bach, 1986: 111)

The first part of *Final Cut* describes how the United Artists' executives attempted to compute the odds and minimize the risks for *Heaven's Gate*; the second half of the book describes why the attempt failed so disastrously. This failure might be seen as a vindication of the belief that Hollywood film production is fundamentally irrational and unpredictable. However, Field's honest accounting for what happened suggests the failure was not inevitable and could have been avoided. It was the product of a particular set of circumstances, some bad judgements and a failure of nerve.

For a variety of reasons, United Artists needed a film such as the one *Heaven's Gate* promised to be. Buoyed up by his success with *The Deer Hunter*, Michael Cimino had enormous confidence in his own artistic talent and little concern for anybody or anything that prevented him from expressing it. From the earliest days of pre-production, Cimino's artistic approach was not properly challenged, even though there was awareness both of the script's limitations and Cimino's choice of actors. Also, financial control was never sufficiently rigorous, even though serious doubts were expressed at the very beginning of the project about the budget Cimino proposed. The debacle that *Heaven's Gate* became was not mysterious and inexplicable; it could have been predicted at a very early stage in the film's production.

Why were the problems not confronted until it was too late? Two crucial reasons emerge from Bach's account. First, large-scale filmmaking, once it gets under way, acquires a momentum that is difficult to halt. Abandoning a production or firing a director is expensive; it is always tempting to continue and hope something can be done to save the situation. Second, the executives had too much respect for Cimino's artistic reputation. Consistently, this respect allowed Cimino to manoeuvre them into compromising positions. If anything, some hard-nosed philistinism might well have had better results both for Cimino and United Artists.

This respect for art emerges strongly from Bach's discussion of the attitudes of the executives. It is clear their lives would have been much simpler if they had been exclusively concerned with profit and loss. Perhaps the conclusive indication of this respect was the decision to back *Raging Bull*. The executives were very aware that a film of this kind, measured by all the usual criteria – it was violent, downbeat and had an unsympathetic protagonist – was unlikely to make money, yet they went ahead and backed it. Hollywood filmmaking is usually portrayed as a conflict between money and art, with studio executives on the money side and directors and writers on the art side. The picture that emerges from *Final Cut* suggests that the relationship between money and art affects everybody involved in film production: heads of studios, studio executives, producers, directors and stars.

Bach also performs an invaluable service in showing how complicated financial issues are in large-scale filmmaking. He makes very clear the problems of putting together a budget for a film:

> Most budgets are honest attempts to say, 'The picture will cost this much', and any evaluation of an honest estimate – or even a 'creative' one – can be only on an if basis: if it doesn't rain, if the leading lady doesn't get a headache; if the ruling military junta isn't overthrown; if the director isn't kidding himself; *if . . .* Safeguards are taken to prevent the more unpleasant ifs, and insurance companies make handsome fees in insuring against their nevertheless frequent enough occurrences to make insurance a costly budget item on every picture made. There is simply no way to eliminate them entirely and vetting a budget is to estimate an estimate.
>
> (Bach, 2000: 181)

As a consequence, once a film is in production, it is not easy to control budgets. There are frequent occasions when a decision has to be made whether to increase the budget or to cut back on the film's ambitions. *Final Cut* demonstrates the disastrous consequences of taking some bad decisions.

We learnt a number of lessons from these descriptions of filmmaking. Three seemed particularly significant. The first was the need to take account of the contribution of studio executives to a film. They regularly play an important role in the early stages of production through decisions they make in areas such as casting and writing. The scripts of both *Bonfire of the Vanities* and *Up Close and Personal* would certainly have been different without the suggestions made by the executives of Warner and Disney. Executives also influence films once they are in production, particularly if the budget becomes a problem. How to deal with an overspend is as much an artistic decision as it is a financial one. Should the director be given extra money? If not, what scenes should be cut from the script to make up for the overspend? Decisions such as these obviously have consequences for the final quality of a film. The evidence we came across about what studio executives contributed made us think that they should be included with cinematographers, editors, writers, etc., as significant contributors to the making of a film.

The second lesson was the importance of the producer in the Hollywood system. Both Julie Salamon and John Gregory Dunne make this explicit in their books. Though Steven Bach does not make it so explicit, the role played by Joann Carelli, the producer of *Heaven's Gate*, emerges as a significant one. Or, rather, it was the role she did not play that was significant. The United Artists' executives believed she was too close to Michael Cimino to exercise control over the budget or the schedule. To counter this they put in their own representatives, which only heightened the tensions with Cimino.

The third lesson was simply the enormous burden a director carries during the making of a film. The director has to make a large number of decisions in many different areas. The decisions are often made under great pressure, with the knowledge that they will have important consequences for the quality of the film. If we put this lesson together with the other two, there is a fourth to be learnt. It is that executives, producers and directors are part of a delicate chain. The success of a film depends significantly on how this chain links together.

chapter six

Criticism: *Jurassic Park, Chinatown, When Harry Met Sally*

Fig 6.1 On the set of *Hannibal,* 2001. (Photo: MGM/Universal/De Laurentiis/The Kobal Collection/Phil Bray)

We thought it would be instructive to develop our exploration of the dynamics of film production by looking in detail at individual films. Our first guideline in choosing the films was, therefore, the availability of substantial information about their production history. Our second guideline was to find films that represented different genres. So we have chosen *Jurassic Park* as an example of the spectacle film, *Chinatown* as an example of film noir and *When Harry Met Sally* as an example of romantic comedy.

Jurassic Park

I never felt the same way about *Jurassic Park*. I didn't think it was a perfect film, and it wasn't so close to my heart that I needed to protect the integrity of a follow-up preventing anybody else from doing one which I certainly had the right to do. Among the films that I really think are good movies that I've directed, it's not even in the top five.

[Steven Spielberg speaking about *Jurassic Park* to Peter Biskind] (Friedman and Notbohm, 2000: 197)

Jurassic Park is an interesting film to explore on many levels: the relationship between Spielberg and the crew, the role of new technologies (both aural and visual), the relationships involved in the writing of the film (from Crichton's book to the many rewrites of the film's script) and the rather schizoid nature of the film's post-production process (when Spielberg was already in Poland filming *Schindler's List*). The latter is a good starting point as it highlights some of the filmmaking dynamics at play in the creation of *Jurassic Park*. Whilst the film was in the post-production stages in California, Spielberg was in Poland filming *Schindler's List*. A rather complex satellite connection between Skywalker Ranch (where the film was being edited and mixed) and Poland allowed Spielberg to keep in touch with developments in California; technologically this clearly helped to bridge the physical distance. Moreover, Spielberg left George Lucas in charge of post-production in California in an attempt to guarantee some measure of control over the process. However, these measures mostly address issues of overall supervision rather than creative input. It mirrors a model of filmmaking that Spielberg has often employed: surround yourself with your most trusted collaborators, give them a detailed brief to work to and then allow them to get on with their work; later, review progress and accept/reject the work already carried out.

Given the nature of the two films, the different teams working on each project, the physical distance and other such factors, it would be disingenuous to suggest that Spielberg could possibly have been entirely responsible, in a creative sense, for both films. The question, then, is who, to what extent and in what way can be identified as having made a crucial creative contribution to the film?

Joseph McBride suggests that this 'cultural dislocation' (Spielberg's own words) actually 'perfectly expressed the duality of his artistic personality' (McBride, 1997: 415). This is an interesting position, one on which many other commentators and Spielberg have expressed agreement. It suggests a clear split between Spielberg the artist (working on *Schindler's List*) and Spielberg the entertainer (working on *Jurassic Park*). At the same time, it keeps Spielberg firmly at the centre of both films: whatever else they may be, sophisticated art or mass entertainment, they belong to Spielberg, creatively and otherwise. The director would seem to concur: speaking of his agreement with MCA president Sid Sheinberg that he would be allowed to film *Schindler's List* only on provision that he would make *Jurassic Park* first, Spielberg remarks: 'He [Sheinberg] knew that once I had directed Schindler I wouldn't be able to do *Jurassic Park*' (McBride, 1997: 416).

Jurassic Park has often been discussed in terms of its financial profitability, of its technological prowess and of its director's authorial presence. These accounts have always been placed firmly within a general understanding of *Jurassic Park* as entertainment, as opposed to *Schindler's List* as art. Indeed, Spielberg himself has readily subscribed to this view, as the opening quote indicates. As a consequence, little of the actual interaction between and contributions of the various people who worked on the film have been explored, with the important exception of the relationship between Spielberg and the visual effects team. We would like to focus on some of these relationships and interactions that we deem to have been central to the creation of the film in order to investigate more closely issues of creative responsibility. In particular two key areas are significant in the case of *Jurassic Park*, namely the scriptwriting process (involving several writers and Spielberg himself) and the relationship involving sound team, visual effects team and director.

The script

Michael Crichton and Steven Spielberg had known each other for some time when Crichton began to write *Jurassic Park*. The two had indeed collaborated on an idea for a TV series, called *E.R. – Emergency Room*, that Crichton had developed from his experience as a hospital doctor and that Spielberg had bought. It was during a meeting on story development that the subject of *Jurassic Park* was first mentioned. As is widely known, Spielberg immediately showed great interest in Crichton's idea (the book was not completely finished at this stage, as Spielberg himself remarks in the book *The Making of Jurassic Park*, Shay and Duncan, 1993), and the two reached an informal agreement whereby Spielberg would direct the movie version of Crichton's book. Crichton recalls that he felt this: 'was going to be a very difficult picture to make . . . Steven is arguably the most experienced and most successful director of this kind of movie. And he's really terrific at running the technology rather than letting the technology run him' (Shay and Duncan, 1993: 8). Despite the inevitable bidding war that followed the publication of Crichton's novel, in which virtually every studio showed an interest, the two eventually did strike an agreement. Part of it was that Crichton would also write the screenplay for the film. Although Crichton agreed to this, he also felt that his prolonged engagement with the *Jurassic Park* material may cause a problem. Having spent over a year writing a book (that had been in gestation for a very long time) Crichton warned Spielberg that he would write a draft but that Spielberg would eventually 'want somebody else to polish his characters' (Shay and Duncan: 1993: 9). Crichton's forecast proved right in many ways. It took him almost seven months to write the first draft of the script. In his own words 'Nobody was happy with it at all' (Shay and Duncan, 1993: 9).

The situation was complicated by Spielberg's attitude towards the book and its story. From very early on in the unusually lengthy pre-production period (two years) Spielberg had formed very specific ideas as to how the film would function. As well as producer Kathleen Kennedy, and Crichton himself, almost immediately Spielberg brought on board production designer Rick Carter. He then set out to work with Carter on the book galleys before Crichton's first draft of the script was anywhere near completion. Clearly, at this stage in the process Spielberg was trying to identify the set pieces that the narrative would be built around and needed Carter to help him get a fuller visual sense of the film. Both Carter and Spielberg have often confirmed this in interviews. Carter says he had: 'many early meetings with Steven where we would break down the scenes in the book and discuss which ones would work best for the film' (Shay and Duncan, 1993: 12). Spielberg also suggests that he wanted to 'boil the book down and choose my seven or eight favourite scenes and base the script around those' (Shay and Duncan, 1993: 12).

This approach inevitably created a difficult situation. Crichton's book, though strong on action, depends essentially on character motivation, especially in the way this helps to illuminate character behaviour when faced with moral dilemmas. In the book a great deal is made of the relationship between man and science and the resulting effects on nature. The very existence of the dinosaurs is a direct consequence of human greed and scientific exploitation rather than genuine scientific interest or accident. By focusing on set pieces Spielberg chose to bypass all these considerations and relegated them to additional plot information rather than a central theme. Given the different approach to storytelling that separated Crichton's book from Spielberg's concept of the film it is hardly surprising that Crichton's first draft met with disapproval and a second writer was brought in.

Malia Scotch Marmo was asked to work on Crichton's script; however, her brief would seem to have been rather vague. Indeed, Marmo's account of her approach to writing the new draft of the script is indicative of her intentions:

> I spent about a week reading everything. I read the first script, and I read the novel again and again. And I looked at the storyboards and production art, which was quite extensive at that point. Steven generates a great deal of thought on subject and he has storyboard artists on hand. As he thinks, they draw . . . I think the structure of Michael's script was pretty close to the final movie. It was after all, the structure of the book. The only differences were the streamlining that one writer might do as opposed to another. Michael had done a brilliant job of presenting the science of biotechnology and raising questions about its harmlessness and the whole issue of science for profit.
>
> (Shay and Duncan, 1993: 40)

Marmo's take on *Jurassic Park* was clearly closer to Crichton's approach in the book than what Spielberg was now asking of her. It is not easy to guess the reasons for this apparent breakdown in communication. What is puzzling about this process is that Marmo and Spielberg continually discussed the new draft of the script while Marmo was writing it. As she recalls:

> Usually writers get an assignment, go home, write it and turn it in. We didn't work that way. I had feedback from Steven all the time. In fact, I would send him my first fifteen pages and he would react to them. Then I'd rewrite them a little in accordance with his wishes and send them back with the next fifteen pages, so he would have thirty. And that was pretty much the process for the whole five-month period.
>
> (Shay and Duncan, 1993: 41)

Yet, after so much communication and collaboration, Marmo's script was in Spielberg's words 'a miss'. This confusion surrounding the nature and character of the script appears even more obvious when Crichton's own views about the book are taken into account. Crichton states that in his book: 'The first thing to do was to make compelling dinosaurs . . . that was my overriding concern' (Shay and Duncan, 1993: 41). This concern with dinosaur believability is driven by the concern that without convincing dinosaurs any other message would be lost: 'Without that it doesn't matter what your message is or who your characters are' (Shay and Duncan: 1993: 41). However, when Spielberg and Crichton discussed the film, Spielberg was adamant that 'Effects are only as good as the audience's feeling for the characters' (McBride, 1997: 421).

Marmo's script focused strongly on character and less on action if compared with either the book or the final version of the film. A good example of this is the surprising decision to break down the tempo and rhythm of one of the film's key set pieces: the 'dinosaurs in the kitchen' sequence. This is a remarkable departure from what Spielberg had envisaged (and had already asked Carter and his team to storyboard) in that the action involving the two kids and two raptors takes place in three different places (the toy shop, the kitchen and the visitor centre's main hall), thus diluting the tension over three different sets rather than focussing on the kitchen alone, as does the film. The fact that Marmo could write this kind of script (it is not a matter of 'quality' here but of 'type') whilst talking regularly to Spielberg and looking at the storyboards is another example of how difficult it can be for key collaborators to communicate efficiently and effectively. The issue of director's vision is particularly relevant here. Spielberg's main preoccupation from very early on in the film was that the dinosaurs should behave like animals, not monsters. However, it is not clear whether there was any kind of agreement on what this actually meant. For some, as in the case of top conceptual artist Mark McGreery, who did the all-important first sketches that would be shown to the studio, this meant moving away from traditional perceptions of dinosaur movement. As he recalls 'I wanted to get as far away from people's perception of dinosaurs as possible . . . the upright bulky, clumsy kind of creatures that have been seen in previous movies' (Shay and Duncan, 1993: 20). The notion of dinosaurs moving more like agile animals than cumbersome beasts is confirmed by Spielberg's attitude during pre-production meetings with the visual effects team, where he spent a considerable amount of time planning how the dinosaurs would move and look in detail. That is to say, the actual difference between animal and monster was never really articulated beyond the notion of movement and looks. In behavioural terms, the main addition was to have the dinosaurs stalk their prey rather than simply attack it. Thus, speaking of this film as being something other than a monster movie might have created more confusion than clarity in the minds of the writers.

Similarly, confusion about theme surfaces from time to time amongst other key collaborators who were involved in the shaping of the film from a very early stage. Speaking of the *Jurassic Park* buildings, Rick Carter says that

Building the perfect *anything* is impossible – especially when one is dealing with nature. The best we can do is never really good enough because we are not God – which is one of the major themes of this movie and one that relates to bioengineering. Just because you *can* do something, does it mean you *should* do it?
(Shay and Duncan, 1993: 45)

Although this is indeed a main theme in Crichton's book (and in Marmo's version of the script) it is not so in the movie, where it is reduced to a brief conversation over dinner during which Malcolm accuses Hammond: 'Your scientists were so preoccupied with whether or not they could that they didn't stop to think if they should. Science can create pesticides, but it can't tell us not to use them. Science can make a nuclear reactor, but it can't tell us not to build it!'

The difficulty in communicating effectively about the project resulted in two unsatisfactory scripts and the need to bring in a third scriptwriter. David Koepp was brought in after he had finished work on Robert Zemeckis's *Death Becomes Her*. In some ways, Koepp, who is now one of the highest paid writers in Hollywood, was a logical choice for Spielberg. At this stage in the process he and long-time collaborator producer Kathleen Kennedy had hired Rick Carter (production designer), William James Teegarden (art director), Michael Lantieri (special effects supervisor) and would soon also bring on board Dean Cundey (director of photography). All of the above, including Koepp and Kennedy, had just finished working on *Death Becomes Her*. Clearly, as they constituted the bulk of the production team, Spielberg and Kennedy went for continuity rather than trying to assemble a new crew, especially as time was now becoming a factor and a workable shooting script had to be delivered quickly. Koepp's choice made sense: he had just rewritten *Death Becomes Her* and most of the production team had worked following his script, so he seemed to be a logical choice. His role in rewriting *Jurassic Park* is very interesting as it confirms Spielberg's approach to the film in more ways than one. Koepp was given what might have looked like *carte blanche*. Koepp felt uneasy about doing a rewrite because he felt that: 'It's very hard to get in the mind of somebody else and try to follow what they were doing' (Shay and Duncan, 1993: 54). However, Spielberg's reassurances that he could start afresh eased those worries: 'I was told that I could start over . . . If you have the world as your canvas it really lets your own ideas run free' (Shay and Duncan, 1993: 54).

Koepp's script reflects changes from both book and the first two drafts in some respects: some of the characters' traits are changed and relationships enhanced (Grant shows profound dislike of children, and is now romantically involved with Ellie; Hammond continues his journey into a much more benevolent character than in either Crichton's book or Marmo's script; the age and role of the children are reversed, with Lex now being the older character). Also a major set piece, the river-rafting chase, is eliminated in Koepp's version of the movie. However, these changes amount more to functional changes than structural: by the time Koepp had come on board the film had been storyboarded. His decision to work from Crichton's book, rather than from either of the first two drafts of the script, was effectively neutralized by Spielberg's insistence that Koepp should also follow the storyboards. As Koepp himself admits, the storyboards were 'enormously helpful. It was like having a large portion of the movie just handed out to you, to be able to walk around and soak up the feel of what the movie was supposed to look like' (McBride, 1997: 418). In a further statement, suggesting once again a lack of clarity on the nature of the film's main drive, Koepp even suggests that: '. . . we didn't want this to be just another slasher movie where the slasher happens to be a dinosaur. We wanted the animals to be really innocent' (Shay and Duncan, 1993: 64).

In light of these facts, it would appear that Koepp's chance to start over was clearly more an attempt on Spielberg's and Kennedy's part to convince the writer to accept the job than a real intent. The existence of the storyboards in particular (with some 'locked' scenes not up for negotiation) posed a considerable limitation on Koepp's margin of independence. A few years later, when Koepp penned the script for *The Lost World*, the sequel to *Jurassic Park*, he candidly admitted that in *Jurassic Park* he had had to throw out 'a lot of detail about the characters because whenever they started talking about their personal lives, you couldn't care less. You wanted them to shut up and go stand on a hill where you can see the dinosaurs' (Friedman and Notbohm, 2000: 1999). This view, action not character, is much closer to the way Spielberg approached *Jurassic Park*.

It would therefore appear that Spielberg showed greater interest in the process of constructing set pieces than actually working on the story or its characters. Koepp's words in this sense explain much about the director's approach to storytelling:

> Steven operates from images. He'll call up and say, 'I had this idea for a shot. It's not even a shot. It's part of a shot. What do you think of that? Is that part of our story?' I'll think, 'Now how does that relate to anything?' And then I try to figure it out. I really like working with directors like that because they tend to leave a lot of the other stuff, dialogue and so on, to you. They provide these sparks.
>
> (Friedman and Notbohm, 2000: 200)

This focus on the set pieces and the look of the film moves attention away from scriptwriting and onto visual production, both in terms of production design and visual effects.

The look

Most reviewers and scholars who have written about *Jurassic Park* have unanimously praised the film for the quality of its visual effects. In particular, the then relatively new computer-generated images (CGI) technology was singled out as a true milestone in the history of cinema. Desson Howe (*Washington Post*, 11 June 1993) comments thus:

> They're dinosaurs and, thanks to the visual mastery of George Lucas's Industrial Light & Magic and special-effects dino-meisters Stan Winston, Phil Tippett and Michael Lantieri, they're extraordinarily beautiful, believable and downright intimidating. In the year's most-awaited movie, they are the MVPs, the box-office draw, the oomph of this picture.

Janet Maslin ('Screen stars with teeth to spare', *New York Times*, 11 June 1993) suggests that:

> They [the dinosaurs] appear only for brief interludes, but the dinosaurs dominate *Jurassic Park* in every way. Amazingly graceful and convincing, they set a sky-high new standard for computer-generated special effects . . . The most important thing about the dinosaurs of *Jurassic Park* is that they create a triumphant illusion. You will believe you have spent time in a dino-filled world.

Even those who had been very critical of the movie, and of its narrative strategy in particular, such as Roger Ebert (*Chicago Sun-Times*), admit that the film's dinosaurs 'are indeed a triumph of special effects artistry.' Some film historians, such as David Cook (2004) go so far as to suggest that *Jurassic Park* is the living proof that: 'From being an embellishment to science-fiction and action films ten years before, CGI had become the driving force of the American cinema.'

Indeed, the exceptional team put together by Spielberg and Kennedy was a who's who of visual effects artistry. Michael Lantieri (visual effects supervisor), Stan Winston (live action dinosaurs), Phil Tippett (Go-motion dinosaurs) and Dennis Muren (CGI dinosaurs) are the most experienced team Spielberg could ever wish to assemble, covering virtually every aspect of the visual effects spectrum and providing an excellent base for publicity and marketing, since these names are very well known both within the industry and amongst fans of Sci-Fi and Fantasy. The relationship between Spielberg and the 'magnificent four' has been widely documented elsewhere. (An unusual source of information in this sense is provided by Spielberg's own home movies documenting pre-production meetings between him, Kennedy and the visual effects team. Some of these are available as extras in the *Jurassic Park* DVD release.) However, despite lavish praise, and the undeniable quality of the visual effects, there were doubts amongst the dinosaurs' creators. Commenting on Spielberg's desire to have lingering shots of the dinosaurs, Phil Tippett worries about a crucial aspect: 'We were going to see the behaviour of these animals for extended lengths of time. But what were they going to be *doing* in all this time? It was fine if they had to perform a specific task, like jumping up on a table or walking. But when they were just standing there, it became a problem to fill the time with interesting action' (Shay and Duncan, 1993: 137). Dennis Muren expressed similar concerns about the relative lifelessness of the dinosaurs when not involved in some kind of action:

> When we started making the computer graphic Tyrannosaurus and Raptors for *Jurassic Park,* I was having trouble getting them to look really alive. Their motions were great. Their skin looked real. But they just weren't as powerful and threatening as they would be if I were standing there looking at real ones. Then I realized that I couldn't 'see' them think. I couldn't 'see' their soul.
> (From *The Making of Jurassic Park* documentary, Columbia Tristar Home Video, 2000)

Muren later suggests that he needed to add a 'soul' to the dinosaurs and that he could do so through lighting, especially of the dinosaurs' eyes.

These expressions of unease go beyond the issue of believability, which remained Spielberg's main concern. In a revealing comment, Tippett candidly admits that: 'For me it was never that important to make things look real, which is pretty much the criteria for computer graphics. I always enjoyed the fact that the dinosaurs looked a little unreal' (Shay and Duncan, 1993: 140).

Lantieri, Tippett, Muren and Winston had created images of dinosaurs that looked and moved in ways that audiences would probably not reject as foolish or laughable: the real yardstick, as Tippett's comments suggest, is less a matter of looking real and more an issue of not looking too unreal. Serious concerns about the life, soul and character of the dinosaurs evidently surfaced amongst their creators. These concerns are important, especially in relation to one of the most interesting and surprising aspects of *Jurassic Park*, namely the rather limited visual exposure that dinosaurs get in terms of screen time. Simply put, dinosaurs are seen for less than ten minutes of the film's two hours and seven minutes running time. Spielberg's comment that he wanted *Jurassic Park* to be '*Jaws* on land' may go some way to explain why dinosaurs appear so little. The choice of not revealing the beast until late in the movie has often been indicated as *Jaws'* main strength (whether this was the result of a conscious narrative decision or a happy by-product of a difficult situation, where the mechanical shark did not meet expectations, is less important). The remarkable cost of CGI shots – like all breakthrough technology in its infancy stage, CGI was extremely expensive – was another important factor. As Spielberg comments, the cost of CGI:

> ... runs you between $250,000 and $500,000 to put anything into a computer, even a small, uncomplicated dinosaur, and that's before you generate a single shot. If you've got a dinosaur just walking around, it's $80,000 for eight seconds. If the dinosaur is splashing in a puddle or kicking up tufts of dirt, it's $100,000. If there are four dinosaurs in the background of that shot, it's $150,000.
>
> (Friedman and Notbohm, 2000: 203)

The question therefore becomes: what gives the dinosaurs 'soul', dynamics and scary value so much that their presence 'dominates the whole picture' and makes experienced writers, such as Ebert, feel that the dinosaurs are 'seen very often' when they are not? The narrative style is very reminiscent of traditional Horror films, where delaying the visual appearance of the 'monster' enhances its presence. In this logic, audiences do not need to see dinosaurs to know that they are there. However, they do need to hear them.

The sound

> *Jurassic*'s animators were creating dinosaurs that looked absolutely real. Yet, they would not be fully brought to life until one crucial element was added [a huge dinosaur roar is heard on the soundtrack] sound.
>
> (James Earl Jones from the *Making of Jurassic Park* documentary, 2000 DVD release)

In many ways *Jurassic Park* marks one of the most remarkable departures from Hollywood sound production patterns of the 1990s. The relationships between the sound team and the visual effects team, the editorial team and the composer all deviate, sometimes substantially, from the norm. As James Earl Jones's words suggest, in filmmaking sound is thought of as an 'add-on', something that comes after the movie has been filmed and edited. Indeed, Richard Hymns, the film's supervising sound editor, would appear to suggest that *Jurassic Park* did conform to traditional sound production patterns when he says: 'My job started from the end of the picture editing period' (Shay and Duncan, 1993: 141). These claims from two 'official'

Jurassic Park sources unwittingly 'hide' one of most meaningful ways in which the film differs from traditional sound production patterns, namely the degree of involvement in the early decision-making period that the key sound people had.

Sound designer Gary Rydstrom was brought on the project very early on. A seven-times Oscar winning sound designer, whose credits include *Titanic, Saving Private Ryan, Terminator 2* and *Toy Story*, and long-time collaborator of Spielberg and Lucas, Rydstrom was the logical choice for the film, as Spielberg had once again chosen to use Lucas's post-production facilities at Skywalker Ranch for *Jurassic Park*. When instructing Rydstrom and his team, Spielberg made suggestions similar to those he had given to his animators as to what the dinosaurs should sound like: 'Make them sound real, but also make them sound big and deep' (Interview with Rydstrom at the Sounding Out Conference, Staffordshire University, July 2002). Once again, the term 'real' is used but not elaborated upon. Indeed, the claim that Spielberg (and virtually all of the visual departments) made about wanting the dinosaurs to be as real as possible in *Jurassic Park* is countered by this quote from Rydstrom that emphasizes the need to be narratively and emotionally effective rather than being literally faithful to the 'original':

> The input I got from Spielberg was just to make all the dinosaurs sound believably animalistic – something that people could relate to. The line we had to walk was to come up with something that was new and different, yet also familiar enough so that people would believe these things actually exist. We couldn't get too far out with the dinosaurs sounds – even if there was scientific evidence to support that – because the audience had to be able to connect with the animals.
>
> (Shay and Duncan, 1993: 142)

Rydstrom clearly chose to focus on the need to establish a 'connection' between dinosaurs and audiences rather than on trying to understand what Spielberg's intentions were when he spoke of realism. This attempt at 'connecting' with audiences translated in a series of important choices regarding sound made early on in the production process, the most important of which concerns dinosaur characterization. Despite attempts to convey difference in visual terms, the difficulty in dealing with dinosaurs as characters stemmed from the simple consideration that traditional means of differentiating characters, namely costume and makeup, could not be used. In terms of facial characteristics and facial movement, the puppeteering element of the animation helped to achieve some degree of characterization, but only in close-up shots. Thus, the task for the sound team was twofold: to provide dinosaurs with 'language' (hence, differentiation) and to provide them with a sense of dramatic action and dynamism. Both of these elements would, in turn, help audiences 'connect' with the dinosaurs, whether they were actually visible (as in the case of the T-Rex attack scene) or not (as in the 'feeding time' scene). Rydstrom confirms the special attention that the sound team devoted to language and vocalization:

> In past dinosaurs movies you would hear the same roar over and over again. What we wanted to do for *Jurassic* was develop a fuller, more natural

vocabulary for these creatures – breathing and grunting and sniffing, even the sound of the eyelids moving or the nostrils flaring. We were striving to make it completely believable.

(Shay and Duncan, 1993: 142)

This quote also emphasizes another aspect connected to the film's soundtrack. The way dinosaurs sound in the film helps articulate mood for the audience in ways that the visuals, no matter how effective, cannot always do, given the limited range of visual expression dinosaurs have. In turn, mood refocuses audience attention away from the 'look' and onto dinosaur behaviour. In other words, whereas the visual department would seem to have concentrated primarily, though not exclusively, on the way the dinosaurs looked, the sound department would appear to have dealt with the issue of giving these creatures 'character'. In this sense, it is perhaps indicative that Stan Winston should comment that 'it's not enough for them to act real, they need to look real'.

Rydstrom and his team designed the key dinosaurs' sounds, including the T-Rex and the various raptors' sounds, before the creatures were animated. The so-called 'animatics' (rough animated sketches that are used to give the filmmakers a sense of how an entire sequence would look because they provide both movement and a sense of depth) provided a basis for the sound designers to work from. That is to say, in some ways *Jurassic Park* followed a certain pattern of production that is more typical of animation than live-action films: the key sounds in a film are designed and recorded first, and animators then follow this aural blueprint for their animation. In short, sound affected the way dinosaurs moved, especially in terms of their jaw and head movement. Figure 6.2 is a spectrum analysis 'snap' of the T-Rex when she is first heard to roar. The sound lasts a remarkable four seconds and clearly this had to be accommodated by animators. (The figures in this chapter are screen grabs of the spectral view of the actual sound recording as it was used in the film. They provide a graphic illustration of how sound operates in terms of frequency, loudness and length. The vertical axis shows frequency (i.e., frequency increases from bottom to top), the horizontal axis shows time (left to right). Black areas in the figures indicate that no sound is present (see, for instance, Figure 6.3 where the black areas separate the seven distinct raptors' sounds.))

The importance of articulating these vocalizations into some kind of language was also very important. There is only one T-Rex in *Jurassic Park*, but several Velociraptors. More importantly, raptors are described in both book and script as having some kind of intelligence and being able to communicate with each other. This was an essential aim for the sound team: 'The raptors had to sound as if they had intelligence – which, vocally, meant that they would make a greater variety of sounds, as if they had some ability to communicate with each other' (Shay and Duncan, 1993: 144). The combination of vocalization and articulation of different voices ultimately helped to create a sense of difference between dinosaurs, as well as contributing to the creation of dramatic action and dynamics. Most noticeably, sound designers on *Jurassic Park* created several different sounds for the raptors that allowed them a certain degree of freedom in attempting to establish 'a language' of sorts. Figure 6.3 is a sound spectrum analysis of seven different raptors' sounds used in the film and it immediately highlights the marked difference in aural characteristics of the various sounds.

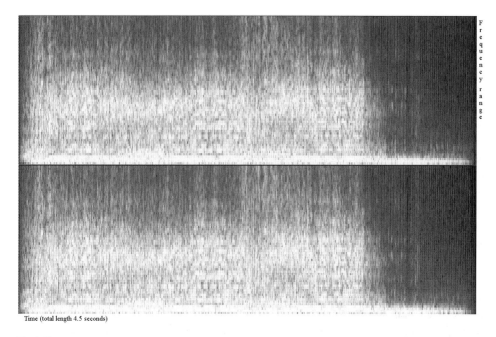

Time (total length 4.5 seconds)

Fig 6.2

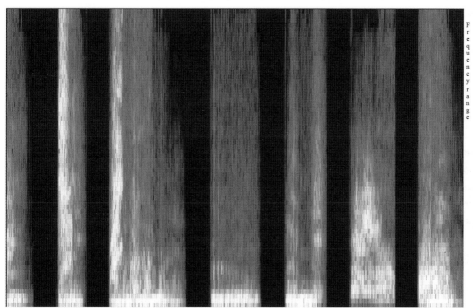

Black spaces signal pauses between the seven different velociraptor sounds (each sound lasts less apx. one second)

Fig 6.3

This ability to articulate dinosaur sounds into much more than simply undefined roaring noises became a storytelling tool that helped some of the choices made by Spielberg and Koepp concerning some key scenes. Perhaps the most striking example of how much filmmakers could rely on sound to do the job is the 'feeding time' scene. In the book, when Grant and the others approach the raptors' paddock into which a cow has just been lowered as food for the dinosaurs, the raptors actually 'hunt' Grant himself, albeit from behind the electrified cage. In the scene, several raptors are seen as they move in and out of the thick foliage. However, in the film, dinosaurs are not seen at all: the sounds they make as they prepare to attack and then devour the poor cow offered to them as food ultimately provide a very dynamic (there is strong sense of movement in the scene) and dramatic instance that serves as a reminder of how dangerous and deadly these beasts actually are.

A further point of departure from convention is the close collaboration between composer and sound team. Traditionally the composer and the sound team work separately, often having very little communication with one another. This was not the case with *Jurassic Park*, where Williams and the sound team collaborated closely. Crucial to this departure from convention is the long-standing collaboration between Spielberg and composer John Williams, and also that between Spielberg and Skywalker Sound (Lucasfilm's post-production facility in Marin County, north of San Francisco) and the film's sound team (Gary Rydstrom, Gary Summers and Richard Hymns are household names at Skywalker Sound and a very experienced team, with a total of 14 Oscars between them to date). John Williams came on board the project in February 1992, once filming had finished. However, by that time the sound team had already assembled a rough version of the sound effects for the key scenes (most crucially, they had dinosaur vocalization already in place). This is probably why Williams's score and the sound effects mesh so well in this film.

Two reasons appear to be key for this successful relationship: one, as we mentioned earlier, is avoiding the customary situation whereby the sound team and the composer work separately and do not get to hear each other's work until very late in the process. The problem in this dominant model of production is a classic situation where the left hand does not know what the right hand is doing. The inevitable clash that happens when the two efforts are brought together in the final mix is indeed a constant cause for argument. It is often mentioned by both sound designers and composers as a rather disheartening process whereby protecting your own material, rather than open collaboration, becomes the name of the game. However, in the case of *Jurassic Park*, John Williams spent far more time than usual communicating with the sound team. Early pre-mixing of sound effects for crucial scenes meant (1) John Williams's score could be tuned into the general soundscape of the film, and (2) music could avoid taking up frequency ranges already occupied by either dialogue or sound effects.

Williams was also often present during the final mix of the film, another uncommon practice (traditionally the composer hands in the score just before the final mix begins and then moves on to the next project, taking virtually no part in the crucial last stage of the creation of a soundtrack). This was aided by the fact that Williams recorded all the music at Skywalker Ranch, next door to where the rest of the sound team was working.

The result is a soundtrack where the three major components, voices, music and sound effects, work together in harmony, both literally and figuratively.

Also, Williams acknowledged early on in his involvement the importance of the sound effects team on this film and that his music should perhaps take a 'back seat'. (Interestingly, Rydstrom and Williams were to collaborate once again with Spielberg on both *Minority Report* and *A.I.* In the case of the latter, it was Rydstrom who suggested that music be the 'leading' factor in that soundtrack and that sound effects would be built around it.) This meant that when necessary, such as in the T-Rex attack, the re-recording mixers could actually focus on sound effects as the driving force without having to find a space for music that was not designed to be there.

A final departure from tradition in *Jurassic Park* is the absence of editor and director from the post-production process. As we mentioned at the beginning of this chapter, both Steven Spielberg and editor Michael Kahn had moved on to *Schindler's List* by the time *Jurassic Park* was in post-production. Spielberg had delegated Kathleen Kennedy to be in charge of the music efforts and entrusted long-time friend and fellow director George Lucas with the post-production sound team. The arrangement was for Kennedy to beam Williams' work to Poland via satellite so that Spielberg could listen to and approve/reject the composer's work. Spielberg had to travel to Paris on a couple of weekends to listen to the final mix of the film's soundtrack that Rydstrom, Hymns, Summer and their team were putting together at Skywalker Sound, and, again, make suggestions, approve or reject the work that had been done thousands of miles away. That is to say, Spielberg's involvement, though significant because he approved the work, was limited. He was not present at the final mix, he was not present at Williams' recording sessions, the editor was not on hand for advice/queries, etc. and this arrangement made dialogue very difficult and sporadic. This reveals a very complex situation from both a creative and organizational point of view. Creatively, Rydstrom and his team were effectively left to their own devices to get on with the job. Similarly, Williams also had less of an input than he would traditionally have had, although Kennedy's frequent discussions with Spielberg would have certainly helped.

Conclusion: the director's vision understood as organization

> As usual, however, the real author was Spielberg . . . Ironically, the man who so tersely rejected the politique des auteurs two decades before had become its most successful example.
>
> [Spielberg as quoted in John Baxter's biography of the director] (Baxter, 1997: 373)

The picture that arises from looking at production patterns in *Jurassic Park* is fascinating. The film was a departure from conventional productions in some significant ways. The complex relationship between production design and scriptwriting, the unusually long (two years) pre-production period, the degree of early involvement and freedom of action that the sound team enjoyed, the absence of both director and editor from the post-production process, the extensive use of new technologies, both aural (DTS digital sound) and visual (CGI), all point to a rather difficult production in organizational terms. In this context, the presumed ability of a director to impose his/her vision becomes a fundamental aspect around which the success or failure of the production hinges. However, this is where things become complicated.

Spielberg is universally acknowledged by commentators as the author of the film. There is evidence to suggest that he was indeed at the core of some key decisions, especially in terms of structuring the film's narrative, casting and, most importantly, selecting his crew. However, there is also clear evidence to suggest that Spielberg's vision, if ever there was one, is very difficult to define. The relationship with the writers on *Jurassic Park* is in this sense indicative. Spielberg's vision would seem to have revolved around three key points: (1) dinosaurs as animals, not monsters; (2) dinosaurs as 'real'; and (3) remove the science bits: dinosaurs are the stars. The concept of dinosaurs as animals rather than monsters is, in many ways, a red herring. *Jurassic Park* is a film about scary dinosaurs, not scary animals. The huge degree of departure from their 'real' behaviour (both in terms of visual and aural characteristics) points, in fact, to the desire to achieve effectiveness: the aim is not to have the audience in awe of the dinosaurs but rather to have audiences scared to death by them.

The concept of making dinosaurs real and believable is also rather unclear. What does real mean in Spielberg's view? He does not seem to be concerned with literal realism: *Jurassic Park* dinosaurs are too fast and agile in their movement, too loud and articulate in the way they sound. Spielberg's use of the term 'real' refers more to issues of making things seem real: *Jurassic Park* dinosaurs should look and sound in a manner that audiences will accept as plausible (or, more importantly, that they will not reject as implausible). However, the latitude that audiences traditionally allow filmmakers in terms of what will be accepted as plausible neutralizes Spielberg's suggestion/comments/instructions. Most importantly, Spielberg's notion of believable and real does not amount to a clear vision that can be easily communicated to cast and crew, as there are too many possible interpretations. The only clues specific enough to be effective remain Spielberg's instructions to the visual effects team on the way dinosaurs should move. Spielberg clearly indicates that movement should be smooth and fluid to signal a departure from (improvement on?) previous dinosaur films where animation is significantly jerky. While this may go some way to explain the choices made by the visual effects team in relation to the dinosaurs' motion, it does not provide any particular sense of direction either in terms of narrative or sound.

In narrative terms the confusion as to what was actually expected of the writers is evident. Despite continuous discussions with Spielberg, both Crichton and Marmo handed in scripts that not only were dismissed by Spielberg as 'a miss' but that also differed significantly in narrative drive and plot direction from Koepp's (final) script. How could Marmo's draft be so different from the film's final script when she had been working so closely with Spielberg during the rewrites? The issue is not one of quantity but rather one of quality of communication. If Spielberg indeed had a vision then neither Crichton nor Marmo understood clearly what it was.

As for Koepp's version of the script, by the time he became involved in the writing process the storyboards that Spielberg and Carter had created had become the real core of the writing process and Koepp worked mostly from them. Some of the storyboards were in fact so detailed as to leave very little to chance. Indeed, despite Koepp's protestation to the contrary, his efforts could be described as having been substantially shaped by what had already been decided by Spielberg. Despite this, however, confusion is still at play somehow when Koepp states that the dinosaurs in *Jurassic Park* are 'innocent' (yet again, even this comment appears to be rather vague and open to interpretation). In the case of the sound team, Spielberg's suggestion to go looking for dinosaur sounds in the animal realm is useful but somewhat superfluous, since the sound team he and Kennedy had assembled comprised people who had built their reputation precisely on working from 'real' sounds (i.e., recorded from actual events rather than manufactured electronically).

Ultimately, Spielberg's vision would appear to amount to little more than generic suggestions open to almost countless interpretations. Whilst some filmmakers actually enjoy this relatively high degree of creative freedom (as opposed to a director such as Cameron who leaves very little open to interpretation), Spielberg's contribution to the film does not reside in some kind of thematic or stylistic vision. In the specific case of *Jurassic Park* the contribution of the director concerns the ability to have a general sense of where the strengths of the film lie and to assemble the various production teams accordingly. In some ways, *Jurassic Park's* greatest asset is that everybody involved in the film, from actors to writers and from visual team to the sound team, was clear about one aspect: dinosaurs are the stars and every creative effort needs to defer to this. Beyond this 'generic' message Spielberg is clearly content to let his team get on with the job and then accept or reject the results. In this sense, the organizational and managerial dimension of *Jurassic Park* also suggest that producers Kathleen Kennedy and Gerry Marshall, as well as George Lucas during post-production, played a very important part in both assembling the production teams and ensuring they worked to the same brief, no matter how vague the brief was.

Does this 'looser than usual' relationship between Spielberg and his key collaborators mean that *Jurassic Park* is a failure? We believe that far from suffering unduly from the relative absence of the director, the post-production teams (both sound and visual) produced a remarkably effective effort that substantially shaped the way in which the film functions. In many respects, the fact that Spielberg virtually refused paternity of the film (as he has often pointed out in interviews, he really did not care that much about this film) acted as a spur for others, especially the visual effects team and the sound team, to make it their own. That the more interesting and stimulating questions concerning the role and effectiveness of the dinosaurs should come from these quarters confirm their engagement with the film. Indeed, the simple fact that these questions should have been asked at all is a testament to their creative effort. We believe that it is thanks to this and the excellent work of the production team (Kathleen Kennedy above all) that the film ultimately achieves exactly what it had aimed at becoming: a spectacular and very scary film about dinosaurs.

The film also remains, to this day, Spielberg's greatest financial success. In this sense, Spielberg's eager dismissal of the film, especially in relation to his more 'serious' work, is a slap in the face of both audiences and all those people who refused to give up on the project. It is also a timely reminder, if ever one was needed, that the art–entertainment dichotomy is alive and well in contemporary Hollywood, even in the mind of the most popular director in film history. Spielberg said that he would not be able to do a film like *Jurassic Park* after *Schindler's List*. However, that is exactly what he did: the fact that Spielberg should return to *Jurassic Park* again after *Schindler's List* in 1997 (and a third and a fourth time in 2001 and in 2005 as

Executive Producer) further complicates Spielberg's attitude to *Jurassic Park*, entertainment and mass appeal.

Chinatown

John Alonzo, Faye Dunaway, Robert Evans, Roman Polanski, Richard Sylbert and Robert Towne have all discussed their work on *Chinatown*. Their accounts cover most of the important contributions: Alonzo was the cinematographer, Dunaway one of the stars, Evans the producer, Polanski the director, Sylbert the production designer and Towne the writer. By matching their accounts against the film it is possible to gain illuminating insights into its production.

The producer

The contribution of the producer, Robert Evans, was central to the eventual success of the film. Evans made three key decisions that shaped its final character: (1) he agreed to fund Towne to develop his idea into a script; (2) he chose Jack Nicholson for the main role, and (3) he hired Roman Polanski to direct the film. All three were risky decisions. Evans admitted he did not understand Towne's original concept and Towne had a reputation as a slow, hard-to-control writer. Nicholson was just establishing himself and there were doubts about his ability to be a leading man. Polanski was Polish while the script was deeply rooted in American history and culture. He had also recently been through the trauma of the Manson murders. Evans also made a number of other contributions to the film. He was involved in the rewriting of the script and in the editing. Perhaps the key decision he took was to fire the musicians Polanski had chosen to write the score and replace them with Jerry Goldsmith. It was a decision that proved crucial for the film's success.

The script

Robert Towne's script was self-consciously a genre script, paying homage to detective stories such as *The Big Sleep* and *The Maltese Falcon*. It employs all the basic conventions of such films: a private investigator as the central figure, a complicated narrative structure, a *femme fatale* and laconic dialogue. He respects these conventions. The script is not smart at their expense. This is especially true of the dialogue. Indeed, the script can be seen as a series of set pieces constructed out of dialogue exchanges. Towne uses jagged rhythms and striking metaphors to create a vivid language for his characters, especially J. J. Gittes. His dialogue shows a great awareness of how, in this kind of fiction, language is used as a form of aggression.

Towne did make some important changes to these elements and it is these changes that make his script especially distinctive. The first change was in the importance of the location for the action. Earlier films of this genre were usually set in specific locations, most frequently Los Angeles, but the settings are not particularly important; the films could be set in any large city. Towne made the setting crucial to the film. He rooted the narrative in the actual history and ecology of Los Angeles. The story emerges out of the struggles to control the water supply, so crucial to the development of the city, that occurred at the beginning of the twentieth century. As a consequence Los Angeles is not simply a backdrop to the action, it is a central character.

The second change was to emphasize the anti-heroic quality of the central character. By the very nature of the work they did, private investigators in earlier films had an anti-heroic character, but the anti-heroism was softened because the nature of the work was left vague. Towne strengthened the anti-heroism by making the work specific. His script opens with a man looking at photographs of a couple having sexual intercourse. The photographs have been provided by J. J. Gittes, a private investigator who makes his living almost exclusively through divorce work. The seediness associated with work of this kind is emphasized by Gittes' vulgar turns of phrase and his coarse sense of humour.

The third change Towne made was in the kind of crime Gittes investigates. The genre often contains suggestions of decadence and perversion but, like the seediness, these suggestions remain vague and unspecific. Towne took advantage of a relaxed censorship and made perversion specific and central by placing an incestuous act at the centre of the drama.

There are, however, problems in the script that were not properly resolved either by Towne or anyone else who worked on it. In the early part of the narrative, a strong sense is created that Gittes has stumbled on a wide-ranging conspiracy, involving politicians, bureaucrats and businessmen. As the script progresses the conspiracy appears much smaller scale, the work of one businessman supported by a few heavies. The complications of plotting diminish the scale even more. In order to join the two strands, the water conspiracy and the family incest drama, it is necessary for Noah Cross to kill Horace Mulwray. Cross makes an improbable murderer. He is too old, especially as there appears to have been a violent struggle before Mulwray dies. In any case, Cross employs people who are much more proficient killers.

The second problem is the character of Evelyn Mulwray, which is not fully developed. What kind of character is she? Is her controlled and enigmatic persona just a disguise? How does she relate to her husband, Horace Mulwray, since she is both much younger and more attractive than he is? Does she have affairs, as she suggests to Gittes? Why does she seem so unmoved by her husband's death?

The director

Roman Polanski's contribution to *Chinatown* was substantial and varied. Apart from staging the action and overseeing the performances, prime responsibilities for any director, there is clear evidence that Polanski worked on the script and contributed ideas for the cinematography.

There is general agreement that initially Robert Towne's script was unwieldy and confusing. Polanski's assessment of the script was that 'It was terribly long and convoluted, it had too many characters, it had a lot of episodic scenes which were not essential' (Biskind, 1998: 161). He worked with Towne (and with Robert Evans and Richard Sylbert) to simplify and clarify the narrative. To a large extent the clarification of the script works well. The basic dramatic situation – a detective begins what appears to be a routine investigation into marital infidelity and finds himself in the middle of something much bigger and more complicated – is clearly and strongly established. Also, as the film concentrates entirely on the detective's investigations (he is present in every scene in the film), a direct form of character identification is offered as a guide through the increasingly complicated narrative developments.

However, because Polanski clarified the story by pruning rather than reworking it, some new problems were created and others left unresolved. A number of details are not explained. Why does Ida Sessions decide to get back in touch with Gittes? Who sends the photographs of Mulwray and the girl to the newspaper? Other details need a fuller explanation, particularly the machinations surrounding the attempt to control the water supply.

Apart from clarifying the narrative, Polanski made two key changes to the script. The first was to give Chinatown a physical presence, not just the metaphorical one it had in early versions of the script. In Towne's original script, Chinatown existed only in the dialogue. Its purpose was to act as a metaphor for the dangers of taking action in a world that is badly known and poorly understood. Polanski thought that Chinatown should have a physical as well as a metaphorical existence in the film. He thought that audiences would be frustrated if a place was frequently referred to but not seen. Accordingly, the last scene in the film is set in an actual Chinatown. But, by doing so, Polanski undermines one of the strengths of Towne's writing. Towne places references to Chinatown strategically in the dialogue throughout the script. Together these references have a powerful metaphorical force, creating the sense not of an actual place but a mythical one, a state of mind perhaps. Polanski was not able to write the actual Chinatown into the script in a way that gives it more than a literal presence.

Polanski's second change was to make the ending bleaker. He rewrote the final scene so that Evelyn is killed instead of her father, a change that led to an estrangement between him and Towne. Justifying the change Polanski said, 'I thought it was a serious movie, not an adventure story for the kids' (Biskind, 1998: 166). The implication of this remark is that the change is a profound one, effectively from a happy ending to an unhappy one. But the ending Towne had originally written is hardly happy. Evelyn walks away from the scene having shot her father. That she is free hardly obliterates what has happened to her. She has killed the father who raped her. Her husband has been murdered and her daughter has been traumatized. This is hardly the conclusion of 'an adventure story for kids'.

A reasonable case can be made for either ending. However, the debate about it seems to have deflected interest from another problem. The final scene that was written is poorly worked out and structured. There is an obvious implausibility in the climactic action. Why should the police fire at a car, driven by a woman with her young daughter as a passenger, in a crowded street? Why not pursue it or set up a roadblock? There are a large number of characters in the scene (12, almost all the important characters in the film). They are involved in a number of different actions that produce the climax. Too much happens too quickly. Polanski clearly was not satisfied with the scene because he (together with Jack Nicholson) rewrote it the night before shooting. But they were not able to solve the problems. The messy structure could have seriously weakened the final impact of the film. The scene is saved, however, by the very last action in it. The pace slows, with Gittes, Walsh and Duffy walking away from the horrific sight of Evelyn's dead body. As they do, the script ends with a perfect line of dialogue that memorably articulates the script's governing metaphor. Duffy says, 'Forget it Jake, it's Chinatown'.

The other area in which clear evidence demonstrates that Polanski made a substantial contribution is cinematography. John Alonzo has spoken in detail about Polanski's contribution. He credits Polanski with having a great deal of technical knowledge of cinematography, which helped him overcome some difficult problems. He also describes the way that Polanski uses the camera dramatically. Overall, the style of the cinematography Alonzo created for *Chinatown* might be described as one designed for 'cool' observation. His basic approach is defined by his choice of a 40 mm lens as the principal one, because he thought it best reproduced human vision and allowed characters to be seen in their environments. The camera is mainly placed at eye level and camera angles are created by the dramatic situation, by how characters are placed in relationship to each other. Camera movement is unobtrusive, the lighting even, the colour palette limited and desaturated. There is a degree of formality about many of the compositions but it is always a restrained, unobtrusive formality. Polanski, according to Alonzo, added what might be called 'visual intensifiers' to this cool style. He did this in different ways; sometimes he placed actors very close to the camera to create an unsettling effect as the conventional spatial relationship between the actor and the frame is suddenly changed. At other times he used self-reflexive images: one image is seen in the lens of a still camera, another through binoculars and another in the wing-mirror of a car.

Obviously the most substantial contribution of all made by Polanski was the staging of the action, where his responsibility was total. He used familiar devices to do this; shot/reverse shot combined with longer, unbroken takes. There is an evident preference for keeping actions whole rather than breaking them up. Certainly, whenever there is movement it is shot in one fluid take. Apart from this, the most distinctive feature of the staging is the way scenes are blocked to highlight depth. Many scenes are played in connecting spaces such as doorways. Some begin with characters facing each other from the extreme ends of a setting; in others, minor characters or incidental actions are placed in the background. Light as well as depth is also emphasized. The action is either staged with windows clearly visible behind the characters or, in reverse, with the characters in bright light against a shaded background. Perhaps the least conventional feature of the staging is the pacing of the action, which for all but the last scenes is slow and controlled. This is particularly the case in dialogue exchanges where the actors are given ample time both to deliver their lines and to react to the responses.

It is only in the last scene where Polanski has problems with the staging. He loses control of the pacing. Crucially, Noah Cross's final triumph is not given the time it needs to register properly. The performances become uncertain, with Jack Nicholson, in particular, suddenly delivering lines so fast that they lose dramatic impact. Also, details of the action are confusing. Where does Evelyn's gun come from? How does Gittes free himself from being handcuffed to the car? What has happened to Cross's shoulder wound when he lifts Catherine out of the car? It is a pity the staging works so badly in such an important scene because everywhere else it is admirably controlled and inventive.

Working with the actors is crucial for Polanski in deciding how to stage the action, 'I always set up with actors, without thinking of the camera. I observe them while they rehearse, and then later I try to film it' (Sherman, 1976: 118). There is plenty of evidence that Polanski worked very closely with the actors during the shooting of *Chinatown*. Some of this evidence does not show him in a good light. In particular, his altercations with Faye Dunaway have become notorious. The account that emerges is of a dictatorial director, attempting to exert close, detailed control over performances. Such a method might constrain actors, producing performances lacking freedom and spontaneity but generally, this is not the case. Crucially, Jack Nicholson gives a relaxed, assured performance. Nicholson was, apparently, able to cope with Polanski's dictatorial tendencies. More importantly, he was playing a role that Towne had written especially for him, one that took account of his speech patterns and mannerisms. However, the general level of performance throughout the film is high, with Perry Lopez and John Huston giving particularly strong performances. Casting is undoubtedly one of the reasons for this, but key is Polanski's appreciation of the quality and importance of Towne's dialogue. As we have already indicated, the pacing of the action allows the actors to get full value from their lines.

The one actor whose performance poses problems is Faye Dunaway. Put simply, it is not always easy to place the nervousness in Dunaway's performance. Is the actor nervous or is the actor playing a nervous dimension in the character? There are good reasons why the actor might have been nervous. Faye Dunaway and Polanski were consistently hostile to each other. Dunaway wrote of their relationship, 'But from the moment I stepped on the set, I felt he was not happy with me. I found him to be a very odd man and I got strange vibes every time I was around him. It was very difficult to pin down exactly what it was, but I was clearly not his cup of tea, ever. Nor he mine' (Dunaway, 1995: 257). But the problem is more than one of temperamental differences. We have already suggested that the character of Evelyn Mulwray is not fully developed. During shooting, Dunaway was frequently uncertain about her character's motivations. Polanski gave her no help and on one occasion is reported to have responded, 'Say the fucking words. Your salary is your motivation' (Biskind, 1998: 189). His anger may well have been fuelled by his awareness that he was not able to offer motivations because the character, as we have suggested, had not been properly worked out.

There is one other area in which Polanski had a big influence on the film. It is a part of directing that is rarely discussed because it is intangible and dependent on inside knowledge. Because of this, John Alonzo's account is worth quoting at length,

> He brought everybody up to a level of competence: the prop man, the production designer, all the heads of departments involved in the movie. He sort of psyched us up to such a degree that we were all putting out top, top efficiency. It gave him a great deal of security to know that when I was going to walk on the set it was going to be perfect ... In other words, none of the little irritations were there like 'I forgot to do this or I forgot to do that: there wasn't enough money to do this.' It was immaculately produced. To everybody involved, that gave us a sense of freedom to really go into the aesthetics or into that realm of trying to create something better in compositions, lighting, and camera moves. We did them with absolute security that everybody else's job had been finished and was complete and we could be brave and try different things.
>
> (Schaefer and Salvato, 1984: 31)

Production design

One of the most distinctive features of *Chinatown* is its production design. The evidence suggests Polanski was not substantially involved in this area. Richard Sylbert was already a very well-established production designer, having won an Oscar for *Who's Afraid of Virginia Woolf?* and worked on a wide range of critically acclaimed and successful films such as *Baby Doll*, *The Fugitive Kind*, *The Manchurian Candidate*, *The Graduate* and *Catch-22*. As a result he had both the authority and confidence to trust his own judgement, to work independently and only to seek general approval from the director.

Sylbert aimed to give *Chinatown* a visual identity and distinctiveness by establishing a series of unities at different levels of the film. At the most general level the film is unified by the use of a limited colour palette. A range of whites, browns and blues dominate. Within this, there are local unities, which are created through choices of colour and/or architecture. Skies are consistently light blue with high white clouds. Brown dominates the interiors. Exterior locations are predominantly white 'Spanish'-style buildings; all the public buildings have a monumental quality and share similar features. Furniture is substantial, windows are strongly featured and glass doors are always opaque.

These unities are interesting simply as organizations of colours, shapes and textures. However, they also have a dramatic impact. Sylbert has responded to the importance of Los Angeles in the script and made sure that it has a powerful visual presence in the film. He achieves this by emphasizing well-known features of the city, in particular its climate and its architecture. By doing this, he does, of course, produce a particular account of Los Angeles – the sky is not always blue, not all buildings are white, low, and in a Spanish style. In terms of its outward appearances, Sylbert's Los Angeles has an ethereal, almost timeless quality that contrasts vividly with the interiors. Interiors are darker and heavier. Blinds and curtains cut down the light. The detailed dressing of rooms with large, dark coloured furniture (book cases, desks, sofas, tables) and numerous pictures and photographs gives them a weighty presence. (Ruby Levitt's set decoration deserves treatment in its own right.) The way space is structured adds to the substantial effect. Rooms are designed so that their connections with other rooms are evident; a particular room is always established as part of a larger, more elaborate structure.

Production design also provides strong support for the establishment of characters. The Mulwray mansion is the set piece. Its setting at the top of a rise, its spaciousness, formal garden and colonnades provide exactly the right kind of environment for the character that Evelyn is trying to project. However, even minor characters get the same kind of support. Ida Sessions's apartment is a small masterpiece. It has a very distinctive setting – two low rows of apartments face each other across a central roofless corridor with an arched entrance – that adds to the mystery of the character. The character of the interior – a set of small, cluttered rooms – is compressed enough to rapidly establish the kind of woman Ida is but sufficiently large to allow the action to take place (Gittes' discovery of Ida's body, the emergence of Escobar and Loach, the confrontation between Gittes and Escobar).

The only place where the production design fails is in the final scene. As an actual place, Chinatown has little visual presence. It is signified by not much more than some neon lighting with Chinese lettering and Chinese bystanders. Apart from these features, Sylbert has designed a 'main street' that could be anywhere. Dramatically the main value of the design is that the street is sufficiently wide and long for the climactic action to be comfortably staged.

Costume design

Anthea Sylbert's costume design also makes an important contribution to the film. The costumes support the characters in a variety of ways; in the case of J. J. Gittes they add another dimension to his character. Gittes wears a variety of elegant suits in the course of the film. They seem at odds with the rest of his character, the grubby kind of work he does, his vulgar turns of phrase and coarse humour. They suggest insouciance in the character, a refusal to be pinned down. Evelyn's costumes are designed to underscore the development of her character. Initially, when she presents herself as assured and in command, they are sophisticated, elegant and in light colours; as Evelyn becomes more open and vulnerable they are simpler and in black. This inventive use of costume does not apply only to the main characters. Gittes' two assistants, Walsh and Duffy, are good examples of how costume helps to establish minor characters. They are marked off by fussiness in Walsh's dress, symbolized by his bow tie. In contrast, Duffy is dressed in more prosaic suit and tie.

Editing

Polanski was not present during the editing of the film so responsibility for it must go principally to Sam O'Steen, though Towne and Evans were also involved. The overall style is simple and unobtrusive. The only device used is the cut (there is only one small exception – a quick fade out and in when Gittes is knocked unconscious). There is, however, an important difference between the editing within a scene and the editing of transitions between scenes. Within a scene, the cuts are smooth and unobtrusive. The rhythm of the cutting is slow (with the obvious exception of the few action scenes). Such a pace supports the production design and the acting. It allows the audience time to appreciate both the settings and the costumes, and the exchanges between the actors. It was a brave choice; the usual rhythm of cutting for films of this kind is quicker. O'Steen avoids the danger of the film developing a rather ponderous rhythm by the way he handles transitions between scenes. Cuts are abrupt; sometimes they are almost jump cuts. The urgency that this creates is strengthened by the fact that a cut is often to a shot containing quick movement: cars being driven, rooms being entered. This difference between the rhythm of the editing within scenes and that between scenes establishes a consistent rhythmic tension throughout the film.

Sound

Since Polanski was not present during the editing, it seems unlikely he had much influence on the construction of the sound track either. Robert Cornett's sound strategy comes from recognition of the importance of the dialogue. It is always highly privileged. Apart from a literal use (water escaping, doors shutting, etc.), sound effects are used only as background suggestions of the larger environment of the city. Only very occasionally is a more dramatic use made of them. The first minute of the film is a good example: the mixture of a man's moans with the scratchy sounds created when glossy photographs are pulled from a pile powerfully establishes Curly's anguish when he is confronted with evidence of his wife's infidelity.

When *Chinatown* was first previewed it was not particularly well received by audiences and the music was given as one of the strongest reasons for disliking it. Music was provided by a small band, chosen by Polanski. Their music had a modernist, dissonant character. Robert Evans decided to replace it with music written by Jerry Goldsmith, a more mainstream Hollywood composer. The next time the film was previewed with Goldsmith's score the audience responded much more sympathetically. Goldsmith's music certainly has a strong presence in the film. A dominant theme is established over the credits. The instrumental combination (lead trumpet supported by strings, piano and percussion) and the sweet melodic character of the sound suggest a 1930s or 1940s dance orchestra. Goldsmith has said that he wrote music in a 1930s style but then arranged it in a contemporary way. It is used, played with different instrumentations at key points in the rest of the film, providing a perfect undertone for the film; romantic, nostalgic and mournful.

The use of music throughout the film is not entirely coherent. While the main theme dominates, there are some signs of the original musical approach. A different kind of musical idiom, closer to what the original must have been like, is also used. Dissonant snatches, played mainly on piano and percussion, are employed to give scenes an eerie, unsettling quality. Towards the end of the film the music is used less as an undertone and more as an overtone. It is employed conventionally to strongly and directly heighten the drama.

Conclusion

How did all of these contributions cohere to produce a successful film? The production history of the film suggests that no single person was responsible. Two people, Robert Evans and Roman Polanski, could make a strong claim for such a responsibility. As producer and director they were in a position to influence the film at a variety of levels. Evans was a central figure in the pre- and post-production stages, Polanski in the pre-production and production stages. However, Evans seems to have had very little influence during the production stage and Polanski very little during post-production. Even at the times when they had most presence, there were areas in which they had little involvement.

The evidence does not suggest that the coherence of the film depends on the 'vision' of one person. The involvement of the contributors with each other is like a spider's web with the script at the heart of it. In the earliest stages, Robert Towne, Jack Nicholson and Robert Evans worked together on the script. Towne and Polanski built on their work. Richard Sylbert and Evans then helped Polanski to further revise the script. The web then reaches out from the script. Polanski worked closely with the actors and the cinematographer, John Alonzo. Sylbert worked closely with Alonzo. Evans and Towne supervised Sam O'Steen's editing. Evans worked with the composer, Jerry Goldsmith. If there is any one element around which all the contributions cohere, it is the script.

We have already pointed to some examples of how this happens. Jerry Goldsmith approached the music in the same way that Towne approached the script. Where Towne brought a modern dramatic sensibility to bear on a traditional genre, Goldsmith composed traditional themes and then scored them in a contemporary way. Richard Sylbert's production design splendidly responds to the centrality of Los Angeles in the drama; the choice of locations, the design of interiors and the colour scheme combine to give Los Angeles a vivid and substantial presence.

The relationship between the script, direction and editing provides another illuminating example. Towne has spoken about how he deliberately wrote 'shoe leather' – scenes that seem to have no obvious dramatic purpose – into the script. He quotes the scene where Gittes first arrives at the Mulwray mansion as an example of this. He thought it was important to spin the scene out, even though nothing significant happens, to establish that the mansion represented a different world. Many directors and editors might have worried that such a scene would bore an audience, but both the way the scene is staged by Polanski and the way it is cut by O'Steen fully respect Towne's intentions. Director and editor give the scene the time and attention it needs for it to have an effect.

Because of the centrality of the script to all of the different contributions, it is tempting to claim Robert Towne as the author of *Chinatown*. However, some qualifications need to be made. Other people made important contributions to its writing and the script had to be articulated in terms of sounds and images. There is another, more complex, qualification worth making. Many of the contributions we have discussed could be predicted from a reading of the script. A good example is Jack Nicholson's performance. Fine though it is, it is not a surprising one, given the strong characterization that exists in the script. The music, however, is more surprising. As we have already suggested Jerry Goldsmith took his cue from the script for the way he approached the music. However, the music also brings something unexpected to the film; the main theme has a strong and direct emotional appeal, the kind of appeal a 1930s orchestra made when it played the last dance. The general emotional tone of the drama is chilly and unsettling. Because feelings are strong and destructive they are kept in check and hidden. The strong and direct appeal of the music enriches the tone and prevents it from becoming oppressive.

We have explored *Chinatown* by way of its production history. Obviously, we approached it in this way because we are interested in general questions about the way film production works. We were not trying to offer a critical evaluation of a particular film. But did our approach lead to any different conclusions from existing critical analyses of the film?

It did not in terms of evaluation. We were not encouraged to challenge the critical consensus that *Chinatown* is an impressive film. We did, however, develop a more shaded estimate of the film's achievements. We became aware of failures that we think have not been properly taken account of before. We have suggested that there are two big problem areas: the inability to develop the character of Evelyn adequately and the poor conception and execution of the final sequence. The failure with Evelyn is the more important one. As far as the final sequence is concerned, it may be that by the time it reaches its climax, the film has developed a sufficiently strong dramatic impetus to override any weaknesses. However, the character of Evelyn is fundamental to the drama; how an audience understands her will determine how it responds to the other characters and, therefore, the film in general. Given our aims in this book, it would be a diversion to examine this failure here, but we suspect an examination would illuminate the problems of creating female characters that the thriller genre, especially in its *film noir* variant, poses for writers, directors and actors.

If our approach made us aware of failures, it also made us more appreciative of the film's richness. We became powerfully aware that the film is as much as anything else a meditation on Los Angeles. A haunting sense of the city's history, geography, climate and architecture permeate the film. Robert Towne's statement that his reading about the city's water scandals in the early twentieth century inspired him to write the script is often quoted. But there is another inspiration he has mentioned that deserves to be better known:

> I don't know how I came to write Chinatown, although I can point to individual steps along the way; I saw a series of photographs by John Waggaman in *West* magazine, appended to an article called 'Raymond Chandler's Los Angeles'. The photographs really affected me; they reminded me of the city I grew up in. I was suddenly filled with a tremendous kind of sense of loss, of what the city once was. And you could see the little pockets of time that could throw you right back into the past. And I knew it was still possible to photograph the city in such a way as to recreate that time, much in the way that those street lamps existed. And I suppose, in a way, that was the beginning.
>
> (McGrath and McDermott, 2003: 141)

The most obvious difference our approach creates is with the many writers who describe the film as 'Roman Polanski's *Chinatown*'. They go on to attribute the horror and bleakness of the film to Polanski's personal history, especially his experiences during the Second World War. Clearly we oppose such an account. We have suggested that the basic horror and bleakness were present in the script from the beginning, before Polanski was involved with the film. They were created by Robert Towne, whose personal history, as a middle-class Angeleno, was much less troubled than Polanski's. This fact encourages us to be wary of critical analyses where films are discussed as the expression of the director's (or anybody else's) personal history.

When Harry Met Sally

The screenwriter and the director

When Harry Met Sally raises some intriguing questions. Virtually all interviews with cast and crew, including director Rob Reiner and screenwriter Nora Ephron, focus on how several key players contributed to the film by pitching in ideas, lines of dialogue or even entire plot changes. To look at the production context of *When Harry Met Sally*, then, means also investigating the genesis and production of a film where writing is clearly indicated by both filmmakers and critics as the key element. Hence the questions: are the dynamics at work in the making of *When Harry Met Sally* any different from other films? Does the writer simply replace the director/producer as the author? Is the collaborative nature of the filmmaking process emphasized more than is customary?

'Everyone who got involved brought something unbelievably special and extra to the movie.' These words by Nora Ephron, from *The Making of When Harry Met Sally: How Harry Met Sally* documentary, suggest strongly that the film was the product of a collaboration between several people. Indeed, she stresses the 'special' nature of this collaboration. This is a good starting point because it raises the central questions: where can we find evidence of this collaboration and what does it suggest? The origins of the film are somewhat foggy. Producer Andrew Scheinman and director Rob Reiner approached screenwriter Nora Ephron about a project they wanted Ephron to script. During the course of the conversation Ephron realized her lack of interest in the proposed project, and declared so to Reiner and Scheinman. Exactly what kind of film it was that Ephron said no to is not known; the only reference Ephron has ever made in relation to that aborted idea is rather vague: 'They told me about an idea they had for a movie about a lawyer, I've forgotten the details' (Ephron, 1999: vii).

Ephron had made her name before *When Harry Met Sally* with two screenplays: *Silkwood* and *Heartburn*. The former is a political drama, the latter a bitter-sweet tale of love, marriage and divorce based on Ephron's own failed marriage with Watergate journalist Carl Bernstein. That is to say, neither of these two films are romantic comedies in the same vein as *When Harry Met Sally* and Ephron's later efforts *Sleepless in Seattle* and *You've Got Mail*.

In the course of the same conversation, Reiner and Scheinman talked about their own lives, especially their love lives. Reiner, who had been divorced for some time from his first wife, talked about the difficulties of the 'dating game' and openly admitted to being depressed about being single. This eventually became the subject for a new film project, and this time Ephron showed interest. In Reiner's own words:

> The whole idea for this film was really born out of my experiences as being a single person having been married a long time . . . trying to figure out whether men and women could be friends, and whether or not if there was sex that would ruin the friendship. It was really the father for the movie and basically Nora sat with me and Andy Scheinman and took notes on our personal lives and made them into this film.
>
> (From the director's commentary on the DVD of *When Harry Met Sally*, MGM, 2001 version)

Reiner's comments do more than simply indicate the source of the idea for the film. They effectively locate the paternity of the movie with Reiner and appear to marginalize Ephron to the role of a glorified note-taker. Having exchanged views and confidences about their personal lives, the two central characters, Harry and Sally, became somewhat extensions of Reiner and Ephron. Although there is general agreement on this point, Reiner and Ephron express rather different views when it comes to describing what the film is really about. Whereas Reiner suggests that the film is about whether men and women can be friends and whether sex always ruins friendship between the sexes, Ephron forcefully claims that the film is: 'about a very interesting subject which is NOT can men and women be friends, but really the difference between men and women'. Indeed, as recently as March 2004, Ephron still contended that: 'I think that's probably my favourite subject. I think that's what *Sleepless in Seattle, You've Got Mail* and most of the romantic movies that I've done are really about' (interview with Norah Ephron in *Loose Ends*, BBC Radio 4, 27 March 2004).

This difference in opinion is significant. On its original release in 1989, the film was accused by critics of suffering from weak characterization that ultimately led, for some critics such as *New York Times*'s Caryn James, to a film that is 'often funny but amazingly hollow' (*New York Times*, 12 July 1989). This criticism is based in particular on the fact that the film never delves into the characters' social background. This is particularly true in relation to Harry's and Sally's jobs. We are told that Harry is a political consultant and that Sally is a journalist (for *New York Magazine*) but that is the extent of what we learn. We never find out exactly who Harry works for and for what political party. Similarly, we never get to know whether he is a scrupulous activist or a cynical operator, and whether he has merely fallen into the job or if it was a life-long ambition. As for Sally, we do not know whether her hope of becoming a journalist (she expresses this desire briefly in the opening section of the film) is based on a desire to do groundbreaking investigative journalism or on other interests, be they fashion, sports or any other topic. Although this lack of information may be used to help avoid pigeonholing the two characters into types, it also drastically reduces our understanding of them and what makes them 'tick'.

If, as Reiner suggests, this film is *specifically* about Harry and Sally, the question of characterization is of paramount importance. We simply need to know more about the characters' backgrounds if we are to care about their relationship. If, on the other hand, we look at Ephron's position (the film is not so much about Harry and Sally, but rather on gender difference in approaching romance, relationships and love) the characters' background becomes less essential, as Harry and Sally need to act less as distinctive individuals and more as representatives of views and behaviour typical of their gender.

This difference of opinion is accentuated by the way in which Reiner and Ephron have articulated their views on the way the film functions in narrative terms. When confronted with the kind of criticism of which James's comment is representative, Reiner's position appears to be less well defined than Ephron's. Indeed, Reiner has often taken a defensive stance on this issue that borders on the elusive. In his DVD commentary to the film he specifically attempts to address the issue of weak characterization:

> One of the comments that people made when they saw this film is that these people [Harry and Sally] are obviously goal oriented, they're upwardly mobile and all of that, yet they never talk about their work, their careers. I used to say 'well, they do talk about it, we just don't turn the camera on during that time'.
> (From the director's commentary on the DVD of *When Harry Met Sally* (MGM, 2001 version)

Conversely, Ephron engages much more effectively with issues of narrative structure and character motivation. In particular, she structures her argument around a discussion of *When Harry Met Sally* as a comedy:

There's two traditions of Romantic Comedy. There's the Christian tradition and there's the Jewish tradition if you will. In the Christian tradition there's a genuine obstacle [to the characters' love]. In the Jewish tradition, pioneered by Woody Allen, the basic obstacle is the neurosis of the character.

(From *The Making of When Harry Met Sally* documentary available on the DVD of the film, MGM 2001 release)

She has reinforced this view on other occasions, as in an intriguing interview with actor Edward Norton at the time of the release of Norton's directorial debut film, *Keeping the Faith*.

Edward Norton: I think that romantic comedies can be marked pre-*Annie Hall* [1977], and post-*Annie Hall*. *Annie Hall* started the romantic comedies that are about romance.
Nora Ephron: Or analyzing romance. To me, *Annie Hall* was the first Jewish romantic comedy in that the obstacle to love was the neurosis of the male protagonist.

. . .

Edward Norton: Do you think that's the key to all romantic comedy: the identifying of the obstacle?
Nora Ephron: I do think it's hard to have one without it.

(Norah Ephron in conversation with Edward Norton, April 2000. Available at: http://articles.findarticles.com/p/articles/mi_m1285/is_4_30/ai_61535329; last accessed 10 January 2004)

It appears from these comments that Ephron has a stronger sense of how the film functions than does Reiner. Both director and writer also acknowledge the role that other key collaborators played in shaping the script. Producer Andy Scheinman is officially awarded a 'Written by' credit on the film. Scheinman's role is not clearly defined: he would appear to have been at the centre of the discussions that went on originally between Reiner and Ephron in the early stages of the project. As Ephron recalls: 'Andy and Rob came to New York and we sat around for several days and they told me some things. Appalling things . . . Rob and Andy and I noodled for hours over the questions raised by friendship, and sex, and life in general' (Ephron, 1999: viii). There is also some evidence that he continued contributing to the film's script after this initial stage. For instance, he worked with Reiner on writing a scene about faking orgasms that was to become the now-famous orgasm sequence at Katz's delicatessen. If Scheinman and Reiner helped mostly with general ideas and plot development, Billy Crystal and Meg Ryan had an important part in contributing to some of the film's more memorable lines and moments. Ryan actually suggested that she should fake an orgasm in the delicatessen sequence, whereas Crystal contributed several one-liners to the script, including the 'I'll have what she's having' line that seals the delicatessen sequence.

All this amounts to what Ephron describes as 'a perfect example of how The Process works on the occasion when it works' (Ephron, 1999: xv). The concept of 'The Process', described by Ephron as a kind of *modus operandi* in Hollywood where 'movies generally start out belonging to the writer and end up belonging to the director' (Ephron, 1999: xv) is a useful way of trying to assess the contributions of all those involved in the screenwriting effort. Although claiming openly that this was the best collaborative effort she had ever experienced, the power struggle over the shaping of the script is still detectable when looking closely at the filmmakers' attempts to claim the film as their own. Reiner is happy to emphasize that the origin of the film rests with him at every possible opportunity. Ephron feels very ambivalent about the whole experience and especially the way in which as she worked on the film with Scheinman and Reiner: 'it became less mine and more theirs'. She refers to The Process as a 'polite expression for the period when, generally, the writer gets screwed'. She suggests that she tried to retain some control over the movie by modelling Harry on Reiner and Sally on herself: 'What made this movie different was that Rob had a character who could say whatever he believed, and if I disagreed, I had Sally to say it for me' (Ephron, 1999: xiv).

The endless lists of titles (Ephron was unhappy with the choice of *When Harry Met Sally* as the title; earlier titles that were eventually discarded included: 'Just Friends'; 'Play Melancholy Baby'; 'Boy Meets Girl'; 'Words of Love'; 'It Had to Be You'; 'Harry, This is Sally'; 'How They Met'; and others), the differences of opinion on what the film is really about, the 'ownership' of the two central characters are, in this sense, symptomatic of a rather complex relationship between writer and director where nobody quite takes over altogether, and that ends up resembling less a full collaboration and more a 'practical' truce. The film's episodic structure and the rather loose characterization owe a great deal to this situation, where perhaps a stronger stance by either director or writer on key choices would have helped in achieving consistency. Indeed, Ephron herself articulates this in her introduction to the book of the screenplay with the help of an amusing culinary metaphor:

> Here is what I always say about screenwriting. When you write a script, it's like delivering a great big beautiful plain pizza, the one with only cheese and tomatoes. And then you give it to the director, and the director says, 'I love this pizza. I am willing to commit to this pizza. But I really think this pizza should have mushrooms on it.' And you say, 'Mushrooms! Of course! I meant to put mushrooms on the pizza! Why didn't I think of that? Let's put some on immediately.' And then someone else comes along and says, 'I love this pizza too, but it really needs green peppers.' 'Great', you say. 'Green peppers. Just the thing.' And then someone says 'Anchovies' . . . And when you get done, what you have is a pizza with everything. Sometimes it's wonderful. And sometimes you look at it and you think, I knew we shouldn't have put the green peppers onto it. Why didn't I say so at the time? Why didn't I lie down in traffic to prevent anyone's putting green peppers onto the pizza?
>
> (Ephron, 1999: xiv)

Other collaborators

Both Reiner and Ephron separately have referred to this movie as a talk piece. Ephron has described *When Harry Met Sally* as a film where 'people sit in a room and go blah, blah, blah' (interview with Norah Ephron, available at:

http://www.hollywoodlitsales.com/archives/ephron.shtml; last accessed 20 April 2004). Reiner has similarly commented that 'Basically this movie is about a lot of people sitting around tables talking' (from the director's commentary on the DVD of *When Harry Met Sally*, MGM, 2001 version). These descriptions raise some interesting questions concerning the demands that a script such as *When Harry Met Sally*'s places on filmmakers. In particular, two sets of questions emerge: the first is about acting. Reiner specifically mentions four attributes that, in his view, both Crystal and Ryan brought to their performances: (1) timing, (2) being 'real', (3) intelligence and sophistication, and (4) chemistry. But what do these terms actually mean? Can we reach any meaningful conclusions as to the contribution that actors made to the film?

Second, how do other members of the crew relate to a script such as *When Harry Met Sally*, which works fundamentally as a series of dialogue set-ups without much movement or action?

On acting in *When Harry Met Sally*

Filmmakers and critics alike were in agreement on one aspect of the film: the on-screen pairing of Billy Crystal and Meg Ryan works very effectively. However, when it comes to defining exactly what that actually meant, both Reiner and Ephron would return to customarily vague remarks. Reiner, for example, claims that 'we wound up with perfect casting . . . Meg was a perfect complement to Billy' and that the actors 'project a lot of intelligence'. Reiner also employs the concept of 'chemistry' when he suggests that: 'The chemistry between Meg and Billy was amazing' (all of these brief extracts are from the director's commentary on the DVD of *When Harry Met Sally*, MGM, 2001 version). He also mentions several times the fact that he thought both Ryan and Crystal were able to play it 'real'. In other words, although some common 'themes' emerge (chemistry, intelligence and so on) there is no actual indication as to where these features can be detected. Critics' comments are mostly along similar lines, but some have tried to go beyond generalization. In his review of *When Harry Met Sally*, Roger Ebert suggests that:

> Harry is played by Billy Crystal and Meg Ryan is Sally, and they make a good movie couple because both actors are able to suggest genuine warmth and tenderness. But what makes it special, apart from the Ephron screenplay, is the chemistry between Crystal and Ryan. She is an open-faced, bright-eyed blond; he's a gentle, skinny man with a lot of smart one-liners. What they both have (to repeat) is warmth.
>
> (*Chicago Sun-Times*, 12 July 1989)

Despite the tentative nature of his remarks, Ebert interestingly points to the physical characteristics of Ryan and Crystal especially as a factor. Both Ryan's and Crystal's physiques are unthreatening. Ryan, though conventionally pleasant (e.g., well-defined cheekbones, versatile hair that can be combed in a variety of fashions, slim) is neither too angular nor voluptuous (she is not very muscular and her bust is relatively small). Crystal has very soft facial features (no square jaw, a wide forehead) and is of average height. There is nothing remarkable about their heights either. They match each other at about 5′8″, which does not attract any particular attention. Matching Ryan and Crystal is very important because Crystal is actually 14 years older than Ryan (Crystal was born in 1947, Ryan in 1961), and this age difference might threaten the believability of the script, which clearly calls for two people of similar age.

Their voices also share similar characteristics. Crystal's voice is rather nasal, but is neither shrill nor deep. It hits mid-frequencies and serves perfectly well the most important requirement of stand-up comedians (or any actor who has to deliver lines quickly and efficiently): it is perfectly intelligible and does not require the audience to strain to hear what is being said. Ryan's voice is higher in frequency, but again very much in the mid range, and thus requiring no particular strain. Neither of the lead actors has a strong accent, nor do they have evident speech peculiarities (e.g., rounded 'r's, sibilant 's's, silent 'h's, etc.).

Acting choices are also interesting. Crystal never mumbles, whispers or raises his voice in ways that might hinder intelligibility. The scene where he 'loses it' after a chance meeting with his former wife Helen is a good example, as Crystal only raises the volume of his voice to shouting level on the last few words of his lines, rather than shouting out the whole scene. Ryan employs a more varied vocal range than does Crystal, and she seems less concerned about maintaining an even tone. That this should be regarded as Crystal's and Ryan's conscious choices is reflected in how their performance differs at times from what the script indicates. In the scene just mentioned, the script indicates that Harry should be shouting throughout a rather long monologue about the perils of divorce:

> Harry [shouting now]: I mean it. I mean it. *Put your name in your books*. Now, while you're unpacking them, before they get all mixed up together and you can't remember whose is whose.
>
> Because someday, believe it or not, you're going to be fighting over who's going to get this coffee table, this stupid wagon wheel coffee table.

However, Crystal ignores instructions and chooses to raise his voice gradually so as to 'peak' on the last line. (Here Crystal's ability as a comedian to select the punch line for maximum effect comes to the fore. Indeed, the stage direction 'shouting now' is actually removed from the published version of the script.)

These aural choices are interesting because they play against character: in the script, Harry is the one who expresses his feelings without social filtering, whereas Sally is the more controlled one. This is spelt out in the moment immediately following the 'wagon wheel' coffee table argument. First Sally admonishes Harry about his unrestricted behaviour: 'Harry, you're going to have to try and find a way of not expressing every feeling that you have every moment that you have them' only for Harry to retort that Sally acts like 'Miss Hospital corners' and that 'nothing ever bothers you'.

Ryan could have chosen to play Sally as an emotionally straight-jacketed woman, employing a very limited acting vocal range, Crystal could have gone the opposite way and portrayed a blabbering buffoon. In this sense, Ryan's and Crystal's acting choices are very effective in the way both employ their physical attributes, acting strengths and understanding of the characters. Crystal's and Ryan's performances work to ensure that the two central characters are neither entirely predictable nor too annoyingly self-centred.

The contributions made by Crystal and Ryan to the film went beyond acting. In particular, Reiner emphasizes the role played by Billy Crystal (and Ephron agrees) to the point of regarding him as the 'fourth' writer on the movie (beyond the Scheinman, Reiner, Ephron trio): 'The script was really a collaboration between the four of us. Then even Meg (Ryan) got into the picture with the idea of the orgasm scene'; and 'The great thing about Billy was that he added so much to the part, he improvised and it was like having another writer on the film' (from the director's commentary on the DVD of *When Harry Met Sally*, MGM, 2001 version). In this sense, it is clear that both Crystal and Ryan made an essential contribution to the film both in terms of acting and involvement with the writing process.

On the look and sound of *When Harry Met Sally*

When Harry Met Sally is a character-led, dialogue-driven film. As we mentioned earlier, both Ephron and Reiner clearly agree on this point. Moreover, Reiner chooses to adopt an unobtrusive camera style for the film (Reiner comments on the DVD's director's commentary that he does not like 'flashy camera work' because in his view camera work 'shouldn't be noticed'). In terms of lighting, director of photography Barry Sonnenfeld (now a very successful director) follows generic romantic comedy conventions: he tends to avoid hard shadows in favour of soft edges in brightly lit set-ups. The script is also rather specific about what 'kind' of day it is, almost invariably described as 'a gorgeous day' or 'a gorgeous fall day' and often suggesting dusk as the time of day. As for editing, Robert Leighton follows closely the rhythms imposed by the dialogue: apart from one montage sequence, the film follows linear editing (e.g., lack of cutaways, matching cuts, avoiding breaking up the space, establishing the geography of the shot clearly so as to give audiences clear bearings).

In other words, filmmakers (1) used mostly long takes, (2) photographed the film in bright sunshine with deep-focus lenses, and (3) avoided fast cutting and breaking up space in a film that employs nearly wall-to-wall dialogue in every scene. The result of this 'equation' raises some useful questions as to the involvement of other members of the filmmaking crew, namely those concerned with setting, costume design and sound. In a film such as *When Harry Met Sally* (where a lot of the action revolves around characters sitting around a table talking and where camera movement and editing are both kept to a minimum) audiences have simply more time to notice detail: what are the characters wearing? Where exactly are they? What do actors look like/sound like?

Production design is particularly effective in the film. In particular, *When Harry Met Sally* belongs to a group of films that use New York as not just a backdrop to the action but more as a character in its own right. Ephron's script is indeed remarkably specific as to where the film should be shot (*When Harry Met Sally* was mostly shot on location). A survey of the script reveals that Ephron's original choices of location were kept virtually unchanged. Her script goes beyond general instructions such as 'Harry and Sally are walking down a tree-lined avenue in the fall.' Ephron's indications are very specific:

Ext. – 77th Street Walk – Dusk
Harry and Sally walking together. The sun is setting.

Later in the film, when Harry and Sally become friends and begin to meet socially, Ephron does not simply suggest that 'they go to a museum'. Her instructions are very specific:

Int. – Metropolitan Museum – Dusk
Harry and Sally are walking through the Egyptian temple exhibit.

Clearly, for Ephron, New York is an integral part of Harry and Sally's romance. In many ways, New York acts as the 'facilitator' for their love story. That this is Ephron's choice rather than Reiner's becomes all the more evident when considering Reiner's rather dismissive remarks about the choice of filming in New York: 'I'm from New York, Norah is from New York so it just seemed like the natural place to set it' (from *The Making of When Harry Met Sally* documentary, DVD, MGM, 2001 version).

On costume design in *When Harry Met Sally*

Reiner is more articulate on this aspect than almost any other area of filmmaking. He specifically mentions costume designer Gloria Gresham: 'What was really tough was for Gloria Gresham to find wardrobe that would be suitable for these characters over a period of many years . . . She did a great job: it's the toughest thing to do to do contemporary wardrobe' (from the director's commentary on the DVD of *When Harry Met Sally*, MGM, 2001 version).

Gresham employs a strategy that revolves around two key aspects and their interaction: (1) the choice of colour schemes for Harry and Sally and (2) the kind of clothing they wore over the period of 11 years covered by the film. The characters' changes in costume, in terms of colour and style, allow audiences to appreciate Harry and Sally's development both as individuals and as a couple. (Obviously, these are conventional, contemporary Western aesthetic judgements. It would be perfectly feasible to imagine a situation where a non-Western audience may interpret the same development in colour schemes very differently. Similarly, issues of 'taste' and 'quality' are even more relative to class and social position of both the characters in the film and the filmmakers themselves.) The two characters go through five main stages: (1) first stage of their relationship, the first meeting; (2) second stage, they meet again, briefly; (3) third stage, they become friends; (4) fourth stage, they develop feelings; (5) final stage, they fall in love.

In each of these stages the characters' clothes work to give a sense of both space and the passing of time (they evolve, as do the hair styles, to suggest the different fashions: late 1970s, early 1980s, late 1980s, etc.). However, they also work to give a sense of Harry and Sally's relationship. In the first stage, Harry and Sally wear clothes that are different from each other without actually clashing. Harry is wearing a grey hooded top under which he has a white, blue-collared baseball shirt and jeans. His clothes are loose. His hair and overall demeanour suggest a certain casual feel, bordering on the unkempt. Sally, on the other hand, has a well-groomed look: knee-length knickerbockers, a yellow shirt and blue cardigan with knee-high socks and a Farrah Fawcett hair style. Harry's blue jeans and his baseball top are different in style from Sally's, but in colour terms there are hints of possible similarities (blue in particular is a colour that both characters wear). In the second stage, the clothes need to reflect their move up the social and professional ladder. They are both in full-time employment and their clothes reflect their desire/need to dress more formally. Once again, Sally appears the more carefully groomed of the two. Her hair style is very studiedly professional woman of the 1980s and her clothes are well cut, with matching accessories. Harry still has a touch of 'casual' about him, especially in the way he wears a waistcoat underneath his otherwise traditional suit and his tie is often loosened. This difference is brought more in to relief by the clothes that Sally's boyfriend (played by the son of former US President Gerald Ford) wears: a very well-cut, tailored suit of expensive fabric. However, once again the colour schemes chosen by Harry and Sally suggest perhaps a greater degree of closeness than might otherwise appear: they both wear schemes with a strong presence of grey (trousers, jacket, waistcoat and tie for Harry, the jacket for Sally – we never get to see what she is wearing below her waist). Again, this is more evident when compared with Sally's boyfriend, who wears primarily a dark-coloured scheme (deep blue tie, jackets, trousers, etc.). The red cravat worn by Sally breaks the similarities so that they both remain considerably distant in outlook, but the choice here is to avoid a complete clash. These first two stages of the relationship occupy a relatively brief amount of screen time. The next three, however, give much more breathing space to Gresham and there is a variety of different outfits on show. Some examples will give a sense of the thinking behind the different choices.

In the third stage, the need to create costumes that suggest a change in Harry and Sally's relationship (from strangers who do not much like each other to close friends) needs to be matched by the awareness that these two characters have just gone through painful relationship break ups (Sally has just broken up her long relationship with Joe and Harry is now separated from his wife Helen). The first time Harry and Sally meet in this stage of the narrative (in the 'Shakespeare & Company' bookshop) is a good example of Gresham's approach. Both Harry and Sally look much more 'mellowed': Sally wears a woollen high-neck jumper underneath a warm casual jacket. Her hair is also more 'relaxed' (there is no complicated style: this is the 'just-got-out-of-bed-looking-like-this' Meg Ryan hairstyle that has been a trademark for her). The glasses that she wears are rather large and not particularly 'trendy', they are functional. Harry also wears somewhat looser clothing than in the previous stage: his jacket (similar in style to Sally's) is worn over a denim shirt with no tie and an open collar. He has also grown a beard that gives him a slightly more mature look. When they go for a walk after their catching-up lunch the camera reveals that Sally is now also wearing jeans. At this point Harry's and Sally's styles of clothing begin to converge: they are in a similar 'place' emotionally but also in terms of maturity and the clothes and colour schemes reflect this.

In the next stage, Gresham needs to suggest even more: Harry and Sally move from being just good friends to realizing they have feelings for each other. The sequence of their walk through Central Park on their way to the Metropolitan Museum is, in this sense, indicative of this development in their relationship. Sally wears what some critics referred to at the time of the film's release as the '*Annie Hall* style' (felt hat, well-cut jacket with matching accessories). The only real update on the costume that Diane Keaton wore in Woody Allen's film is that Meg Ryan wears trousers rather than a skirt. It is an elegant but understated style.

Similarly, Harry has now moved on to wearing something other than just jeans in his spare time. He now also wears a brown leather jacket. Both look comfortable in these clothes. More importantly, their colour schemes are complementary, with close attention being paid to avoid any kind of clash: Harry and Sally now look like a (screen) couple. It is at this point that Gresham's work becomes perhaps most incisive: the two outfits just described paint an interesting 'picture', where the two characters are becoming more attuned not just to each other, but also to their own environment. In the Central Park walk, a long shot of the two characters walking together emphasizes the degree to which both Harry and Sally blend in with their surroundings: the earth colours of their clothes match perfectly the deep greens and browns of the park. The fact that this famous shot has only the two characters in it (no passing jogger, dog walker or any other figure disturb their walk) emphasizes their relationship. From this moment on, Harry's and Sally's outfits mostly match in all departments: style, fabric, colours, etc.

Perhaps the most evident example of Gresham's excellent work comes in the restaurant scene when Harry and Sally (who have not yet acknowledged their feelings for each other) go to dinner with their two best friends Marie and Jess in the hope that romance may blossom. Marie (played by Carrie Fisher) sits next to Harry. Opposite Harry is Jess with Sally at his side. This seating arrangement is clearly designed to facilitate conversation between the two 'possible' couples. But it is undermined by Gresham's costumes: both Marie and Harry and Jess and Sally wear rather different clothes and colour schemes (Marie sports a green top with a boat neck whereas Harry wears a simple jacket on a black polo shirt; Sally opts for a plunging neck black dress with a white scarf whereas Jess wear a rather more casual jacket with a blue-ish shirt and tie). What appears almost immediately obvious is that, in fact, it is Jess and Marie, and more importantly, Harry and Sally, who wear complementary clothes. Visually, through Gresham's costumes, before the narrative spells it out, the film suggests Harry and Sally's future: not with Jess or Marie but with each other.

The sound in *When Harry Met Sally*

The most striking choice concerning the use of sound in *When Harry Met Sally* revolves around the characterization of New York in aural terms and the use of music. We have mentioned earlier how specific Ephron was in terms of choosing locales in New York as the setting for some of the key sequences in the film. The role that New York plays visually (i.e., a very constant presence, creating a sort of frame within which Harry and Sally live and love) is counterbalanced by the way New York is depicted aurally. In some sense, the strategy employed is virtually the opposite of that used for the film's images. The traditionally loud and vibrant New York soundscape is eschewed in favour of a much softer and rarefied sound environment. From when Harry and Sally first reach New York (when they part for the first time in Washington Square) the sounds that would normally be expected (traffic, people, the usual business of the metropolis) are discarded in favour of a rather neutral, quiet aural background against which both voices and music play undisturbed. In terms of city sounds, all we hear is the distant humming of the city. It is very much in the background and never intrudes in the exchanges between the two characters. This basic but crucial strategy, to leave dialogue virtually undisturbed, is confirmed almost immediately afterwards in the airport scene. Whilst the visuals suggest a very busy airport the sounds of the announcements, sounds of people (e.g., children crying, people calling out to each other, families passing by, etc.) are muted so that the dialogue between Harry, Sally and Joe is perfectly audible and very much in the foreground.

Later, on the plane, we hear no sound from the engines, no chatter amongst passengers: all sounds are again muted except for a very soft background hum that serves as ambience. (It is a well-recognized necessity for films to have some kind of background ambient sound: audiences have been known to notice if this is lacking and have found its lack distracting and puzzling. This, of course, is not surprising since there is no equivalent in real life, where there is always some measure of ambient sound.) This approach is repeated throughout the film. The main aim is to bestow New York with a very soft, non-aggressive aural character. There is nothing of New York's harsh and discordant soundscape, that is present in other romantic comedies such as *Frankie & Johnny*: this is a version of New York that, in aural terms, is as soft and unthreatening as a cotton ball.

One of the consequences of this choice is that dialogue is not just audible, it has the kind of 'cleanness' in terms of intelligibility and clarity that it is rarely found in contemporary cinema, as dialogue ordinarily fits within a more articulated context where music and sound effects are more present than in *When Harry Met Sally*. This cocooning of the two main characters' dialogue allows audiences to hear every nuance in Crystal's and Ryan's voices and this gives a strong sense of intimacy to the film: audiences hear Harry's and Sally's voices as if they were with them on the same pavement, sitting by them on the same bench, lying next to them on the same bed.

The attention given to voices and dialogue in *When Harry Met Sally* is emphasized by the way music is used in the film. The use of standards as the backbone to the film's score was quite unusual at the time, as Reiner emphasizes: 'I was talking about doing something different . . . you hear a lot of rock 'n roll, you hear a certain kind of traditional classical score and at the time nobody had used old standards' (from *The Making of When Harry Met Sally* documentary, DVD, MGM, 2001 release).

In *When Harry Met Sally* standards are employed as a means to support the dialogue and give the film the feel almost of a musical: the characters' voices, in this sense, become almost singing voices. Rarely is music employed in a more traditional way to suggest mood or anticipate danger/surprise, etc. In the 77th Street Walk (Central Park) scene mentioned earlier, the music rises from a very low level to support the dialogue. Marc Shaiman's rearrangement of the standards used in the film helps the filmmakers to strengthen the integration between the way the music is phrased and the tempo of the dialogue: they blend almost seamlessly. *When Harry Met Sally* partly resuscitated the use of standards in movies. However, the way standards are used in the film does not work to create something 'new', quite the opposite. Their familiar feeling (Western audiences would probably be familiar with at least some of them – *It Had to Be You* and *Let's Call The Whole Thing Off* are classics) contributes to creating a sense of comfort and warmth about Harry and Sally: there is nothing unsettling or particularly unusual about their situation, setting and lifestyle.

Ultimately, the sonic world that Harry and Sally inhabit is an idealized world where whispering and sighing can muffle the harsh sounds of the city. Rarely had New York City sounded so harmonious in movies.

Conclusion

When Harry Met Sally has often been described either as a 'Rob Reiner film' or as the first in Nora Ephron's trilogy of romantic comedies (*When Harry Met Sally, Sleepless in Seattle* and *You've Got Mail*). Although Reiner clearly played a central role in providing the original idea for the film, helping to shape the way the script developed and generally being engaged with the project, it is difficult to see how it could be possible to suggest that this is 'his' film. In particular, Nora Ephron's contribution would seem to extend beyond merely being one of three screenwriters. Her take on New York, understanding of what 'kind' of romantic comedy *When Harry Met Sally* is, and ability to articulate her thoughts on these subjects strongly suggest that her contribution was essential to the film.

However, the contribution of other key collaborators appears to be equally important. In particular, given the choices that were made in terms of directing style, lighting and camera movement, the contribution of both costume designers and actors are essential. Both Crystal and Ryan do an excellent job at playing off each other, especially in terms of timing and rhythm. Crystal's downbeat, slow tempo is counter-pointed effectively by Ryan's pulsating, stop-and-start pace. This creates an interesting creative tension in relation to their characters, Harry, the restless one of the two, plays against Sally, the more apparently cerebral of the pair. The rhythm of their exchanges, especially in aural terms, is one of the pleasures of the film and the two actors clearly make the most of Ephron's dialogue, thus compensating, in part at least, for deficiencies in plot structure and character development. In this they are aided substantially by Gresham's choice of costumes. The way they progressively converge in terms of colour schemes (Harry and Sally go from wearing clashing outfits to sporting almost perfectly complementary colours) and the way their clothes become progressively looser and more comfortable reflect the evolution of the characters both individually and as a couple. Finally, the way the score is used in supporting some of the key dialogue exchanges between them in the film confers a certain lightness of touch and intimacy to the film.

Ultimately, *When Harry Met Sally* is an interesting example of how complex the politics of filmmaking can be, even when everyone involved claims it was a very collaborative project. Reiner never misses an opportunity to remind us that this is 'his' film, whilst Ephron claims that this was an excellent collaboration only to proceed to compile what amounts to a list of things she was not happy with (ending, title, several scenes) that ultimately would appear to underline her view that in the power struggle between director and screenwriter the latter 'usually gets screwed'.

Perhaps the most revealing aspect to come out of a study of the production of *When Harry Met Sally* concerns the issue of compromise. In many ways all of the key contributors make noises about the fact that they had to compromise but were happy to do so. The evidence, however, would seem to point to an uncomfortable truth, namely that filmmaking is not a perfect democracy and perhaps ought not to be approached thus. Ephron's soul-searching comment about giving in to other people's demands only to realize that perhaps she should have stood her ground more is, in this sense, the key to understanding the criticism that was levelled at the film.

Indeed, we agree with most of this criticism. The film has a rather episodic structure and is ultimately very uneven in tone. Although the various scenes/moments in the movie have Harry and Sally's relationship as their common thread, it is a rather thinly woven thread. In an article for *Variety*, William Goldman once wrote that films are about 'moments' (*Variety*, 18 January 2004). Indeed, he quotes the orgasm scene from *When Harry Met Sally* as one of such memorable moments that audiences remember. However, *When Harry Met Sally* is precisely only that, a collection of moments, often very different in tone and effectiveness.

However, the film still retains warmth and this needs to be accounted for. Critics have often indicated Reiner as the reason for this. As one *Variety* reviewer once suggested: 'Rob Reiner directs with deftness and sincerity, making the material seem more engaging than it is, at least until the plot mechanics begin to unwind and the film starts to seem shapeless' (*Variety*, 1 January 1989).

We disagree: most of the considerable degree of charm and affection that the film achieves owes less to its director and more to the film's setting, its actors, music, costumes and witty one-liners.

chapter seven

Conclusion – authors, entertainers and other issues

Fig 7.1 On the set of *I Spy*, 2002. (Photo: Columbia/The Kobal Collection/Joe Lederer)

Authors

While writers often acknowledge the collective nature of filmmaking, their acknowledgement is usually a token one. Typically, the collective nature of filmmaking is declared to be obvious but, in the discussion that follows, the obvious is ignored and the focus is on the director. We wanted our acknowledgement to be more than token. To ensure it was we have tried to establish the collective nature of filmmaking in a concrete and detailed way. As we said in our introduction, one of our chief ambitions has been to call attention to filmmakers, other than the director; who make significant contributions to a film. If we have achieved this, we will be satisfied. We did, however, have other ambitions also. In our introduction we raised some general issues about the nature of filmmaking. The essential one was the position of the director, how does that role emerge from our investigations? Should the director still be regarded as the film's author in a cinema such as Hollywood's?

Two main reasons are given to support the belief that the director is the author of a film. That cited most often is the one given by David Bordwell and Kristin Thompson: '*the director has most control over how a movie looks and sounds*' (Bordwell and Thompson, 2001: 33; our emphasis).

It is important to note exactly what is being claimed for the director. It is not that they have *total* control; the claim is a qualified one – the director has *most* control. However, it is not nit-picking to say that it is important to be clear about what 'most' entails. It could entail that the director has *much* more control than anyone else, or that they have a *little* more control than anyone else. There is an important difference between the two situations. If the director has much more control than anybody else, then the claim they are the author of the film has more weight than if they only have a little more control.

In practice, the amount of control varies enormously. There are films where the director has almost total control (e.g., *Titanic* – James Cameron). There are films where the director has substantial control but with obvious limits (e.g., *Bonfire of the Vanities* – Brian De Palma). There are films where control is clearly divided (e.g., *Great Expectations* – between the director, Alfonso Cuarón, and the producer, Art Linson), and there are films where control is in the hands of the producer, not the director (e.g., *Top Gun* – or any other film produced by Jerry Bruckheimer and Don Simpson). These are only some of the most obvious situations. There are many others: where, for example, the star (e.g., *Rhinestone* – Sylvester Stallone) or the writer (e.g., *Bowfinger* – Steve Martin) has to be taken into account. It is also necessary to recognize that the amount of control any one director has will vary throughout their career, depending on box-office success and critical reputation.

Any generalization about the amount of control a director has in making a film has to be qualified so much that it becomes vacuous. Therefore, we do not accept the claim that 'the director has most control over how a movie looks and sounds'. The belief that the director is the author of the film cannot be supported on these grounds.

The second main reason for the belief that the director is the author of a film is a modification of the first. The director may not have control over all phases of the making of a film but *they have control over the key phase, which is the shooting of the film.*

This belief combines a theoretical proposition with an empirical one. The theoretical proposition is that a film is created through its images. The empirical proposition is that directors control the creation of the images. If the theoretical proposition were true, one would expect directors to support it, especially as many of them have been exposed to arguments of this kind. Our evidence does not suggest that they do. They vary in the commitment they show to creating images. As we have mentioned, Steven Soderbergh feels the process is so important that he has become his own cinematographer. Jonathan Demme, on the other hand, says he leaves the creation of the images entirely to his cinematographer. In general, directors say that shooting is the least enjoyable part of filmmaking – Steven Spielberg says it is the part he most dislikes. It is not enjoyable because it is the time when they feel least in control, burdened as they are by the need to make hundreds of decisions, without being sure of the consequences of those decisions. The majority view amongst filmmakers is that the script is the most important part of filmmaking.

Directors could be wrong. In the end, the proposition has to be addressed in its own terms. One of our strongest objections to it is that it ignores the place of sound. Since the earliest days of the cinema, films have been a combination of images and sounds. The cinema is an *audio-visual* medium not just a *visual* one. It's no accident that *mise-en-scène*, the concept coined to express the dominance of images, takes no account of sound. Our objection to the proposition is strengthened by the confusing way *mise-en-scène* is used. It originally indicated what was in front of the camera; sets, costumes and actors constituted a film's *mise-en-scène*. Its current use often includes the camera as well as what is in front if it. To add to the confusion, *mise-en-scène* is sometimes used in a more expansive way, as a synonym for the overall style of a film. Our biggest objection, as far as the aim of this book is concerned, is that it disguises the collective nature of filmmaking. The *mise-en-scène* of a film is discussed as if it were the property of the director. The contributions of the art director, costume designer, production designer and actors are ignored.

Our evidence does not support the empirical proposition that directors control the creation of images. What it does suggest is that directors are likely to suffer less interference during the shooting of a film than in other phases. However, they do not have complete freedom. They get interference that ranges from the minor (according to Dawn Steel, Michael Eisner did not like smoke or dust in images) to the substantial. The interference is likely to be substantial if a film goes over budget, a not infrequent occurrence. If it does, a director may be asked to speed up the shooting. If shooting is speeded up, it will have consequences for the quality of the images. Much of the conflict in the *Heaven's Gate* affair was caused by this situation.

Before we state our own conclusions, there is a clarification we would like to make. In discussing authorship we are, in the first place, talking about who should be held responsible for a film. The film itself may be good or bad – the question of its quality has to be established separately. The concept of the *auteur* blurs this distinction. To say that Robert Altman is an *auteur* is not the same as saying that Anne Tyler is an author. The word *auteur* implies quality; author does not. To call Robert Altman an *auteur* is to claim that he is the author of good films. Why? Because an individual personality – an Altman presence – can be detected in the films he directs. It is this presence that separates a good film from a bad one. The position depends on identifying most films as anonymous; a personality cannot be detected in them. This is the cinema version of a familiar position; mass culture products are designed according to formulae and created by machines. We do not share this position.

Our own conclusions about authorship are:

1   It's not appropriate to talk about authorship of films in a cinema such as modern Hollywood in the same terms as the authorship of novels, paintings, poems or symphonies. Therefore, any credit such as 'a film by' is inaccurate and misleading. It would be better to return to the old version of credits with only a 'directed by' credit for the director.

2   The authorship of a film always has to be established, it cannot be taken for granted. It is likely to be collective; the most likely candidates for inclusion are director, producer, star and writer. Other candidates are always possible.

3   The script is the key element in the making of a film. Most of the accounts we have come across suggest that the creative dynamics of filmmaking are best understood in terms of the opportunities offered by the script and how directors, producers, stars, etc., respond to those opportunities.

4   Filmmaking is a collaborative effort but it is as strongly marked by disagreement as it is by cooperation. The existence of conflict, tension and egotism in Hollywood filmmaking is hardly an unknown fact. For us, the interesting thing is the conclusions that are drawn from it. Usually they are negative ones that lead to condemnations of the whole process. It is certainly true that the consequences are often over-budget, incoherent films. But our explorations suggest that conflict and tension can be productive, generating energy and inventiveness. Carl Gottlieb provides a vivid description of how this happens in his account of the making of *Jaws*.

5   The idea that filmmaking should be judged in terms of personal expression is completely inappropriate for commercial cinema. Personal expression is always strongly mediated through interaction with other filmmakers. That mediation often blocks or reshapes the personal expressiveness of a director (or a writer, actor, cinematographer or others). It would be more appropriate to talk about collective expressiveness, much as that goes against the grain of a culture that places such a high value on personal expressiveness.

Entertainers

When we explored the question of authorship in modern Hollywood, there were, obviously, other issues that demanded our attention. A crucial one was the status of entertainment because it raised questions about our overall perspective on the films that were made.

In contemporary cultural discussion the distinction between art and entertainment is a familiar one. Although it is regularly used, the distinction is rarely expanded on. It works by a kind of shorthand. Both terms are given a set of attributes. Art is demanding, substantially engages with human experience, is critical, has depth and is formally complex and innovative. It makes you think, it is personally expressive. Entertainment is undemanding, escapist and shallow, accepts the world as it is and is formally simple and conservative. It discourages you from thinking, it is impersonal and anonymous. Artists and entertainers differ in their sense of responsibility. Artists believe their first responsibility is to their art; entertainers believe their first responsibility is to their audience. This is to put the distinction in its strongest form; it is often weakened – people will admit that art can be boring and self-important, that entertainment can be unpretentious and refreshing. However, the basic value judgement is rarely disturbed.

As we have already suggested, the art/entertainment distinction has a strong presence in filmmakers' reflections. Generally they discuss their work with the implicit assumption that they are talking about art. The concept of 'the director's vision' is an obvious example of this. (William Friedman ironically said, 'If it's a film *by* somebody instead of *for* somebody, I smell art'; (Biskind, 1998: 223). However, there is an uncertainty about this sense of filmmaking as art that unsettles many filmmakers, especially writers and directors. The uncertainty can be detected by the number of times they feel compelled to define their work against entertainment. We have already quoted some examples of this but we will highlight the issue by quoting Jonathan Demme's discussion of *Married to the Mob*.

> I am very concerned with themes and psychological subtext in movies, but the thing that attracted me to *Married to the Mob* was the complete absence of themes and subtext, on one level. I liked the idea of trying to do a movie that was a complete escapist fantasy, which didn't pretend it had anything profound to say about anything. It was fun to do, and very cathartic, revivifying.
>
> *Do you really mean it when you say* Married to the Mob *has nothing profound to say?*
>
> Let's face it, *Married to the Mob* is a blatant attempt at a full tilt, crassly commercial entertainment – let's make no bones about that. Nevertheless, I did hope that if people liked the picture, part of their experience would be seeing this white person leave their comfortable, suburban, fully equipped home and become an absolute outsider – Angela moves into profoundly more difficult living circumstances, surrounded by people who, through their ethnic definition or what have you, are relegated to a certain outsider status. Without beating it on the head, the audience sees: well, what do you know, down there people are people. When someone gives her a chance at a job and sticks by her, because she's blessed with the absence of a racial distinction – she doesn't like people on the basis of what race they are – she's available to be reached out to. The fact that she's not a racialist proves to be an asset down there and helps her to get started on a new and positive path.
>
> OK, that's probably corny, and it's not very well executed, but I feel it's as important an arena of thinking as exists in the world today. I mean, it's killing our society in a zillion ways, and it's so hard not to get sucked into the awfulness and the violence of racism, whether as an observer or a participant. Even when doing escapist movies like *Married to the Mob* you desperately want to try to get something positive, informationally, in there.
>
> (Boorman and Donohue, 1992: 184)

Demme defines entertainment in a limiting way. It lacks depth and profundity (no subtext or themes), it is 'escapist fantasy'. However, he begins by taking a positive attitude to making a film of this kind but, challenged by his interviewer, he feels unable to continue justifying the film in this way. He retreats to a familiar position. He claims that *Married to the Mob* does deal with important issues. By the end of his answer he claims that it is a statement about racism.

Demme is not the only one to get caught up in this way. We have quoted a number of examples in a similar vein: Bruce Joel Rubin's claim that while films can be 'wonderful entertainments' they should also serve 'a higher purpose', Joel Silver's defensiveness when he tries to justify his films as entertainments. The uncertainty is created by awareness that Hollywood's primary purpose is to provide entertainment but that entertainment in itself is a limited goal.

The effects of this conflict seem to us to be mixed. Some are undoubtedly negative. One of the worst is a cynicism that leads to a belittling of the cinema as a medium. This attitude, for obvious reasons, is most strongly expressed by screenwriters. Richard Price's comment that 'screenwriting – there's no reason to do it except to make money' is one of the most aggressive statements of this. A similar attitude can be detected in *Monster*, where it appears that John Gregory Dunne and Joan Didion regard their novels and journalism as of much more consequence than their screenwriting. Cynicism of this kind can produce jaded films.

However, there are also positive effects, which we think are more important. The contradictory pulls of art and entertainment invigorate Hollywood filmmaking. The impulse towards entertainment is clearly dominant: the best and worst of that impulse are on display in the films. The films may have energy and accessibility, along with impressive spectacle, powerful, direct emotional appeal, vivid, large-scale characters and broad humour. They may express populist sentiments and be unsympathetic to convention and authority (for example – *Jaws*, the *Lord of the Rings* trilogy, *The Silence of the Lambs*, *Alien*, *Star Wars* and the *Terminator* films). Or, they may be predictable and stale, full of repetitive situations, with over-familiar characters, cheap emotional effects and obvious jokes. They may display crude cultural prejudices (there are many examples on offer – *Basic Instinct* and *Charlie's Angels* would be high on our list). We should not, perhaps, present the situation in the form of a direct contrast, because the good and the bad features regularly appear in the same film. In *Titanic*, to take a very obvious example, a simplistic story and characters are combined with imposing spectacle.

While it is much weaker, the art impulse is also evident. Again, the best and the worst of the impulse are on display. On the one hand the films may be complex and substantial, they may offer sharp social criticism, refined emotions, substantial characterization and be formally unorthodox (for example – *Being John Malkovich*, *Six Degrees of Separation*, *Punch Drunk Love*). On the other hand the films may be intellectually vacuous, or opaque and constricted, or emotionally undernourished, or formally sterile or all of these together! (For example *Eyes Wide Shut*, *Prêt a Porter*, *Bring out your Dead*.)

The most interesting territory is where entertainment and art meet (for example – *Chinatown*, *Body Heat*, *Magnolia*, *Godfather 1 and 2*, *Manhattan* and *Do the Right Thing*). Overall, the majority of Hollywood films are undoubtedly of limited interest. There is certainly plenty of dross, but that has always been true of popular culture. It has always attracted hucksters, fortune seekers, con men and charlatans. The intriguing thing about Hollywood is that sometimes the hucksters produce some surprising films.

For us, the tension between art and entertainment expressed by filmmakers has been fruitful. We do not think it has been fruitful for critics. We claimed in the introduction that there was myopia about entertainment that we attributed to the framework created by *Cahiers du Cinema*. We pointed out that *Cahiers'* writers set out to give the cinema the same status as the established, high prestige arts. The conservatism of this project was initially disguised because of their preoccupation with Hollywood cinema. It seemed to be a radical move to look for art in such an unlikely place. However, the move only masked a conservatism that, with time, has become more and more obvious. To treat the cinema in the same terms as painting or classical music or poetry encourages an evasion of all the things that makes it, especially in its Hollywood form, different from those art forms: the power of capital, the collective form of production, the centrality of technology, the need for large audiences and the commitment to entertainment.

Entertainment has been a very significant evasion. With the enormous expansion of television, the huge impact of pop music, the globalization of sport and the emergence of video games, it has become a central phenomenon of Western capitalist societies in the second half of the twentieth century. The cinema, as the first example of the phenomenon, was an ideal object to investigate it thoroughly. However, the desire to establish cinema as art precluded this.

As a more critical political attitude developed towards the USA, provoked, first by the Vietnam War, then by the election of Ronald Reagan and now George Bush, entertainment has increasingly been judged to be bad, a way of disguising political realities. It became a synonym for ideology. In his book, *Hollywood from Vietnam to Reagan*, Robin Wood writes:

> One of the functions of the concept of entertainment – by definition, that which we don't take seriously, or think about much ('Its only entertainment') – is to act as a kind of partial sleep of consciousness. For the filmmakers as well as the audience, full awareness stops at the level of plot, action and character, in which the most dangerous and subversive implications can disguise themselves and escape detection.
>
> (Wood, 1986: 78)

If we wanted something to demonstrate why a more substantial discussion of entertainment is necessary, a statement like this provides it. Who defines entertainment as something we do not take seriously? The dictionary certainly does not. How can 'one of the functions of a concept' act as 'a kind of partial sleep of consciousness'? It is a sloppy formulation of the traditional belief that entertainment acts as a narcotic. What evidence is there for this? If filmmakers and audiences are not fully aware of 'the most dangerous and subversive implications' of films, is such awareness confined to film academics?

The same failure to engage with entertainment is also evident in the critical judgement made of modern Hollywood cinema. The judgement is that in the late 1960s and 1970s it was a vibrant cinema, full of the work of artists such as Martin Scorsese, Robert Altman, Hal Ashby, Frances Ford Coppola and Bob Rafelson. A cinema dominated by entertainers such as George Lucas and Steven Spielberg displaced it. The result was an infantilization of filmmaking: vacuous films whose main feature was empty spectacle.

If we begin from the assumption that entertainment is an inferior form, it is easy to dismiss films such as *Star Wars* and *E.T.*, but such an easy dismissal prevents serious analysis. Such an analysis would need to take into account the cinema's change of status from the dominant form of mass entertainment to being one of a number, all competing for audiences. It would also need to take into account the fact that films such as *Star Wars* and *E.T.* were crucial in making the cinema competitive. They saved it from becoming a marginal form, like theatre. The analysis would also need to address the audience's experience of 'entertainment' films. Is that experience an empty one? If it is, why have audience figures been so buoyant over the last 20 years? If children are included in the audience, why should cinema not be infantilized?

For us, art and entertainment are not separate things but two ends of a continuum. One is not inferior to the other. They need each other.

Other issues

However well or badly we may have communicated it, we have learnt a lot about filmmaking: its dynamics, structures and politics. We have also learnt some things about film criticism. We will highlight some of the things that struck us most forcefully.

The burden on directors is too great. This is one of the most frequent complaints made by directors. During shooting, Spike Lee says the director is asked '5 million questions a day'. To this must be added all the decisions that need to be made before and after the film is shot: about the script, the cast, the crew, locations, costumes, schedules, editing, music, sound. If confirmation of the oppressiveness of the burden is required, Julie Salamon's portrait of Brian De Palma provides it. She gives a disturbing account of the impact of all the stresses and strains on a director.

This is a particular phenomenon of modern Hollywood. The widespread acceptance of the *auteur* theory by filmmakers as well as critics has elevated the importance of the director. But the collapse of the studio system has left the director more isolated, without the support systems the studios provided. The editor, Carol Littleton, points to one of the most significant consequences of the new situation.

> Editors, cinematographers, production designers, and so on essentially have more experience than directors do. Making a movie can be a terrorizing experience for a first time director, or for a second or a third or a fourth, you know. Cutting your teeth as a film director is difficult because directors now have to generate their own material, generate interest, get the actors, raise the funds and so forth. So directors now have to do a whole lot more than directors in the past. It's easy for editors to have a body of work because we're on a film probably every nine months, and before you know it, you've worked on quite a few. But directors simply don't have the opportunity to work on that many films if it takes them two or three years to put a project together, direct it, and get it released.
>
> (Oldham, 1995: 76)

The context has been made even more difficult by the increased scale of filmmaking. The introduction of new technologies has made new demands on the director. The visual effects artist, John Van Vliet, has, for example, pointed to the complications the demands of visual effects create for actor-oriented directors

There is no common aesthetic amongst moviemakers. We were hugely impressed by the depth and sophistication with which moviemakers discussed their own crafts. However, a common aesthetic position did not emerge from these discussions. There is one strongly held belief – direction is the creative centre of filmmaking. However, there is also a belief, almost as strongly held, that the script is crucial to the quality of a film. The possible contradiction between these two beliefs is not explored. Another belief that has some presence is transparency: that the effects created by cinematography, editing, sound, etc., should not be obvious to an audience. We have already pointed out that this has the appearance of a formal belief that is contradicted in practice. Realism is frequently referred to but, as our discussion of *Jurassic Park* indicates, it is a vague term and usually turns out to be a synonym for plausibility or believability.

Is the absence of a common aesthetic surprising? Should we expect a common aesthetic from filmmakers who are working in diverse genres with different ambitions? Would we expect modern American novelists to have a shared aesthetic?

Cinematographers, editors, production designers and sound designers are not technicians. There is almost always a quality of condescension when somebody is described as a technician. It suggests the person has knowledge but of a limited and, probably, inferior kind. In the context of filmmaking, it also suggests people who, given orders, apply pre-existing knowledge in a straightforward way. None of this makes sense in terms of what we discovered. The technical knowledge of cinematographers, editors, production designers and sound designers was hugely impressive. Every film we came across was dependent on it. Sometimes the evidence was very obvious – *Jaws* or *Titanic* are prime examples. Sometimes it was less obvious – the contribution of the production designer's knowledge to the success of *Seven* is easy to miss. Whether it was obvious or not, we developed a great respect for technical knowledge. It did not exist on its own but was always intimately related to other kinds of knowledge. Most cinematographers, for example, have a strong sense of art history. In the accounts of filmmaking we came across, technical knowledge rarely emerges as something that could be applied in a simple and direct fashion. There was always a dialogue between it and dramatic demands – the animation of the dinosaurs and the creation of sound for them in *Jurassic Park* being prime examples. Technician is an inadequate word for describing cinematographers, editors, production designers and sound designers. A better word is needed.

The producer and the studio executive need to be written into the script. Certainly one of the most straightforward discoveries we made was how much producers contributed to filmmaking. It is not easy to place them in the overall structure of filmmaking, for reasons we have already mentioned: they do not all perform the same role, their titles are frequently misleading, and the stereotype of producers as gross men with big cigars and vulgar minds is still pervasive. However, with a little research, it is not impossible to give them their due.

Studio executives also suffer from a stereotype. They are characterized as 'suits', uncreative bureaucrats preoccupied with the bottom line. Our research on them was limited and studios have layers of bureaucracy the function of which is not clear. From what we did discover, however, they did not fit the stereotype, except that they were actively interested in budgets and box office returns. A thought occurred to us: if sums of US$100 million are being spent on a film, should somebody not be concerned with the bottom line? Whatever view is taken of studio executives, our main concern is that their contribution to the making of films should be properly taken account of. If account is taken of what they contribute, it is usually in a dismissive, off-hand way. Our investigations have encouraged us to resist this kind of dismissal.

We have sketched the various ways in which studio executives do influence the character of particular films. It is clear that their interventions are motivated by some general ideas about what audiences want from films: there should be main characters with whom the audience can sympathize, the overall effect of a film should not be a depressing one and there should be some uplift at the end. It is easy to dismiss such ideas and certainly they are often crassly applied. But, taken seriously, is this assessment of the audience wildly wrong? Do judgements based on them necessarily make a film worse?

William Goldman is wrong. Goldman's statement that in Hollywood nobody knows anything is endlessly quoted. It is a smart-ass statement of the kind Goldman is fond. It appears iconoclastic but, in fact, anybody can sign up to it. Critics can happily do so because it confirms their sense of superiority over Hollywood. Hollywood insiders can sign up just as happily; Goldman gives them an 'out' for their failures.

Despite its sweeping nature, the statement really means that nobody can predict the success of a particular film. But that's one piece of knowledge that everybody in Hollywood has. The problem for filmmakers is what you do once you recognize this. The obvious strategy is to minimize the overall risk as much as possible. To do so, there is a wide variety of knowledge that is helpful. Do not put all your eggs in one basket, for example. Do not make more than one mega-budget film at the same time. Make a variety of films. Get Harrison Ford, Julia Roberts or Tom Hanks to star and Steven Spielberg or James Cameron to direct. Publicize your films as much as possible. Knowledge of this kind is obvious. It is also provisional and limited and comes with no guarantees. But the sum of human knowledge would be very small if it was only confined to obscure, eternal truths!

A final comment about politics. When we began work on this book, George Bush had just been elected President of the USA. As we finish it, he is coming up for re-election. In between, the Twin Towers have been destroyed, Afghanistan and Iraq invaded. Not since Vietnam have more questions been asked about the role the US is playing in the world. At the same time, and closely related, more and more opposition is being expressed to the growth of economic and cultural globalization. It is impossible to write about a major feature of American society, such as Hollywood, with its global presence, without reflecting on its relationship with those developments. We have felt the challenge particularly strongly because we have offered what is, in many respects, a sympathetic account of Hollywood.

This is not the place to describe a full-blown political position. There are indications of where we stand at various points in our discussion: our interest in collective activity, enthusiasm for the cinema as popular entertainment and lack of sympathy for the conventional critique of mass culture. The one point we want to elaborate upon may seem paradoxical in this context. Ever since Jean-Luc Godard offered inane slogans such as 'Paramount-Nixon', Hollywood cinema and developments in American politics have been indivisible. Hollywood films are seen as representative of the values of the Bush (or, previously, the Reagan) administration. We believe that, in any analysis, Hollywood films and American politics should be held apart as long as possible. The critic's first task is to create as strong a sense as possible of their differences. There are connections between the two; we do not believe they are umbilical ones.

Intellectually, the attempts to make connections have not impressed us. They depend on simplistic accounts of society as a monolith or dubious notions such as the existence of a collective unconscious. Politically, a view of the USA as a monolithic society has proved attractive. However, the consequence of this view is either an impractical revolutionary politics – the system must be overthrown – or political passivity – what is the use?

We wrote this book in the belief that the way in which politics, just as much as aesthetics, is thought about in film scholarship needs refreshing.

Any collaborative art succeeds by virtue of the positive contributions made by all the participants. Wittingly or not, the successful end product reflects the hands of dozens of artists and craftsmen. Movies, for all their size, are big celluloid mosaics – editors, actors, painters, cameramen, writers, producers, a director, all of us can point at the finished picture and pick out bits and pieces of our individual work . . . In the order dictated by their art, their lawyers, their agents, and their unions, the collective contributors to *Jaws* are summarized here. If you enjoy the picture, if you laugh or scream, or jump in your seat, all of us thank you. If, in addition, you've paid cash for your ticket, the producers and studios especially thank you. All of us, and hundreds more un-named, made *Jaws*.

(Carl Gottlieb – writer and actor)

Appendix 1: Filmmakers' grids

The grids below are meant to provide readers with a quick opportunity to notice any meaningful patterns in the production teams of the directors who worked on the three films we chose to analyse: Steven Spielberg, Roman Polanski and Rob Reiner. In addition, we have included a similar grid for Nora Ephron in recognition of her role in the making of *When Harry Met Sally* and especially in relation to the fact that the film has often been described as the first one in a 'Nora Ephron' romantic comedy trilogy (the others being *Sleepless in Seattle* and *You've Got Mail*).

To retain some degree of control over the material, we chose to include five films in each grid. In the cases of Spielberg, Polanski and Reiner, we placed the films included in the book as the fourth entry out of five. This is to ensure that the grids show any pattern in the period leading up to the film in question. The fifth film is included to provide some continuity. In the case of Ephron, we chose to include five films that received wide international distribution and are readily available on home video or DVD. They are all romantic comedies to some degree and we thought that this would also ensure that readers can form some opinion over issues of authorship and collaboration in relation to her reputation as a romantic comedy specialist.

These grids are obviously not meant to be exhaustive. We included data concerning nine key areas:

- Director
- Screenplay
- Music
- Sound [a) supervising sound editor b) sound re-recording mixers]
- Production design [a) production designer & b) art direction]
- Editing
- Costume design
- Cinematography
- Producers.

The division of sound and production design into two sub-categories each reflects the creative input of two rather different though related roles: those of production designer and art director in the latter case, and those of supervising sound editor and sound re-recording mixer in the former. We hope that this material will provide some useful elements for further analysis.

Table A1.1: Steven Spielberg

	Indiana Jones and the Last Crusade (1989)	Always (1989)	Hook (1991)	Jurassic Park (1993)	Schindler's List (1993)
Director	Steven Spielberg	Steven Spielberg	Steven Spielberg	Steven Spielberg	Steven Spielberg
Screenplay	George Lucas & Philip Kaufman (characters) George Lucas & Menno Meyjes (story) Jeffrey Boam (screenplay)	Chandler & David Boehm (story A Guy Named Joe) Dalton Trumbo (screenplay A Guy Named Joe) Frederick Hazlitt Brennan (screenplay adaptation A Guy Named Joe) Jerry Belson (screenplay)	J.M. Barrie (books & play) James V. Hart & Nick Castle (screen story) James V. Hart & Malia Scotch Marmo (screenplay)	Michael Crichton (novel) Michael Crichton & David Koepp (screenplay) Malia Scotch Marmo (screenplay, uncredited)	Thomas Keneally (book) Steven Zaillian (screenplay)
Music	John Williams	John Williams	John Williams	John Williams	John Williams
Sound: a) supervising sound editor	a) Richard Hymns	a) Richard Hymns	a) Charles L. Campbell Richard Franklin	a) Richard Hymns	a) Charles L. Campbell Louis L. Edemann
b) sound re-recording mixers	b) Ben Burtt Shawn Murphy Gary Summers	b) Ben Burtt Shawn Murphy Gary Rydstrom Gary Summers Randy Thom	b) Shawn Murphy Andy Nelson Steve Pederson	b) Shawn Murphy Gary Rydstrom Gary Summers	b) Scott Millan Andy Nelson Steve Pederson
Production design: a) production designer	a) Elliot Scott	a) James D. Bissell	a) Norman Garwood	a) Rick Carter	a) Allan Starski
b) art direction	b) Stephen Scott	b) Christopher Burian-Mohrb)	b) Andrew Precht Thomas E. Sanders	b) John Bell William James Teegarden	b) Ewa Skoczkowska Maciej Walczak
Editing	Michael Kahn	Michael Kahn	Michael Kahn	Michael Kahn	Michael Kahn
Costume design	Joanna Johnston Anthony Powell	Ellen Mirojnick	Anthony Powell		Anna Biedrzycka-Sheppard
Cinematography	Douglas Slocombe	Mikael Salomon	Dean Cundey	Dean Cundey	Janusz Kaminski
Producers	George Lucas Frank Marshall Arthur F. Repola Robert Watts	Kathleen Kennedy Frank Marshall Steven Spielberg Richard Vane	Kathleen Kennedy Malia Scotch Marmo Frank Marshall Gerald R. Molen Gary Adelson Craig Baumgarten Bruce Cohen Dodi Fayed James V. Hart	Kathleen Kennedy Gerald R. Molen Lata Ryan Colin Wilson	Irving Glovin Kathleen Kennedy Branko Lustig Gerald R. Molen Robert Raymond Lew Rywin Steven Spielberg

Table A1.2: Roman Polanski

	Rosemary's Baby (1968)	Tragedy of Macbeth, The (1971)	What? (1972) [aka Diary of Forbidden Dreams (1973)]	Chinatown (1974)	Locataire, Le [The Tenant] (1976)
Director	Roman Polanski	Roman Polanski	Roman Polanski	Roman Polanski	Roman Polanski
Screenplay	Ira Levin (novel)	Roman Polanski	Gérard Brach	Robert Towne	Gérard Brach
	Roman Polanski	Kenneth Tynan	Roman Polanski	Roman Polanski	Roman Polanski
		William Shakespeare (play)		(uncredited)	Roland Topor (novel)
Music	Christopher Komeda	The Third Ear Band	Claudio Gizzi	Jerry Goldsmith	Philippe Sarde
Sound:					
a) supervising sound editor	N.A.	N.A.	N.A.	a) N.A.	a) N.A.
b) sound re-recording mixers				b) Bud Grenzbach	b) Jean Nény
Production design:					
c) production designer	a) Richard Sylbert	a) Wilfred Shingleton	a) Aurelio Crugnola	a) Richard Sylbert	a) Pierre Guffroy
d) art direction	b) Joel Schiller	b) Fred Carter	b) Franco Fumagalli	b) W. Stewart Campbell	b) Claude Moesching
					Albert Rajau
Editing	Sam O'Steen	Alastair McIntyre	Alastair McIntyre	Sam O'Steen	Françoise Bonnot
	Bob Wyman				
Costume design	Anthea Sylbert	Anthony Mendleson	Adriana Berselli	Anthea Sylbert	Jacques Schmidt
Cinematography	William Fraker	Gilbert Taylor	Marcello Gatti	John A. Alonzo	Sven Nykvist
			Giuseppe Ruzzolini		
Producers	William Castle	Andrew Braunsberg	Carlo Ponti	C.O. Erickson	Hercules Bellville
	Dona Holloway	Timothy Burrill		Robert Evans	Andrew Braunsberg
		Hugh M. Hefner			Alain Sarde
		Victor Lownes			

Table A1.3: Rob Reiner

	Sure Thing, The (1985)	Stand by Me (1986)	Princess Bride, The (1987)	When Harry Met Sally... (1989)	Misery (1990)
Director	Rob Reiner	Rob Reiner	Rob Reiner	Rob Reiner	Rob Reiner
Screenplay	Steven Bloom Jonathan Roberts	Stephen King (novel) Raynold Gideon Bruce A. Evans	William Goldman	Nora Ephron	Stephen King (novel) William Goldman
Music	Tom Scott	Jack Nitzsche	Mark Knopfler	Marc Shaiman	Marc Shaiman
Sound: a) supervising sound editor	N.A.	a) Lon Bender	a) Lon Bender	a) Charles L. Campbell	a) Charles L. Campbell
b) sound re-recording mixers		Wylie Stateman b) Gregg Rudloff John T. Reitz David E. Campbell	Wylie Stateman b) Gregg Rudloff John T. Reitz David E. Campbell	Louis L. Edemann b) David J. Hudson Mel Metcalfe Terry Porter	Donald J. Malouf b) Rick Kline Gregg Landaker Kevin O'Connell
Production design: a) production designer b) art direction	a) Lilly Kilvert	a) J. Dennis Washington	a) Norman Garwood b) Richard Holland	a) Jane Musky	a) Norman Garwood b) Mark W. Mansbridge
Editing	Robert Leighton	Robert Leighton	Robert Leighton	Robert Leighton	Robert Leighton
Costume design	Durinda Wood	Sue Moore	Phyllis Dalton	Gloria Gresham	Gloria Gresham
Cinematography	Robert Elswit	Thomas Del Ruth	Adrian Biddle	Barry Sonnenfeld	Barry Sonnenfeld
Producers	Roger Birnbaum Andrew Scheinman Jeffrey Stott Henry Winkler	Bruce A. Evans Raynold Gideon Andrew Scheinman	Norman Lear Steve Nicolaides Rob Reiner Andrew Scheinman Jeffrey Stott	Nora Ephron Steve Nicolaides Rob Reiner Andrew Scheinman Jeffrey Stott	Steve Nicolaides Rob Reiner Andrew Scheinman Jeffrey Stott

Table A1.4: Nora Ephron

	Heartburn (1986)	When Harry Met Sally (1989)	Sleepless in Seattle (1993)	Michael (1996)	You've Got Mail (1998)
Director	Mike Nichols	Rob Reiner	Nora Ephron	Nora Ephron	Nora Ephron
Screenplay	Nora Ephron (novel & screenplay) Delia Ephron (screenplay)	Nora Ephron	Jeff Arch (story) Nora Ephron David S. Ward Jeff Arch (screenplay)	Peter Dexter Jim Quinlan (story) Nora Ephron Delia Ephron Peter Dexter Jim Quinlan (screenplay)	Nikolaus (Miklós) Laszlo (play) Nora Ephron Delia Ephron (screenplay)
Music	Carly Simon	Marc Shaiman	Marc Shaiman	Randy Newman	
Sound: a) supervising sound editor b) sound re-recording mixers	a) Stan Bochner b) Michael J. Cerone Richard Vorisek	a) Charles L. Campbell Louis L. Edemann b) David J. Hudson Mel Metcalfe Terry Porter	a) Michael Kirchberger b) Lee Dichter	a) Michael Kirchberger b) Lee Dichter	a) Ron Bochar b) Ron Bochar
Production design: a) production designer b) art direction	a) Tony Walton b) John Kasarda	a) Jane Musky	a) Jeffrey Townsend b) Charley Beal Gershon Ginsburg	a) Dan Davis b) Michael Scheffe James E. Tocci	a) Dan Davis b) Ray Kluga Beth Kuhn
Editing	Sam O'Steen	Robert Leighton	Robert Reitano	Geraldine Peroni	Richard Marks
Costume design	Ann Roth	Gloria Gresham	Judy Ruskin	Elizabeth McBride	Albert Wolsky
Cinematography	Néstor Almendros	Barry Sonnenfeld	Sven Nykvist	John Lindley	John Lindley
Producers	Robert Greenhut Mike Nichols Joel Tuber	Nora Ephron Steve Nicolaides Rob Reiner Andrew Scheinman Jeffrey Stott	Jane Bartelme Patrick Crowley Delia Ephron Gary Foster Lynda Obst James W. Skotchdopole	G. Mac Brown Alan Curtiss Sean Daniel Delia Ephron Nora Ephron Ralph Horan James Jacks Jonathan D. Krane Donald J. Lee Jr	G. Mac Brown Dianne Dreyer Julie Durk Delia Ephron Nora Ephron Donald J. Lee Jr Lauren Shuler Donner

Appendix 2: Film credits (*Jurassic Park, Chinatown, When Harry Met Sally*)

We thought it important in a book of this kind to include the credits of the films we talked about in depth in Chapter 6. Credits serve as a reminder of both the number of people involved in any Hollywood film project and the filmmakers' hierarchy that shapes them. Wherever possible, we have tried to keep the same order of appearance as in the original credits. We have used several sources from a variety of different media: *Sight and Sound* magazine, the *Film Index International* CD-ROM, the *Internet Movie Database* (http://www.imdb.com), and the credits as listed on DVDs and videos have proven to be particularly useful – and we are grateful to all those people who painstakingly compile film credits for lazier scholars such as ourselves!

Jurassic Park (1993)

Directed by
Steven Spielberg

Written by
Michael Crichton
David Koepp
Based on the novel by
Michael Crichton

Produced by
Kathleen Kennedy . . . producer
Gerald R. Molen . . . producer

Cast
Sam Neill . . . Dr. Alan Grant
Laura Dern . . . Dr. Ellie Sattler

Jeff Goldblum . . . Dr. Ian Malcolm
Richard Attenborough . . . John Hammond
Bob Peck . . . Robert Muldoon
Martin Ferrero . . . Donald Gennaro
Joseph Mazzello . . . Tim Murphy
Ariana Richards . . . Lex Murphy
Samuel L. Jackson . . . Ray Arnold
B.D. Wong . . . Henry Wu
Wayne Knight . . . Dennis Nedry
Gerald R. Molen . . . Gerry Harding (as Jerry Molen)
Miguel Sandoval . . . Juanito Rostagno
Cameron Thor . . . Lewis Dodgson
Christopher John Fields . . . Volunteer #1
Whitby Hertford . . . Volunteer Boy
Dean Cundey . . . Mate
Jophery C. Brown . . . Worker in Raptor Pen (as Jophery Brown)

Tom Mishler . . . Helicoptor Pilot
Greg Burson . . . Mr. D.N.A. (voice)
Adrian Escober . . . Worker at Amber Mine
Richard Kiley . . . Jurassic Park Tour Voice
  (voice)

Director of Photography
Dean Cundey

Production Design by
Rick Carter

Edited by
Michael Kahn

Original Music by
John Williams

Associate producers
Lata Ryan
Colin Wilson

Visual effects supervision
Dennis Muren . . . visual effects supervisor
Stan Winston . . . live action dinosaurs
Phil Tippett . . . dinosaur supervisor
Michael Lantieri . . . special dinosaur effects

Casting by
Janet Hirshenson
Jane Jenkins

Art Direction by
John Bell
William James Teegarden

Set Decoration by
Jackie Carr

Makeup Department
Fríða Aradóttir . . . assistant hair supervisor
Lynda Gurasich . . . hair styles supervisor
Christina Smith . . . makeup supervisor

Julie C. Steffes . . . body makeup
Monty Westmore . . . assistant makeup supervisor

Production Management
Paul Deason . . . unit production manager
Jules Tippett . . . production supervisor: tippett
  studio

Second Unit Director or Assistant Director
John T. Kretchmer . . . first assistant director
Carla McCloskey . . . first assistant director:
  second unit
Michele Panelli-Venetis . . . second assistant
  director
Frederic Roth . . . DGA trainee
Kenneth J. Silverstein . . . second second assistant
  director

Art Department
John Berger . . . set designer
Jeff Brown . . . greensman
Janine Cavoto . . . set dressing coordinator
Lauren Cory . . . assistant art director
Tom Cranham . . . illustrator
Tim Donelan . . . lead man
John R. Elliott . . . construction foreman
Anthony Feola . . . tool foreman
Nancy Gomes . . . paint foreman
Beth Hathaway . . . art department: Stan Winston
  Studio
Hugo Herrera . . . greensman
Tom Hrupcho . . . paint foreman
Kay Jordan . . . construction accountant
Martin A. Kline . . . assistant art director
Maureen Kropf . . . set painter
Tony Leonardi . . . stand-by painter
Scott W. Leslie . . . swing gang
David Lowery . . . illustrator
Kevin Mangan . . . greens foreman
Masako Masuda . . . set designer
Jerry Moss . . . property master
Dan Ondrejko . . . head greensman
Dan Pemberton . . . construction foreman

Ken Peterson . . . assistant property master

Lauren E. Polizzi . . . set designer

Caroline Quinn . . . art department coordinator

Craig Raiche . . . assistant property master

David Robbie . . . plaster foreman

Brian Rock . . . head laborer

Bob Skemp . . . greensman

Paul M. Sonski . . . assistant art director

Dave Trevino . . . paint foreman

John Villarino . . . construction coordinator

Mike Villarino . . . construction foreman

Sound Department

Sandina Bailo-Lape . . . foley editor

Sara Bolder . . . dialogue editor

Christopher Boyes . . . assistant sound designer

Christopher Boyes . . . foley recordist

Greg Dennen . . . scoring crew

Dean Drabin . . . ADR mixer

Teresa Eckton . . . sound effects editor

Mark Eshelman . . . scoring crew

Ken Fischer . . . sound effects editor

Douglas Greenfield . . . stereo sound consultant: Dolby

J.R. Grubbs . . . assistant sound effects editor

Scott Guitteau . . . assistant sound effects editor

Ann Hadsell . . . ADR recordist

Ruth Hasty . . . assistant supervising sound editor

Tim Holland . . . sound effects editor

Richard Hymns . . . supervising sound editor

Robert Jackson . . . boom operator

Donna Jaffe . . . assistant dialogue editor

Ron Judkins . . . sound mixer

Laurel Ladevich . . . ADR editor

Mary Helen Leasman . . . foley editor

Robert Marty . . . assistant ADR editor

Marnie Moore . . . foley artist

Shawn Murphy . . . music scoring mixer

Shawn Murphy . . . sound re-recording mixer

Susan Popovic . . . assistant foley editor

Gary Rydstrom . . . sound designer

Gary Rydstrom . . . sound re-recording mixer

Michael Silvers . . . dialogue editor

Gary Summers . . . sound re-recording mixer

Bill Talbott . . . scoring crew

Dennie Thorpe . . . foley artist

Tove Blue Valentine . . . cable person

Maia Veres . . . assistant dialogue editor

Kenneth Wannberg . . . music editor

Special Effects by

Francesca Avila . . . art department: Stan Winston Studio

Lloyd Ball . . . hydraulic engineer: Stan Winston Studio

Craig Barr . . . technical coordinator: T-Rex, Stan Winston Studio

Bill Basso . . . key artist: Stan Winston Studio

David Beneke . . . art department: Stan Winston Studio

Evan Brainard . . . mechanical designer: Stan Winston Studio

Steve Bunyes . . . special effects

Len Burge . . . art department: Stan Winston Studio

Sebastien Caillabet . . . art department: Stan Winston Studio

Craig Caton . . . mechanical department coordinator: Stan Winston Studio

Mitchell J. Coughlin . . . art department: Stan Winston Studio

Richard Davison . . . dinosaur skin fabricator: Stan Winston Studio

Jon Dawe . . . mechanical designer: Stan Winston Studio

Kim Derry . . . special effects

Marilyn Dozer-Chaney . . . dinosaur skin fabricator: Stan Winston Studio

Matthew Durham . . . mechanical department: Stan Winston Studio

Jeff Edwards . . . mechanical designer: Stan Winston Studio

Donald Elliott . . . special effects foreman

Cory Faucher . . . special effects

Greg Figiel . . . key artist: Stan Winston Studio

Nathalie Fratti-Rapoport . . . art department: Stan Winston Studio

Anthony Gaillard . . . art department: Stan Winston Studio

Rick Galinson . . . mechanical designer: Stan Winston Studio

Joss Geiduschek . . . special effects

Armando González . . . master welder: Stan Winston Studio

Dave Grasso . . . key artist: Stan Winston Studio

Erik Haraldsted . . . special effects

Beth Hathaway . . . art department: Stan Winston Studio

Rich Haugen . . . mechanical designer: Stan Winston Studio

Rob Hinderstein . . . key artist: Stan Winston Studio

Adam Jones . . . art department: Stan Winston Studio

Mark Jurinko . . . art department: Stan Winston Studio

Eileen Kastner-Delago . . . art department: Stan Winston Studio

Terry W. King . . . special effects

Brad Krisko . . . art department: Stan Winston Studio

Richard J. Landon . . . mechanical department coordinator: Stan Winston Studio

Louie Lantieri . . . special effects

Michael Lantieri . . . special dinosaur effects

Mark Lohff . . . production coordinator: Stan Winston Studio

Frank Charles Lutkus III . . . mechanical designer: Stan Winston Studio

Lindsay MacGowan . . . art department: Stan Winston Studio

Shane Mahan . . . art department coordinator: Stan Winston Studio

Greg Manion . . . mechanical department: Stan Winston Studio

Jules Mann . . . assistant model maker

Nick Marra . . . art department: Stan Winston Studio

Karen Mason . . . dinosaur skin fabricator: Stan Winston Studio

Tony McCray . . . master mold maker: Stan Winston Studio

Mark 'Crash' McCreery . . . concept artist: Stan Winston Studio

Matt McDonnell . . . special effects

Kevin McTurk . . . art department: Stan Winston Studio

Tara Meaney-Crocitto . . . production coordinator: Stan Winston Studio

Paul Mejias . . . key artist: Stan Winston Studio

Bruce Minkus . . . special effects

Tim Moran . . . special effects rigging foreman

Brian Namanny . . . mechanical department: Stan Winston Studio

Mark Noel . . . special effects

Tim Nordella . . . mechanical designer: Stan Winston Studio

Joey Orosco . . . key artist: Stan Winston Studio

Dan Ossello . . . special effects

Eric Ostroff . . . art department: Stan Winston Studio

Tom Pahk . . . special effects shop supervisor

Jeff Periera . . . art department: Stan Winston Studio

Kevin Pike . . . special effects: custom props

Jon Porter . . . special effects

E. Wayne Rabouin . . . special effects

Robert Ramsdell . . . art department: Stan Winston Studio

Joe Reader . . . key artist: Stan Winston Studio

Andy Schoneberg . . . key artist: Stan Winston Studio

Alan Scott . . . mechanical designer: Stan Winston Studio

Shannon Shea . . . key artist: Stan Winston Studio

Patrick Shearn . . . mechanical designer: Stan Winston Studio

Alfred Sousa . . . mechanical designer: Stan Winston Studio

Bruce Stark . . . mechanical department: Stan Winston Studio

Ian Stevenson . . . key artist: Stan Winston Studio

Christopher Swift . . . key artist: Stan Winston Studio

Michiko Tagawa . . . art department: Stan Winston Studio

Pierre-Olivier Thevenin . . . art department: Stan Winston Studio

Brian Tipton . . . special effects

Mike Trcic . . . key artist: Stan Winston Studio

Scott 'Gwidge' Urban . . . art department: Stan Winston Studio

Kimberly Verros . . . production assistant: Stan Winston Studio

Kevin Willis . . . art department: Stan Winston Studio

Chuck Zlotnick . . . production assistant: Stan Winston Studio

Visual Effects by

Barbara Affonso . . . chief model maker

Eric Armstrong . . . computer graphics animator

Joel Aron . . . computer graphics technical assistant

Paul Ashdown . . . computer graphics software developer

Bill Barr . . . stage technician: ILM

Randall K. Bean . . . scanning operator

Kathleen Beeler . . . digital artist

John Andrew Berton Jr. . . . CG department operations manager

Ken Beyer . . . computer graphics systems supporter

Mike Bienstock . . . animatics: Tippett Studio

Nicholas Blake . . . engineer: Tippett Studio

Kim Blanchette . . . animatics: Tippett Studio

Patricia Blau . . . executive in charge of production: ILM

Mike Bolles . . . camera engineer: ILM

Conrad Bonderson . . . engineer: Tippett Studio

Barbara Brennan . . . digital artist

Geoff Campbell . . . computer graphics animator

Dave Carson . . . digital artist

Terry Chostner . . . visual effects camera operator

Charlie Clavadetscher . . . computer graphics camera matchmover

Michael Conte . . . computer graphics technical assistant: ILM

Jean M. Cunningham . . . computer graphics artist

Gail Currey . . . CG department production manager

Mark A.Z. Dippé . . . co-visual effects supervisor

Lisa Drostova . . . digital artist

Sheila Duignan . . . production coordinator: Tippett Studio

Edwin Dunkley . . . computer graphics technical assistant

Randy Dutra . . . senior animator: Tippett Studio

TyRuben Ellingson . . . visual effects art director

John Ellis . . . optical supervisor

Mike Ellis . . . scanning operator

Eric Enderton . . . computer graphics software developer

Douglas Epps . . . computer technician: Tippett Studio

Christopher Evans . . . matte artist

Stefen Fangmeier . . . lead computer graphics supervision

Scott Farrar . . . additional plate photographer

Robert Finley Jr. . . . stage technician: ILM

Pat Fitzsimmons . . . stage technician: ILM

Carl N. Frederick . . . computer graphics artist

George Gambetta . . . scanning operator

Steve Gawley . . . chief model maker

Tim Geideman . . . optical lab technician

Bart Giovanetti . . . digital artist

Michael Gleason . . . visual effects editor: ILM

Jeffrey Greeley . . . camera assistant: ILM

Timothy Greenwood . . . projectionist: ILM

Craig Hayes . . . computer interface engineer: Tippett Studio

Janet Healy . . . visual effects producer

Robert Hill . . . camera assistant: ILM

Diane Holland . . . digital matte coordinator

John Horn . . . computer graphics software developer

Sandy Houston . . . digital artist

Wade Howie . . . computer graphics artist

Tom L. Hutchinson . . . computer graphics artist

Keith Johnson . . . optical camera operator

Zoran Kacic-Alesic . . . computer graphics software developer

Douglas S. Kay . . . senior CG department manager

Pam Kaye . . . production accountant: ILM

Ira Keeler . . . chief model maker

Brian Knep . . . computer graphics software developer

Peter Konig . . . animatics: Tippett Studio

Jay Lenci . . . computer graphics systems supporter

Joe Letteri . . . computer graphics artist

Jeffrey B. Light . . . computer graphics artist

James Lim . . . optical camera operator

Nancy Luckoff . . . computer graphics coordinator

Greg Maloney . . . digital artist

Tina Matthies . . . production assistant: ILM

Mark 'Crash' McCreery . . . concept artist

Roberto McGrath . . . assistant editor: ILM

Gary Meyer . . . video engineer: ILM

Fred Meyers . . . video engineer: ILM

Mark S. Miller . . . plate producer: ILM

Jim Mitchell . . . computer graphics artist

Curt I. Miyashiro . . . computer graphics technical assistant

Steve Molin . . . computer graphics technical assistant

Tim Morgan . . . stage technician: ILM

Jim Morris . . . general manager: ILM

George Murphy . . . computer graphics supervisor

Patrick T. Myers . . . computer graphics camera matchmover

Michael J. Natkin . . . computer graphics software developer

Patrick Neary . . . computer graphics technical assistant

Joe Pasquale . . . computer graphics artist

Lorne Peterson . . . chief model maker

Josh Pines . . . scanning supervisor

Gary Platek . . . engineer: Tippett Studio

Ellen Poon . . . computer graphics artist

Steve Price . . . computer graphics animator

Steve Reding . . . computer technician: Tippett Studio

Christopher Reed . . . chief model maker

Carolyn Ensle Rendu . . . digital artist

Louis Rivera . . . negative cutter: ILM

Stephen Rosenbaum . . . computer graphics artist

Rebecca Schiros . . . production: Tippett Studio

John Schlag . . . computer graphics artist

Alex Seiden . . . computer graphics supervisor

Linda Siegel . . . computer graphics systems supporter

Jerry Simonsen . . . courier coordinator: ILM

Tom St. Amand . . . animator: Tippett studio

James Straus . . . computer graphics animator

Duncan Sutherland . . . camera engineer: ILM

Eric Swenson . . . animatics: Tippett Studio

Dave Tanaka . . . editorial coordinator: ILM

Ginger Theisen . . . computer graphics coordinator

Kristen D. Trattner . . . optical line-up

Bart Trickel . . . engineer: Tippett Studio

Tien Truong . . . computer graphics artist

Pat Turner . . . visual effects camera operator

Yusei Uesugi . . . matte artist

Lisa Vaughn . . . optical coordinator

Lisa Vaughn . . . scanning coordinator

Don Waller . . . computer graphics animator

Judith Weaver . . . visual effects coordinator: ILM

John Whisnant . . . optical line-up

Steve 'Spaz' Williams . . . CG animator

Tom Williams . . . supervisor of software and digital technology

Suzanne Niki Yoshii . . . production: Tippett Studio

Stuart Ziff . . . engineer: Tippett Studio

Rita E. Zimmerman . . . digital artist

Dennis Muren . . . visual effects supervisor: ILM

Stunts

Nathalie B. Bollinger . . . stunts

Laura Dash . . . stunts

Larry Davis . . . stunts

Gary Epper . . . stunts

Donna Evans . . . stunts

Rusty Hanson . . . stunts

Norman Howell . . . stunts

Gary Hymes . . . stunt coordinator

Les Larson . . . stunts

Gary McLarty . . . stunts

Pat Romano . . . stunts

R.A. Rondell . . . stunts

Myke Schwartz . . . stunts

Brian Smrz . . . stunts

Patricia Tallman . . . stunts

Other crew

Todd J. Adelman . . . first aid/safety coordinator

Lloyd Ahern II . . . additional photographer

Yarek Alfer . . . chief sculptor

Lance Anderson . . . coat and body parts supplier

Dolores Ayala Olivares . . . lyricist

Michael Backes . . . display graphics supervisor

Lloyd Ball . . . puppeteer

Craig Barnett . . . production assistant

Craig Barr . . . puppeteer

Bill Basso . . . puppeteer

David Beneke . . . puppeteer

Larry Bolster . . . puppeteer

Evan Brainard . . . puppeteer

Judith M. Brown . . . teacher

Gary Burritt . . . negative cutter

Beth Cahn . . . assistant: Ms. Kennedy

Denny Caira . . . transportation coordinator

Tino Caira . . . driver

Dale Caldwell . . . color timer

Brian Callier . . . 24 frame computer sync

Lynne Cannizzaro . . . production secretary

Ron Cardarelli . . . key grip

Steven Cardarelli . . . grip

Craig Caton . . . puppeteer

Rebecca Chaires . . . assistant: Ms. Ryan

Steve Chandler . . . assistant chief lighting technician

Henry Charleston . . . lighting technician

Leslie Cheatham . . . assistant: Ms. Kennedy

David Chevalier . . . picture pilot: aerial unit

Murray Close . . . still photographer

Alan Cody . . . assistant editor

John Coker . . . grip

John Connell . . . assistant camera: aerial unit

Mitchell J. Coughlin . . . puppeteer

Alexander Courage . . . orchestrator

Patrick Crane . . . assistant editor

Don Crow . . . driver

Bonnie Curtis . . . assistant: Mr. Spielberg

Richard Davison . . . puppeteer

Jon Dawe . . . puppeteer

Richard De Armas . . . scoring crew

Sandy DeCrescent . . . music contractor

Stefan Dechant . . . computer design

Greg Dennen . . . scoring crew

Marty Dobkousky . . . grip

Judy Drosd . . . special thanks

Jeff Edwards . . . puppeteer

Michael Fallavollita . . . apprentice editor

Peter Fandetti . . . assistant editor

Don Feldstein . . . stand-in

Andre Fenley . . . apprentice editor

Greg Figiel . . . puppeteer

Jim Frear . . . driver

Rick Galinson . . . puppeteer

Jane Goe . . . production controller

Tim Gonzales . . . craft service

Armando González . . . puppeteer

René González . . . projectionist: Amblin

Ben O. Graham . . . lighting technician

Dave Grasso . . . puppeteer

Susanna Griffith . . . casting assistant

John Gurche . . . dinosaur specialist

Art Halissi . . . color timer

Mark Hallett . . . dinosaur specialist

Barbara Harris . . . voice casting

Beth Hathaway . . . puppeteer

Rich Haugen . . . puppeteer

Angela Heald . . . production office coordinator

Michael Ronald Heath . . . grip

Bud Heller . . . key rigging grip

Deborah Henderson . . . assistant production accountant

Doug Henderson . . . dinosaur specialist

Michael Hirshenson . . . casting associate

Elena Holden . . . assistant accountant

Jack Horner . . . consultant: paleontology

Gordon Jernberg . . . driver

Johnny Johnson . . . stand-in

Lorin Jordan . . . driver

Ian Kelly . . . video engineer

Deborah Kelman . . . additional video assist operator

Mitchell Ray Kenney . . . costumer

J.M. Kenny . . . production assistant

Bob Kurtz . . . movement designer: 'Mr. D.N.A.' animation

Karen Bittenson Kushell . . . second assistant: Mr. Spielberg

Richard J. Landon . . . puppeteer

Hal Lary . . . transportation captain

Sam Lee . . . assistant location manager: Hawaii

Don Lessem . . . special thanks

Ken Levine . . . location manager: Hawaii unit

Tim Litchauer . . . safety coordinator

George Lucas . . . special thanks

Steve Luce . . . driver

Sid Lucero . . . best boy grip

Frank Charles Lutkus III . . . puppeteer

Cynthia Madvig . . . stand-in

Shane Mahan . . . puppeteer

Patrick Marshall . . . rigging gaffer

Sherry Marshall . . . assistant production coordinator

Karen Mason . . . puppeteer

Victoria Mattson . . . assistant production coordinator: Hawaii

Patrick McArdle . . . assistant camera: plate photography

Mark 'Crash' McCreery . . . puppeteer

Susan McLean . . . scoring crew

Paul Mejias . . . puppeteer

Simon Millar . . . assistant: Sam Neill

John Monsour . . . 24 frame computer sync

Sue Moore . . . costume supervisor: women

Dennis Muren . . . full-motion dinosaurs

David Nakabayashi . . . display graphics

John Neufeld . . . orchestrator

Stuart Neumann . . . location manager

Tim Nordella . . . puppeteer

David B. Nowell . . . director: aerial unit

Kristen J. Nye . . . payroll accountant

John O'Grady . . . grip

Joey Orosco . . . puppeteer

Gregory Paul . . . dinosaur specialist

Robert Peluce . . . layout designer: 'Mr. D.N.A.' animation

Jeff Periera . . . puppeteer

Patti Podesta . . . slide show coordinator

Kelly Porter . . . costumer

Ana Maria Quintana . . . script supervisor

Becky Raiche . . . driver

Joe Reader . . . puppeteer

Leroy Reed . . . driver

Calmar Roberts . . . first assistant camera

Marsha Robertson . . . unit publicist

John Rosengrant . . . puppeteer

Keith Roverud . . . lighting technician

Eric H. Sandberg . . . costume supervisor: men

Jack S. Schlosser . . . gaffer: second unit

Andy Schoneberg . . . puppeteer

Alan Scott . . . puppeteer

Stephen Sfetku . . . camera loader

Shannon Shea . . . puppeteer

Patrick Shearn . . . puppeteer

John Smith . . . production assistant

Steve Sorkin . . . driver

Mark Soucie . . . lighting technician

Alfred Sousa . . . puppeteer

Raymond Stella . . . camera operator

Ian Stevenson . . . puppeteer

Christine Stewart . . . assistant accountant

Christopher Swift . . . puppeteer

Jules Sylvester . . . animal trainer

Michiko Tagawa . . . puppeteer

Traci Tateyama . . . office assistant: Hawaii

Edward R. Thompson Jr. . . . lighting technician

Roger Thompson . . . electrician: Hawaii

Phyllis Thurber-Moffit . . . textile artist

Diana Tinkley . . . assistant: Mr. Molen

Phil Tippett . . . dinosaur supervisor

Arlene Trainoff . . . assistant: David Koepp

Mark Travis . . . security: Hawaii

Mike Trcic . . . puppeteer

Jim Turner . . . production accountant

Harry Ueshiro . . . transportation captain: Hawaii
unit

Davida Vaccaro . . . stand-in

Adam Valdez . . . animator

Adam Valdez . . . computer systems: Tippett
Studio

Ruben Vasquez . . . grip: Hawaii

Bill Venegas . . . grip

Dave Wachtman . . . dolly grip

O'Shana Walker . . . assistant chief lighting
technician

Mark Walthour . . . chief lighting technician

Mark Wescott . . . driver

Robert West . . . post-production assistant

Wayne Williams . . . driver

Matt Winston . . . puppeteer

Stan Winston . . . live action dinosaurs

Jolanda R. Wipfli . . . second assistant camera

Anthony Wong . . . lighting technician

Ron Woodside . . . lighting technician

Mark Yacullo . . . driver

Mayor Joan Yukimora . . . special thanks

Cynthia Zajonc . . . safety coordinator: aerial unit

Robert 'Bobby Z' Zajonc . . . aerial coordinator:
aerial unit

Joe Zimmerman . . . stand-in: Mr. Goldblum

Chinatown (1974)

Jack Nicholson . . . J. J. (Jake) Gittes

Faye Dunaway . . . Evelyn Cross Mulwray

A Robert Evans Production

Directed by
Roman Polanski

Cast

John Huston . . . Noah Cross

Perry Lopez . . . Lt. Lou Escobar

John Hillerman . . . Russ Yelburton

Darrell Zwerling . . . Hollis I. Mulwray

Diane Ladd . . . Ida Sessions

Roy Jenson . . . Claude Mulvihill

Roman Polanski . . . Man with knife

Richard Bakalyan . . . Det. Loach

Joe Mantell . . . Lawrence Walsh

Bruce Glover . . . Duffy

Nandu Hinds . . . Sophie

James O'Rear . . . Lawyer

James Hong . . . Kahn

Beulah Quo . . . Mulwray's maid

Jerry Fujikawa . . . Mulwray's gardener

Belinda Palmer . . . Katherine Cross

Roy Roberts . . . Mayor Bagby

Noble Willingham . . . Councilman

Elliott Montgomery . . . Councilman

Rance Howard . . . Irate farmer at council meeting

George Justin . . . Barney

Doc Erickson . . . Banker at barbershop

Fritzi Burr . . . Mulwray's secretary

Charles Knapp . . . Morty

Claudio Martínez . . . Boy on horseback

Federico Roberto . . . Cross' butler

Allan Warnick . . . Clerk at Hall of Records

John Holland . . . Farmer in the Valley

Jesse Vint . . . Farmer in the Valley

Jim Burk . . . Farmer in the Valley

Denny Arnold . . . Farmer in the Valley

Burt Young . . . Curly

Elizabeth Harding . . . Curly's wife
John Rogers . . . Mr. Palmer
Cecil Elliott . . . Emma Dill
Paul Jenkins . . . Policeman
Lee de Broux . . . Policeman
Bob Golden . . . Policeman

Art Direction by
W. Stewart Campbell

Re-recording mixer
Bud Grenzbach

Production Design by
Richard Sylbert

Edited by
Sam O'Steen

Costume Design by
Anthea Sylbert

Original Music by
Jerry Goldsmith

Associate producer
C.O. Erickson

Director of photography
John A. Alonzo

Written by
Robert Towne

Produced by
Robert Evans

Directed by
Roman Polanski

Other crew:
Casting by
Jane Feinberg

Mike Fenton

Set Decoration by
Ruby R. Levitt

Makeup Department
Hank Edds . . . makeup artist
Susan Germaine . . . hair stylist
Lee Harman . . . makeup artist
Vivienne Walker . . . hair stylist

Production Management
C.O. Erickson . . . unit production manager
Second Unit Director or Assistant Director
Michael Ader . . . second assistant director
Hawk Koch . . . assistant director

Art Department
Bill MacSems . . . property master
Gabe Resh . . . set designer
Robert Resh . . . set designer

Sound Department
Clint Althouse . . . boom operator
Bob Cornett . . . sound editor
Bud Grenzbach . . . sound re-recordist
John C. Hammell . . . music editor
Larry Jost . . . sound mixer

Special Effects by
Logan Frazee . . . special effects

Stunts
Jim Burk . . . stunts

May Wale Brown . . . script supervisor
Richard Bruno . . . wardrobe
Gary Chazan . . . assistant to producer
Wayne Fitzgerald . . . title design
Hugh K. Gagnier . . . camera operator
Earl Gilbert . . . gaffer
Jean Merrick . . . wardrobe
Bernie Schwartz . . . key grip
Florence Williamson . . . assistant editor

When Harry Met Sally (1989)

A Rob Reiner film

Cast
Billy Crystal . . . Harry Burns
Meg Ryan . . . Sally Albright
Carrie Fisher . . . Marie
Bruno Kirby . . . Jess

Associate producer
Nora Ephron

Music adapted and arranged by
Marc Shaiman

Costume Design by
Gloria Gresham

Co-producers
Steve Nicolaides
Jeffrey Stott

Casting by
Janet Hirshenson
Jane Jenkins

Edited by
Robert Leighton

Production Design by
Jane Musky

Director of photography
Barry Sonnenfeld

Produced by
Rob Reiner
Andrew Scheinman

Written by
Nora Ephron

Directed by
Rob Reiner

Other cast and crew:
Set Decoration by
George R. Nelson
Sabrina Wright-Basile

Other cast:
Steven Ford . . . Joe
Lisa Jane Persky . . . Alice
Michelle Nicastro . . . Amanda Reese
Gretchen Palmer . . . Stewardess
Robert Alan Beuth . . . Man on aisle
David Burdick . . . Nine-year-old boy
Joe Viviani . . . Judge
Harley Jane Kozak . . . Helen Helson
Joseph Hunt . . . Waiter at wedding
Kevin Rooney . . . Ira Stone
Franc Luz . . . Julian
Tracy Reiner . . . Emily
Kyle T. Heffner . . . Gary
Kimberley LaMarque . . . Waitress
Stacey Katzin . . . Hostess
Estelle Reiner . . . Older customer in orgasm scene
John Arceri . . . Christmas-tree salesman
Peter Day . . . Joke teller at wedding
Kuno Sponholz . . . Documentary couple #1
Connie Sawyer . . . Documentary couple #1
Charles Dugan . . . Documentary couple #2
Katherine Squire . . . Documentary couple #2
Al Christy . . . Documentary couple #3
Frances Chaney . . . Documentary couple #3
Bernie Hern . . . Documentary couple #4
Rose Wright . . . Documentary couple #4
Aldo Rossi . . . Documentary couple #5
Donna Hardy . . . Documentary couple #5
Peter Pan . . . Documentary couple #6
Jane Chung . . . Documentary couple #6

Makeup Department
Stephen Abrums . . . makeup artist: Meg Ryan
Joseph A. Campayno . . . makeup artist: Meg

Ryan

Ken Chase . . . makeup artist: Billy Crystal

William A. Farley . . . hair stylist

Barbara Lorenz . . . hair stylist

Peter Montagna . . . makeup artist: Billy Crystal

Production Management

Mark A. Baker . . . unit manager

Steve Nicolaides . . . production manager

Second Unit Director or Assistant Director

Aaron Barsky . . . first assistant director

Forrest L. Futrell . . . additional second assistant director

Lucille Ouyang . . . additional second assistant director

Michael Waxman . . . second assistant director

Charles Zalben . . . additional second assistant director

Art Department

James J. Archer . . . props

David L. Glazer . . . property master

Billy Puzo . . . scenic artist

Harold Thrasher . . . art department co-ordinator

Dick Tice . . . property master

Frank Viviano . . . construction coordinator

Sound Department

George Baetz . . . boom operator

Charles L. Campbell . . . supervising sound editor

Paul Timothy Carden . . . sound editor

Larry Carow . . . sound editor

Dean Drabin . . . foley mixer

Robert Eber . . . sound mixer

Louis L. Edemann . . . supervising sound editor

Richard C. Franklin . . . sound editor

John Fundus . . . boom operator

David Gertz . . . dubbing recordist

David J. Hudson . . . sound re-recording mixer

Pamela G. Kimber . . . assistant sound editor

Mel Metcalfe . . . sound re-recording mixer

Chuck Neely . . . sound editor

Terry Porter . . . sound re-recording mixer

John Richards . . . music scoring mixer

Rod Rogers . . . assistant ADR editor

Larry Singer . . . supervising ADR editor

Joshua Abeles . . . production assistant

Robin Joy Allan . . . casting associate

Brian W. Armstrong . . . assistant camera

Nicole Barnum . . . production secretary

Judy Bauer . . . production accountant

Bruce Birmelin . . . still photographer

Donna E. Bloom . . . location manager

Carlyn Bochicchio . . . production assistant

Kathy Bond . . . production secretary

Norman Buckley . . . assistant editor

Gary Burritt . . . negative cutter

Jason Charles . . . production assistant

Harry Connick Jr. . . . singer: 'It Had To Be You'

Harry Connick Jr. . . . special musical performances and arrangements

Leslie Cornyn . . . assistant accountant

Victoria Cullingham . . . production assistant

Angelo Di Giacomo . . . assistant camera

Christopher Duskin . . . assistant camera

Russell Engels . . . gaffer

Iddo Lampton Enochs Jr. . . . production assistant

James Fanning . . . transportation coordinator

Eddie Fickett . . . production assistant

Linda Folsom . . . production coordinator

Dennis Gamiello . . . key grip

Don Garrison . . . location manager

J. Kathleen Gibson . . . second assistant editor

Lynn Goldman . . . assistant accountant

Debbie Goldsmith . . . assistant editor

Shell Hecht . . . production secretary

M. Todd Henry . . . camera operator

Michael Hirshenson . . . casting associate

Dave Jenkins . . . production assistant

Kevin Kelley . . . gaffer

Emily Maupin . . . assistant: Mr. Reiner

Kerry Lyn McKissick . . . script supervisor

Gregory L. McMurry . . . video: Video Image

Hwei-Chu Meng . . . production coordinator

Thomas Miligan . . . assistant camera

Maura Minsky . . . production secretary

Michael Neuman . . . production assistant

Steve Nevius . . . assistant editor

Jennifer L. Parsons . . . costume supervisor

Jane Raab . . . production coordinator

Tim Roslan . . . transportation coordinator

Donna Santora . . . assistant accountant

Andrew D. Schwartz . . . still photographer

Marc Shaiman . . . orchestrator

Thom Sharp . . . orchestrator

Scott Stambler . . . music supervisor

References

A note on references

We wanted to make this book as accessible and economical as possible so, as an experiment, we have presented our references in a different manner than usual. To provide something more than a long list of books and articles, we have combined acknowledgement of our sources with suggestions for further opportunities for research about the topics and films we discuss. We have not tried to provide an exhaustive account of everything we looked at. What follows contains expanded information about the most relevant primary sources we have employed. It also includes a list of the Internet sites that were particularly useful, as they provided official information on several topics (see, for example, the sites officially run by the various Guilds). These notes are organized by chapter.

Feel free to contact us by e-mail if you have any queries. Alan Lovell's address is: alovell730@aol.com; Gianluca Sergi's is: gianluca.sergi@nottingham.ac.uk.

Chapter 1: Introduction

The accounts of the making of *Blade Runner, Up Close and Personal* and *Titanic* are drawn from:

Sammon, P. M., 2000, *Future Noir – The Making of Blade Runner*, London: Orion.
Dunne, J. G., 2000, *Monster – Living off the Big Screen*, London: Pan.
Parisi, P. 1998, *Titanic and the making of James Cameron*, London: Orion.

Although they are written from different perspectives, all three books contain enough detailed information to be helpful guides to how the production system works.

In the second part of the Introduction, the quote about the director's role comes from Bordwell, D. and Thompson, K., 2001, *Film Art – An Introduction*, New York: McGraw-Hill. This book is designed for students and provides a systematic and exceptionally well-presented account of the orthodox view of the nature of film production. For a different view, it is well worth reading Schatz, T., 1998, *The Genius of the System – Hollywood Film-making in the Studio Era*, London: Faber and Faber. There's a good representation of writings from *Cahiers du Cinema* in Hillier, J., 1985, *Cahiers du Cinema. Vol. 1, 1950s: Neo-Realism, Hollywood, New Wave*, London: British Film Institute.

Chapter 2: The politics of filmmaking

The quotation from Walter Murch comes from Ondaatje, M., 2002, *The Conversations – Walter Murch and the Art of Editing Film*, London: Bloomsbury.

To gain an understanding of what the different members of the crew do and how their roles relate to each other, we have been enormously helped by Brouwer, A. and Wright, T. L., 1990, *Working in Hollywood*, New York: Avon. Sidney Lumet provides a comprehensive and sympathetic account of filmmaking from the point of view of the director in Lumet, S., 1995, *Making Movies*, London: Bloomsbury. The book of the television series, *Naked Hollywood*, is also informative about the work filmmakers do: Kent, N., 1991, *Naked Hollywood*, London: BBC.

William Goldman gives his take on the collective nature of filmmaking in Goldman, W., 1985, *Adventures in the Screen Trade*, London: Futura; and Goldman, W., 2000, *What Lie Did I Tell?*, London: Bloomsbury.

For our accounts of filmmakers' backgrounds, apart from our own research, we have drawn upon:

Campbell, D., 2002, 'Hollywood's Women Directors Hit Celluloid Ceiling', London: *The Guardian*, 5 July, 14.

Levy, E., 1984, 'The Democratic Elite: America's Movie Stars', *Qualitative Sociology*, vol. 12, no. 1, 29–52.

Powers, S., Rothman, D. J. and Rothman, S., 1996, *Hollywood's America – Social and Political Themes in Motion Pictures*, Oxford: Westview Press.

Duncan Campbell's article is a report of research done by Martha Lauzen of the University of San Diego. *Hollywood's America* is mainly a study of content in films. Written by three sociologists, it's particularly interesting for its critique of the way critics examine the social and political implications of films. Levy's article is also the work of a sociologist.

Chapter 3: What do filmmakers think of filmmaking?

In this chapter, we are exclusively concerned with depicting filmmakers' attitudes. We are not interested in critical judgements about their work. We learned most from interviews and autobiographical materials.

Sources for producers

Fleming, C., 1998, *High Concept: Don Simpson and the Hollywood culture of Excess*, London: Bloomsbury.

Kent, N., 1991, *Naked Hollywood*, London: BBC.

Linson, A., 2002, *What Just Happened – Bitter Hollywood Tales from the Front Line*, London: Bloomsbury.

Obst, L., 1996, *Hello, He Lied & other truths from the Hollywood Trenches*, New York: Broadway.

Solman, G., Smith, K. and Smith, G., 2002, 'Star Wars – Interview with George Lucas', *Film Comment*, vol. 38, no. 4, 22–32.

Thomas, P., 1992, 'No Ordinary Joel', *Empire*, September, 72–78.

Art Linson's and Lynda Obst's books provide the best general accounts of how producers function. They are also frustrating to read because illuminating insights are not fully developed.

Sources for writers

Goldman, W., 1985, *Adventures in the Screen Trade*, London: Futura.

Goldman, W., 2000, *What Lie Did I Tell?*, London: Bloomsbury.

McMurtry, L., 2001, *Film Flam – Essays on Hollywood*, Touchstone: New York.

Schanzer, K. and Wright, T. L., 1993, *American Screenwriters – The Insiders' Look at the Craft and the Business of Writing Movies*, New York: Avon.

Taylor, T., 1999, *The Big Deal*, New York: William Morrow.

Both William Goldman and Larry McMurtry drew on their own experiences as screenwriters to provide informed and intelligent accounts of the trials and tribulations of screenwriting. *American Screenwriters* is valuable because it contains interviews with a range of writers.

Sources for directors

Breskin, D., 1997, *Inner Views: Filmmakers in Conversation*, New York: Da Capo Press.

Burton, T., 1995, *Burton on Burton*, London: Faber and Faber.

Friedman, L. D. and Notbohm, B. (eds), 2000, *Steven Spielberg Interviews*, Jackson MI: University of Mississippi Press.

Kagan, J. (ed.), 2000, *Directors Close Up*, Boston MA: Focal Press.

Kaufman, A. (ed.), 2002, *Steven Soderbergh Interviews*, Jackson MI: University of Mississippi Press.

Lippy, Tod, 2000, *Projections Volume 11*, Boorman, J. and Donohue, W. (eds), London: Faber and Faber.

Lumet, S., 1995, *Making Movies*, London: Bloomsbury.

Sammon, P. M., 2000, *Future Noir – The Making of Blade Runner*, London: Orion.

Schrader, P., 1990, *Schrader on Schrader*, London: Faber and Faber.

Sherman, E. (ed.), 1976, *Directing The Film*, Los Angeles CA: Acrobat.

Smith, G., 1992, 'That's the way it happens' – Interview with Sidney Lumet, *Film Comment*, vol. 28, no. 5, 50–61.

Smith, G., 1999, Mike Nichols – Interview. *Film Comment*, vol. 35, no. 3, 10–30.

Soderbergh, S., 1999, *Getting Away With It – Or The Further Adventures of the Luckiest Bastard You Ever Saw*, London: Faber and Faber.

Thompson, D. (ed.), 1992a, *Levinson on Levinson*, London: Faber and Faber.

Thompson, D., 1992b, 'Demme on Demme', in J. Boorman and W. Donohoe (eds), *Projections*, London: Faber and Faber, 1, 158–97.

Thompson, D. and Christie, I. (eds), 1989, *Scorsese on Scorsese*, London: Faber and Faber.

As might be expected, there is a wide range of materials available about directors. Most take the interview form. There is little to choose between most of the books and articles. The interviews in the magazine *Film Comment* and the book *Inner Views* are the most sustained and probing.

Sources for stars

Cardullo, B., Geduld, H., Gottesman, R. and Woods, L., 1998, *Playing to the Camera – Film Actors Discuss their Art*, New Haven CT: Yale.
Lee, S., with Wiley, R., 1993, *By All Means Necessary*, London: Vintage.
Norman, B., 1989, *Interview with Meryl Streep*, London: BBC 1.
Smith, G., 1990, Midnight Heart – Interview with Jennifer Jason Leigh, *Film Comment*, vol. 26, no. 2, 55–8.
Smith, G., 1997, Robert Duvall – Interview, *Film Comment*, vol. 33, no. 6, 30–41.
Thomson, D., 1990, His Royal Hyphenate – Interview with Michael Douglas, *Film Comment*, vol. 26, no. 1, 16–22.
Zucker, Carole, 1990, An Interview with Lindsay Crouse, *Post Script*, vol. 12, no. 2, 4–28.

Although there is a huge amount of material available about stars, little of it is relevant to questions about acting. This short list represents the best material we came across. *Playing to the Camera* has interviews with a good selection of stars. Spike Lee's account of the making of *Macolm X* is useful for what it reveals about Denzel Washington's approach to acting.

Sources for production designers

Brouwer, A. and Wright, T. L., 1990, *Working in Hollywood*, New York: Avon.
Heisner, B., 1997, *Production Design in Contemporary American Film: a Critical Study of 23 American Films and their Designers*, London: McFarland.
LoBrutto, V., 1992, *By Design*, Westport CT: Praeger.

The Heisner and LoBrutto books provide substantial interviews with a range of production designers. The extras on the DVD of *Seven* (Region 2 – 1997) (Entertainment in Video) are very illuminating about the approach of the production designer, Arthur Max, to the film.

Sources for cinematographers

Schaefer, D. and Salvato, L., 1984, *Masters of Light – Conversations with Contemporary Cinematographers*, London: University of California Press.

Although it is a little dated, this is by far the most impressive book we came across for the light it throws on filmmakers' attitudes. Schaeffer and Salvato are well informed about the technical details of cinematography and are also able to place technical issues into a broader artistic context. These qualities enable them to conduct very enlightening conversations with cinematographers.

Rogers, P., 1998, *Contemporary Cinematographers on their Art*, Boston MA: Focal Press.

Although more up to date, the book is also more restricted in its questioning of contemporary cinematographers.

Almendros, N., 1985, *A Man with a Camera*, London: Faber and Faber.
Almendros, N., 1992, 'Matters of Photogenics', in J. Boorman and W. Donohue (eds), *Projections, Volume 1*, London: Faber and Faber, 198–211.

Nestor Almendros's autobiography and the article provide insights into the approach of one of the most influential cinematographers of the last 50 years.

Bailey, J., 2003, 'An Eye for Outsiders', *American Cinematographer*, vol. 5, 68–71.
Hall, C., 2003, 'Hall on Hall', *American Cinematographer*, vol. 5, 56–67.
Silberg, J., 2004, Honoring a (Reluctant) Vanguard, *American Cinematographer*, 2, 32–41.

The *American Cinematographer* is obviously an invaluable source for anyone wanting to know about the attitudes of cinematographers.

Sources for editors

LoBrutto, V., 1991, *Selected Takes: Film Editors on Editing*, New York: Praeger.
Oldham, G., 1995, *First Cut – Conversations with Film Editors*, London: University of California Press.

Both of the above books provide substantial interviews with a range of editors.

Bronwer, A. and Wright, T. L., 1990, *Working in Hollywood*, New York: Avon.
Murch, W., 2001, *In the Blink of an Eye – A Perspective on Film Editing*, Los Angeles CA: Silman-James Press.
Ondaatje, M., 2002, *The Conversations – Walter Murch and the Art of Editing Film*, London: Bloomsbury.

Murch's attitudes to editing, as revealed in these books, are a mixture of good sense and some less convincing philosophizing.

Saada, N., 1997, 'Thelma Schoonmaker Interviewed', in J. Boorman and W. Dononhue (eds), *Projections, Volume 7*, London: Faber and Faber, 22–8.

Sources for visual effects artists

Chell, D., 1987, *Moviemakers at Work – Interviews*, Redmond WA: Microsoft Press.
Rogers, P. B., 1999, *Art of Visual Effects – Interviews on the Tools of the Trade*, Boston MA: Focal Press.

The materials on visual effects are, as might be expected, much more limited than those for other areas. These books are welcome for the help they give in establishing a better understanding of the attitudes of visual effects artists.

Sources for Sound Designers

LoBrutto, V. (ed.), 1994, *Sound-on-Film – Interviews with the Creators of Film Sound*, Westport CT: Praeger.

Another in Vincent Lo Brutto's series of substantial interviews.

Sergi, G., 2004, *Film Sound in the Dolby Era*, Manchester: Manchester University Press.

The book is principally a theoretical and historical exploration of the role of sound but it contains extended interviews with two contemporary sound designers, Gary Rydstrom and Bruce Stambler.

Sources for Composers

Morgan, D., 2000, *Knowing the Score*, New York: Harper Entertainment.
Schelle, M., 1999, *The Score – Interviews with Film Composers*, Los Angeles CA: Silman-James Press.

Both of these books provide substantial interviews with a range of composers.

Lippy, T., 2000, 'Interview with Carter Burwell', in Boorman, J. and Donohoe, W. (eds), *Projections, Volume 11*, London: Faber and Faber, 36–52.

Carter Burwell is a very good interviewee. His thoughtful responses illuminate both big budget and independent filmmaking.

Chapter 4: Oscars and Aesthetics

Virtually all of the Guilds and large associations of filmmakers have rather comprehensive web sites that contain all relevant information (these sites are, in most cases, the first port of call for filmmakers themselves). As such, they are a true goldmine of information, although a considerable amount of 'sifting' through the, at times gargantuan, amount of material contained in them may be testing, even for the most enterprising scholar. Although the list of web sites below is not comprehensive, we believe that these are the most relevant sites available and cover virtually all of the key areas of filmmaking that we discuss in the book, including the key labour organizations involved in the negotiation of contracts (all sites were accessed 24 September 2004).

http://www.dga.com (The Directors Guild of America)
http://www.wga.org (The Writers Guild of America)
http://www.sag.org (Screen Actors Guild)
http://www.editorsguild.com (Motion Picture Editors Guild)
http://www.mpse.org (Motion Picture Sound Editors)
http://www.thescl.com (The Society of Composers & Lyricists)
http://www.ascap.com (The American Society of Composers, Authors and Publishers)
http://www.cameraguild.com (International Cinematographers Guild)

http://www.costumedesignersguild.com (Costume Designers Guild)
http://www.artdirectors.org (Art Directors Guild)
http://www.producersguild.org (Producers Guild of America)
http://www.amptp.org (Alliance of Motion Picture & Television Producers)

As for the Academy Awards (Oscars), the Academy of Motion Picture Arts and Sciences has two main sites, both of which hold all the necessary information and data to gain a sense of perspective on how the Academy and its members understand their role in relation to both the filmmaking community and the outside world at large:
(1) http://www.academyawards.com and (2) http://www.oscars.org. The former is the 'official front' of the Academy, and has information and material about the Oscar ceremony, the voting system and related topics. The latter is more relevant to scholars as it contains the recently created Academy Awards Official Database. This is a searchable database (free at time of writing) of all past winners. The way it is organized means that scholars can customize searches by category or combination of categories, making it possible to carry out the kind of systematic comparisons in this book that otherwise would have been a substantially more demanding effort, given the amount of data available. Perhaps in anticipation of possible scholarly interest, the Academy has also begun compiling a series of statistics that will be useful for further research.

Magazines such as *Variety* and *Screen International*, to quote only two of the most well known, are also a very useful source of information and material on filmmakers' views and opinions. They both offer online services, but the majority of their more interesting areas are for subscribers only and subscription rates can be costly. We used *Variety*, but there are other sources that offer similar services.

Other useful sources, especially for information on the Guild Awards and Academy Awards, are O'Neil, T., 2003, *Movie Awards*, New York: Perigee; and Kinn, G. and Piazza, J., 2002, *The Academy Awards*, New York: Black Dog & Leventhal Publishers.

Chapter 5: Observations

The three books discussed in this chapter are:

Salamon, J., 1993, *The Devil's Candy*, London: Picador.
Dunne, J. G., 2000, *Monster – Living off the Big Screen*, London: Pan.
Bach, S., 1986, *Final Cut*, London: Faber and Faber.

As we make clear in the text, we have high regard for Julie Salamon's book. It was just the kind of book we were looking for. It is a fine example of what a journalist can achieve through careful and sympathetic observation.

Chapter 6: Criticism

Jurassic Park

The opening, disparaging remarks on *Jurassic Park* made by Spielberg in an interview with Peter Biskind are contained in an interesting collection of interviews with Spielberg: Friedman, L. and Notbohm, B. (eds), 2000, *Steven Spielberg Interviews*, Jackson MI: University Press of Mississippi. Although there is no interview on *Jurassic Park* itself (the remarks about the film were actually expressed by Spielberg in an interview about *The Lost World: Jurassic Park*), this book is useful as a means of getting acquainted with the development of Spielberg's ideas about filmmaking, Hollywood and entertainment, as it contains interviews dating back to 1974 and *Sugarland Express*.

Joseph McBride's often-cited biography of Spielberg spans virtually the whole career of the director, up to and including *Schindler's List*, although, once again, *Jurassic Park* is only treated incidentally, within the context of McBride's chapter on *Schindler's List* and Spielberg's 'coming of age'. This creates some interesting friction in relation to notions of Spielberg as a serious filmmaker versus Spielberg the entertainer. Many of the extracts that refer to *Jurassic Park* being secondary in Spielberg's view to serious films such as *Schindler's List* are taken from this thorough biography of the director. McBride, J., 1997, *Steven Spielberg – A Biography*, New York: Simon and Schuster.

A further interesting biographical account is John Baxter's unauthorized biography. Baxter takes a strong *auteurist* position and that makes for some interesting reading, especially in terms of how the films Spielberg directed are understood as examples of the presence of an author. Baxter, J., 1997, *Steven Spielberg: The Unauthorised Biography*, London: HarperCollins.

Undoubtedly, the most significant source of material for this chapter comes from the book on the making of the film: Shay, Don and Duncan, Jody, 1993, *The Making of Jurassic Park*, London, Boxtree. This is one of those officially endorsed 'Making of' books that, inadvertently perhaps, reveal more than the authors had envisaged. In particular, Shay and Duncan's book is illuminating about the early stages of pre-production and the mammoth effort of the visual effects team. In the case of the former, the relationship between Spielberg and Crichton and the early storyboarding of the film are of particular relevance (this is, for example, where Spielberg reveals his interest in the film before the book was even published). In the case of the latter, the creative effort of the Lantieri, Tippet, Winston and Muren team is brought to the fore in great detail. Most importantly, Shay and Duncan's book provides a remarkable insight in the dynamics of the filmmaking process in the case of *Jurassic Park*.

The novel itself, and David Koepp's official script of *Jurassic Park*, are widely available from booksellers and specialized film script retailers. Their usefulness is particularly evident when compared with Malia Scotch Marmo's failed script. The latter is available at the time of writing from http://www.scifiscripts.com/scripts/JurassicPark_1stDraft.txt. (accessed 20 July 2004). We are aware of the potential pitfalls in using material that was not officially published so we decided early on to use only scripts and other material bearing some official reference, especially to date and script version in the case of early drafts of scripts. Marmo's script bears these reference marks. Those of you wishing to look at other scripts from the film and its sequels could also visit http://www.script-o-rama.com/snazzy/table2.html (accessed 20 July 2004).

Information about the sound team can be found especially in two interviews with sound designer Gary Rydstrom in two books: (1) LoBrutto, V. (ed.), 1994, *Sound-on-Film – Interviews with the Creators of Film Sound*, Westport CT: Praeger; (2) Sergi, G., 2004, *The Dolby Era: Film Sound in Contemporary Hollywood*, Manchester: Manchester University Press. Both books deal with the issue of sound, especially in terms of its overall contribution to the filmmaking process, and post-production in particular.

The quote from David Cook concerning the computer-generated dinosaurs comes from his book *A History of Narrative Film*, fourth edition, 2004, London: W. W. Norton & Company Ltd.

Finally, the DVD version of *Jurassic Park* contains some very interesting material about both the making of the film (contained in a 50-minute documentary) and some early pre-production meetings shot on video (including location shooting and early discussions about dinosaurs' movement). The documentary is mostly relevant in terms of gaining a sense of the development of the film in its various stages, although it is not as effective and revealing as Shay and Duncan's book. It is the 'home movie' of the pre-production meeting between Winston's team and Spielberg and Kennedy that is most interesting, despite its short duration (it is only a few minutes long). The discussion about movement in the short film is revealing of Spielberg's ability in thinking about dynamics and how to relate these to behaviour. In this sense, it is a fascinating insight into the way Spielberg relates to his collaborators and how he communicates with them. We used two main sources for the film for viewing material: (1) *Jurassic Park* – THX mastered edition Laserdisc (NTSC – 1997 release) (MCA/Universal Home Video) and (2) *Jurassic Park* – DVD (Region 2 – 2000 release) (Columbia TriStar Home Video).

Chinatown

There is substantial information available about the making of the film. Unfortunately, it is piecemeal and to be found in a variety of sources. It takes quite a bit of detective work to track it down and put it together into a coherent picture.

Three of the people involved have written autobiographies that have informative sections about the making of the film:

Dunaway, F., 1995, *Looking for Gatsby*, New York: Simon and Schuster.
Evans, R., 2003, *The Kid Stays in the Picture*, London: Faber and Faber.
Polanski, R., 1984, *Roman/by Polanski*, London: Heinemann.

John Alonzo and Richard Sylbert are particularly illuminating about their contributions to the film in interviews in *Masters of Light* (pp. 23–46) and *By Design* (pp. 49–62).

LoBrutto, V., 1992, *By Design*, Westport CT: Praeger.

Schaefer, D. and Salvato, L., 1984, *Masters of Light – Conversations with Contemporary Cinematographers*. London: University of California Press.

Sherman, E. (ed.), 1976, *Directing the Film*. Los Angeles CA: Acrobat.

Robert Towne has discussed his work on the script in a variety of places. They include:

- a BBC Television interview, *Writing Chinatown*, February 1997;
- a Masterclass on *Chinatown* at the Edinburgh Film Festival, August 1995;
- Towne, R., 2003, Interview, in D. McGrath and F. MacDermott (eds), *Screenwriting*, Hove: RotoVision.

A script of the film is in Towne, R., 1997, *Two Screenplays* – Chinatown *and* The Last Detail, New York: Grove Press. This has been identified as the third draft of the script and has some significant differences from the script that was shot.

There is also illuminating background information about the making of the film in: Biskind, P., 1998, *Easy Riders, Raging Bulls*, New York: Simon and Schuster.

When Harry Met Sally

The material available on *When Harry Met Sally* is rather different in tone and type from that of *Jurassic Park*. It is fundamentally divided into two categories: (1) interviews with Rob Reiner and/or Nora Ephron; and (2) officially released material about the film, such as DVD commentaries, 'Making of' material and the published screenplay. The Internet is an excellent resource for newspaper and magazine interviews with Nora Ephron especially. A former journalist, Ephron has regularly appeared in both newspaper features and radio and television interviews over the years since the release of *When Harry Met Sally*. This ranges from features in publications such as *The New York Times* – see, for example, James, C., 1989: 'It's Harry loves Sally in a Romance of New Yorkers and Neuroses', *The New York Times*, Wednesday 12 July 1989 – to radio interviews on the film as late as 2004 (*Loose Ends*, BBC Radio 4, air date: Saturday 27 March 2004). These interviews are interesting in that they clearly indicate that the views of the film held by both Reiner and Ephron at the time of its release have remained mostly unchanged over the years. Most of these reviews, articles and features are available in their entirety free of charge on searchable indexes of most large-circulation newspapers and the main tabloids. As for radio and television interviews, it is often difficult to find material, but perusing online archives and past TV and Radio listings can sometimes provide unexpected results.

The best source of information and material on the film came from two key sources. The first one was the official screenplay: Ephron, N., 1999: *When Harry Met Sally*, New York: Knopf. The screenplay provides an interesting contrast to one of the final drafts of it, dated 23 August 1988, available at:

http://www.dailyscript.com/scripts/whenharrymesally.pdf (accessed 28 July 2004). Although these two are late versions of the script, they are very useful, especially in view of Nora Ephron's insightful comments on the writing process and the making of *When Harry Met Sally* contained in the introductory section to the aforementioned book of the screenplay. Her most revealing comments about the filmmaking process and the relationship between writer and director come from this book.

The other key source is the additional material in the special edition DVD, which contains a director's commentary by Rob Reiner and 'The Making of When Harry Met Sally: How Harry met Sally' documentary. Both are available in the DVD Special Edition re-release of the film: *When Harry Met Sally* – DVD (Region 2 – 2001 release) (MGM). In the former, Reiner speaks, if reluctantly at times, about the way he approached the film and his relationship with both Ephron and producer Andy Scheinman. Although Reiner does not appear to be particularly engaged with the commentary process, he nonetheless offers some very useful insights on his approach to the film, his relationship with the other filmmaker and his overall attitude towards the filmmaking process. Similarly, but in a much more expanded and articulate manner, Reiner, Ephron, Crystal and others offer some useful comments in the 'Making of' documentary. In it, Gresham is interviewed, as are other collaborators, although the documentary fundamentally revolves around Ephron and Reiner, once again highlighting the central relationship at the core of the film.

The same material is also available in the Region 1 version of the DVD: *When Harry Met Sally* – DVD (Region 1 – 2001 release) (MGM Contemporary Classics Special Edition). To track possible changes – an everyday event with re-releases of DVDs (it is not uncommon for the soundtrack of a film to be remastered or changed altogether in a new DVD release) – we also used an earlier 1995 VHS release of the film as a reference copy.

A further useful reference is the CD of the music for the film. Although the official release of the music score from *When Harry Met Sally* is not an actual compilation of the standards used in the film (they are arrangements sung by Harry Connick Jr), it remains a useful starting point to consider the ways in which music works in the film. (Connick, Harry Jr, 1999: 'When Harry Met Sally', Columbia.) In particular, this release 'hides' the real agency of the arrangements, Marc Shaiman. Shaiman was brought on to the project by Billy Crystal, with whom he had worked previously on *Saturday Night Live*, and who arranged all the standards used in the film.

Chapter 7: Conclusion

There are two thoughtful discussions of authorship by Paisley Livingstone and Berys Gaut in Allen, R. and Smith, M., 1997, *Film and Philosophy*, Oxford: Clarendon.
The quotation about entertainment comes from Wood, R., 1986, *Hollywood from Vietnam to Reagan*, New York: University of Columbia Press.

The absence of any serious discussion of entertainment is alarming. Richard Dyer's article, 'Entertainment and Utopia', published nearly 40 years ago, still remains the only attempt to provide one. It can be found in Dyer, R., 1992, *Only Entertainment*, London: Routledge.

Biskind, P., 1998, *Easy Riders, Raging Bulls*, New York: Simon and Schuster.
Boorman, J. and Donohue, W. (eds), 1992, *Projections Volume 1*, London: Faber and Faber, 198–211.

Bordwell, D. and Thompson, K., 2001, *Film Art – An Introduction*, New York: McGraw-Hill.

Oldham, G., 1995, *First Cut: Conversations with Film Editors*, London: University of California Press.

The final quotation comes from Gottlieb, C., 2001, *The Jaws Log*, London: Faber and Faber.

Index